D1258921

THIS

INCOMPARABLE

LAND

THIS

INCOMPARABLE

LAND

A GUIDE TO AMERICAN NATURE WRITING

Thomas J. Lyon

MILKWEED EDITIONS

Published 2001 by Milkweed Editions
Printed in Canada
Cover and interior design by Dale Cooney
Cover art by Randy Scholes
The text of this book is set in Minion.
01 02 03 04 05   5 4 3 2 1
Revised and Updated Edition

Milkweed Editions, a nonprofit publisher, gratefully acknowledges support from World As Home program funder Lila Wallace-Reader's Digest Fund as well as operating support from the Elmer L. and Eleanor J. Andersen Foundation; Bush Foundation; Faegre and Benson Foundation; General Mills Foundation; Marshall Field's Project Imagine with support from the Target Foundation and Target Stores; McKnight Foundation; Minnesota State Arts Board through an appropriation by the Minnesota State Legislature and a grant from the National Endowment for the Arts; Norwest Foundation on behalf of Norwest Bank Minnesota; Lawrence and Elizabeth Ann O'Shaughnessy Charitable Income Trust in honor of Lawrence M. O'Shaughnessy; Oswald Family Foundation; Ritz Foundation on behalf of Mr. and Mrs. E. J. Phelps Jr.; John and Beverly Rollwagen Fund of the Minneapolis Foundation; St. Paul Companies, Inc.; U.S. Bancorp Foundation; and generous individuals.

Library of Congress Cataloging-in-Publication Data

Lyon, Thomas J. (Thomas Jefferson), 1937–
    This incomparable land / Thomas J. Lyon.
       p. cm.
    Rev. ed. of: This incomperable lande. 1989.
    Includes bibliographical references (p.).
    ISBN 1-57131-256-0 (alk. paper)
       1. Nature. 2. Natural history—United States.   I. This incomperable lande.   II. Title.
    QH81.T355 2001
    508.73—dc21

                                                                                    2001018683

To Jan

THIS INCOMPARABLE LAND

Complete instructions on how to live, how to govern, even how to die—everything is around us in nature, in the tides, in the storm, in the way the sea grass, moved back and forth by the wind, etches a curve in the sand.

—JOHN A. MURRAY, "THE PACIFIC COAST OF CALIFORNIA," IN
  The Nature of Nature

PREFACE

IN THIS BOOK'S FIRST edition, I grumbled about the lack of attention given nature writing, but the twelve years since its publication have erased my complaints. It now seems almost beside the point to mention the academic riskiness, to take one example, of publishing a book about nature writing, for what has happened in recent years makes such dissatisfaction seem historical only. Books such as Max Oehlschlaeger's *The Idea of Wilderness* (1991), Sherman Paul's *For Love of the World* (1992), Lawrence Buell's *The Environmental Imagination* (1995), not to mention Marcia Bonta's *Women in the Field* (1991)—and I mention only a few, as a reader of the second part of the bibliography will soon discover—have taken nature writing seriously indeed and have not wasted time bemoaning a lack of interest. And books of primary engagement (which constitute the first part of the bibliography) have simply exploded. Terry Tempest Williams's *Refuge* (1991), Jack Turner's *The Abstract Wild* (1996), and Carolyn Servid's *Of Landscape and Longing* (2000)—again for just three examples—show how capacious nature writing is; these books stretch the limits, and no one complains. During the past decade, the most alive writing is taking place in nature writing.

The revised edition of *This Incomparable Land* no longer includes an anthology. Since the first edition, numerous anthologies about the natural world have been published, and it no longer seemed useful to introduce writers whose claim on the attention of readers has been made. However, I have had many requests from readers for what they seem to have found valuable in the book—namely a taxonomy of nature writing and the annotated bibliography, which I have been told is the most complete and detailed listing of works dealing with the natural world. Some 170 new books, likely to last, have been published in these twelve years. Along with the bibliography, I have updated the chronology to reflect events through 2000.

As far as events on the academic side go, deconstruction, poststructuralism, and narrative criticism have all reached a pinnacle of popularity and have been practiced upon the writing that has been done. They have affected mainly professors of literature and have shown some new ways to look at the primary literature. The culture-wide phenomenon of feminism is the one movement whose effect is palpable, enlivening the tone of the writing considerably and resulting in a wave of new women writers. However, the fundamental themes of nature writing itself have been little disturbed by any new critical movements; they emerge in the new millennium with utter simplicity.

The crucial point about nature writing is the awakening of perception to an ecological way of seeing. "Ecological" here is meant to characterize the capacity to notice pattern in nature, and community, and to recognize that the patterns radiate outward to include the human observer. There is nothing exclusivist about nature writing. The perception of pattern has been the moving spirit of American nature writing almost from the beginning; this is why, for example, it is concerned with ethical questions. It is not primarily concerned with self or with strictly human society. It may be that this body of literature will be looked at in a truly new and more complete way.

Not all nature writing, of course, is philosophical. Some of it seems merely to record the facts of nature; some, at the other extreme, appears to be founded on impression or sentiment alone. I would argue, though, that just the turning of our attention to the natural world tends to subvert our anthropocentric heritage. The nature essay may even be seen as reflecting a general human stirring over the past two or three centuries, a movement in thinking toward what may be a great watershed. We may be on a halting journey toward understanding the world, and ourselves within it, as one system. No one, to my knowledge, has spoken of the death of the nature essay.

I have limited this book to essays on natural history and experiences in nature, believing that in fiction and poetry, though there are often beautiful descriptions of nature, other themes and intentions tend to predominate. There is, to be sure, a most interesting gray area here: some works classified as novels, such as the Adventures series by David Grayson (Ray Stannard Baker's pen name), may be nature essays in light disguise, and many nature essays use fictional techniques of narration and characterization. Perhaps it would be more accurate to say that I have arbitrarily confined this book to materials I consider primarily nonfictional.

For the first edition, I was greatly indebted to Annemarie Dietzgen of Berkeley; Mardy Murie of Moose, Wyoming; Lyn and Robert Paton of Kelly, Wyoming; and Gary and Masa Snyder of Kitkitdizze, California, for hospitality, for the use of their personal libraries, and for the opportunity to talk about nature writing. These good friends opened their homes to me. I thank too my colleagues Glenn R. Wilde and Patricia Gardner of Utah State University; Glenn for leading me to sources in the agrarian literature, and Pat, Head of the English Department, for services, materials, and accommodations too numerous to detail. At the University of California, I have been grateful for the efficiency and helpfulness of the staffs of the Bancroft Library and the Biology Library, and for a sponsorship to the Faculty Club kindly provided by James D. Hart, Director of the Bancroft Library. Constance Hatch and Suzan McBride of the Reference and Interlibrary Loan Department of the Merrill Library, Utah State University, gave me very special assistance, for which I thank them heartily. I am much obliged to Emily Jordan of Colorado State University for aid on some particularly obscure research. Max Lyon gave me helpful criticism; Ernest Duncan, a special boost at a crucial time; and Barbara R. Stratton of Houghton Mifflin Company clarified the manuscript at several points. I thank each of them. Jack Turner called many sources to my attention and gave me the benefit of his judgment on several points. My wife, Janis, has continued to walk, read, and think with me during the whole time of this study.

For the second edition of the book, I thank Jane Reilly of Utah State University for scanning the first edition. Thanks too to the staffs of the Carlsbad Public Library, particularly Audrie Clark, Lenore Bouras, Wendy Sears, and Patty Clark, and the University of California at San Diego Geisel Library.

I want to thank Laurie Buss and Ben Barnhart, of Milkweed Editions, for shepherding the book all along the way—a tremendous job.

THIS
INCOMPARABLE
LAND

AN AMERICAN CHRONOLOGY

THIS IS A QUICK history of the invasion and transformation of a portion of the New World, covering about five hundred years. No list of mere dates and happenings, of course, can do justice to the enormous complexity involved, nor can it do more than suggest the tragic overtones or the persistent hope. What I have tried for, in this selection, is truth.

1492   Columbus makes landfall in the Bahamas. "All is so green that it is a pleasure to gaze upon it."

1524   Giovanni da Verrazzano, cruising the eastern coast of North America, stops in present-day Rhode Island for two weeks. He goes inland and sees "champaigns [great meadows] twenty-five to thirty leagues in extent, open and without any impediment of trees. . . ."

1528   Cabeza de Vaca begins a journey across much of the Southwest. In eight years and something over two thousand miles of wandering, he is out of sight of Indians for only a few days.

1539   Hernando de Soto begins his expedition into the Southeast. Accompanying him are six hundred troops, 213 horses, a pack of fighting hounds, and thirteen pigs, to be bred along the way as a source of food.

1542   De Soto dies on the banks of the Mississippi River. His share of the swine herd is reckoned at seven hundred animals.

1562   Jean Ribaut coasts along Florida and South Carolina, looking
        for a site for a dissenters' colony. He responds with joy to the
        abundance of wildlife.

1585   Thomas Heriot, member of a voyage to Virginia sponsored by
        Sir Walter Raleigh, makes observations in his "briefe and true
        report of the new found land of Virginia," cataloging some of
        the prominent trees and wildlife species.

1624   Thomas Morton arrives in New England and begins a survey of
        natural resources.

        The first cattle ("three Heifers and a Bull," according to John
        Josselyn) are brought to New England.

1629   William Wood begins a four-year residence in New England.
        He keeps notes on trees, soil, wildlife, and Indian methods of
        land use.

1634   William Wood's *New England's Prospect* is published.

1637   Thomas Morton's *New English Canaan* is published.

1638   John Josselyn makes his first voyage to New England.

1639   According to Josselyn's chronology (published in 1672), "This
        year a strange multitude of caterpillars in New England."

1672   Josselyn's *New England's Rarities Discovered* is published. It
        includes a list of twenty-two weeds introduced into the New
        World by the Europeans, including dandelion and plantain.

1678   John Banister ("America's first resident naturalist," according to
        his biographer) arrives in Virginia. He begins collecting plants
        and insects and sending them back to England.

1691   In England, John Ray publishes *The Wisdom of God Manifested in the Works of the Creation,* signaling a new, higher status for scientific nature study and promoting a nonanthropocentric view.

1709   John Lawson, a surveyor, publishes *A New Voyage to Carolina,* which has been described as "the first major attempt at a natural history of the New World."

1712   Mark Catesby arrives in Virginia from England and begins a seven-year visit to the colonies.

1718   Massachusetts declares a three-year moratorium on deer hunting.

1722   Catesby begins a four-year study of the natural history of Carolina, Florida, and the Bahamas, including expeditions to areas uninhabited by Europeans.

1731   Catesby, having returned to England, begins serial publication of *The Natural History of Carolina, Florida, and the Bahama Islands.* The artistic quality is praised, and the natural history accounts are regarded as the most detailed and comprehensive attempted to date in the colonies.

1734   John Bartram of Pennsylvania (William Bartram's father) begins collecting plants for his English patron, Peter Collinson.

1735   The Swedish naturalist Linnaeus publishes *Systema Naturae,* rationalizing the nomenclature of natural history and stimulating its study.

1743   Benjamin Franklin proposes the organization of the American Philosophical Society, saying that "the first drudgery of settling new colonies" is now "pretty well over," leaving leisure for the pursuit of knowledge.

1748   Peter Kalm, one of Linnaeus's best pupils, begins his travels in the colonies, making extensive natural history notes over the next two and a half years.

1749   Pennsylvania pays bounties on 640,000 gray squirrels.

1755   John Bartram proposes a geological map of the colonies. By making systematic "borings" into the earth, he suggests, "we may compose a curious subterranean map."

1759   William Bartram (John's son) writes to the British ornithologist George Edwards that "many animals, which abounded formerly in settled parts, are now no more to be found, but retire to the unsettled border of the province; and that some birds, never known to early settlers, now appear in great numbers, and much annoy their corn-fields and plantations."

1773   William Bartram begins four years of travel into the wilds of the Southeast.

1782   Crèvecoeur publishes *Letters from an American Farmer* in London, an evocative appreciation of rural life, nature, and America.

1784   Thomas Jefferson's *Notes on the State of Virginia* is published in Paris. It includes natural history information and dismisses certain theories of the Comte de Buffon on New World animals.

1790   The first United States census records a white population of 3,929,214.

1791   William Bartram's *Travels* is published to lukewarm reviews, but several British and European editions and translations follow.

1794   Samuel Williams, a Rutland minister, publishes *A Natural and Civil History of Vermont.*

1799   The last bison in the East is killed in Pennsylvania.

1802   Alexander Wilson, who arrived in America in 1794, begins his study of American birds.

1803   John James Audubon, eighteen, arrives in Pennsylvania.

1804   Lewis and Clark begin their expedition to the Pacific with thirty men. On the way, they will collect several hundred specimens of western flora and fauna.

1807   Cedar waxwings sell for twenty-five cents a dozen in Philadelphia meat markets.

1808   Thomas Nuttall arrives in Philadelphia. He begins botanizing the day after his arrival.

        William Maclure completes the first geological survey of the United States.

        Volume 1 of Alexander Wilson's *American Ornithology* is published. When complete in 1814, the study fills nine volumes and covers 260 species in prose both precise and affecting.

1821   *A Journal of Travels into the Arkansa Territory, During the Year 1819,* by Thomas Nuttall, is published.

1825   The Erie Canal opens, facilitating midwestern and Great Lakes development.

1826   John D. Godman's *American Natural History*, a text with a progressive view of predation, is published.

1829   The first locomotive in America proves too heavy for the tracks during a trial run in Pennsylvania.

1831   John James Audubon commences publication of the *Ornithological Biography*, which includes essays on American scenes and citizens.

1832   Thomas Nuttall's *Manual of the Ornithology of the United States and Canada*, a handbook that will be in use throughout the nineteenth century, is published.

1834   Nuttall crosses the continent in company with a commercial expedition. The natural history studies he undertakes in California in 1835 are the first conducted there by an American.

        The last elk in the Adirondacks is killed.

1836   Ralph Waldo Emerson publishes his immensely influential *Nature*.

1841   The artist George Catlin, after a venture into the western wilderness, proposes a "nation's Park."

1845   On July 4, Henry David Thoreau moves into the "tight shingled and plastered" 10' x 15' house he had built at Walden Pond for $28.12 $^1/_2$.

1849   The Gold Rush begins the rapid transformation of much of the accessible California landscape.

        John Muir's father brings his young family from Scotland to wild Wisconsin and begins clearing land for a farm.

1851   Henry David Thoreau delivers his lecture on "the wild" for the first time.

1854   Henry David Thoreau's *Walden* is published.

1859   In England, Charles Darwin publishes *On the Origin of Species.*

1860   The population of the United States is 31,443,321.

        United States railroad tracks total thirty thousand miles.

1862   Henry David Thoreau dies. His last words are ". . . moose . . . Indian."

1864   George Perkins Marsh publishes *Man and Nature,* a study of the decline of cultures following the abuse of their environment.

1867   Alaska is purchased.

        The last elk in Pennsylvania is killed.

1869   John Wesley Powell, with a crew of nine men in four boats, descends the Green and Colorado Rivers. On his explorations of the West, Powell describes the Escalante and the Henry Mountains (both in Utah Territory), the last river and mountain range to be discovered.

        In this year of the "Golden Spike," American locomotives are estimated to have burned nineteen thousand cords of wood per day.

        John Muir spends his first summer in the Sierra.

1871   John Burroughs's first book of nature essays, *Wake-Robin,* is published.

1872   Yellowstone National Park, the first such reserve in the world, is established.

From this year to 1883, the last bison hunts are conducted in something very like frenzy. Theodore Roosevelt remarks, "Never before in all history were so many large wild animals of one species slain in so short a space of time."

1875   The last Labrador duck is killed on December 12 on Long Island.

1878   Barbed wire comes to Texas.

1882   Clarence Dutton's *Tertiary History of the Grand Cañon District* is published.

1883   The gasoline engine is developed.

1884   Hydraulic mining is outlawed.

1890   The United States Census Bureau declares the frontier closed. Yosemite National Park is created, drawn on boundaries suggested by John Muir.

The population of the United States is 62,947,714.

1893   Frederick Jackson Turner delivers his influential thesis, "The Significance of the Frontier in American History."

1894   The last pair of wild whooping cranes to have nested in the United States is seen at a marsh near Eagle Lake, Iowa.

John Muir's first book, *The Mountains of California*, is published.

1900   On March 24, the last passenger pigeon to be seen in the wild is killed at Sargents, Ohio.

1901   John C. Van Dyke's *The Desert* is published.

1903   The nation's first federal wildlife refuge is created in Florida. Mary Austin's first book, *The Land of Little Rain*, is published.

The "nature-fakers" controversy begins with an article by John Burroughs attacking anthropomorphism.

1904   The last Carolina parakeet is seen in the wild.

The American chestnut blight breaks out in the Brooklyn Botanical Garden following an importation of Oriental plants, and quickly spreads.

1906   *The Writings of Henry David Thoreau* are published, in twenty volumes.

The United States Forest Service is established.

1911   Enos Mills's *The Spell of the Rockies*, one of the comparatively small number of natural history books from that region, is published.

1914   The last passenger pigeon dies in the Cincinnati Zoo.

1915   Liberty Hyde Bailey publishes *The Holy Earth*, a radical agrarian text.

1916   The National Park Service is established.

1920   John Burroughs's *Accepting the Universe* is published.

Rockwell Kent's *Wilderness* is published.

1921   John Burroughs dies on a train somewhere in Ohio. His last words are "How far are we from home?"

1924   The first wilderness reserve within a national forest is established in New Mexico, in part due to the efforts of Aldo Leopold.

1925   The last cougar in Yellowstone to be killed in the Park Service's "control" program is dispatched.

1928   Henry Beston's *The Outermost House* is published.

1930   The population of the United States is 123,202,624.

1932   The last heath hen is seen on Martha's Vineyard, Massachusetts.

1934   Hawk Mountain, Pennsylvania, a ridge on a noted raptor migration route, is leased by conservationists, and two wardens are hired.

        Over this year and the next, predator control within Yellowstone National Park comes to an end.

1935   Donald Culross Peattie's *Almanac for Moderns* is published.

1938   Hawk Mountain, Pennsylvania, is purchased by conservationists and becomes the world's first sanctuary for birds of prey.

1939   In Mount McKinley National Park, Adolph Murie begins the first scientific study of wolf behavior in the wild.

1944   Sally Carrighar's *One Day on Beetle Rock* is published.

        Adolph Murie's *The Wolves of Mount McKinley* is published.

1948   Fairfield Osborn's *Our Plundered Planet*, one of the first post–World War II environmental alarm calls, is published.

1949   Aldo Leopold's *Sand County Almanac* is published.

        J. Frank Dobie's *The Voice of the Coyote* is published.

1951   *The Sea Around Us,* by Rachel Carson, is published. The book
        becomes a major best-seller.

        Edwin Way Teale's *North with the Spring,* the first of the
        American Seasons series, is published.

1954   *The Voice of the Desert,* by Joseph Wood Krutch, is published.

1956   Robert Marshall's *Arctic Wilderness* is published.

1959   Peter Matthiessen's *Wildlife in America,* a comprehensive his-
        tory of extinctions and protective measures, is published.

1960   John Graves's *Goodbye to a River* is published.

1962   Rachel Carson's *Silent Spring* is published. The book inaugu-
        rates a new era of environmental concern.

        Margaret Murie's *Two in the Far North* is published. The final
        section directs attention to Alaskan wilderness concerns.

1964   The Wilderness Act, establishing a National Wilderness
        Preservation System, becomes law after eight years of legislative
        struggle. By 2000, slightly more than 4 percent of the United
        States is under protection as legal wilderness, with more than
        half of that located in Alaska.

1967   Roderick Nash's *Wilderness and the American Mind* is pub-
        lished, helping to establish wilderness as a field for historical
        scholarship.

1968   Edward Abbey's *Desert Solitaire* is published.

The National Wild and Scenic Rivers System is created.

1969   A notable year for the literature of nature: Wendell Berry's *The Long-Legged House*, John Hay's *In Defense of Nature*, Edward Hoagland's *Notes from the Century Before*, Josephine Johnson's *The Inland Island*, Gary Snyder's *Earth House Hold*, and John and Mildred Teal's *Life and Death of the Salt Marsh* are published.

1970   On January 1 the National Environmental Policy Act of 1969 becomes law, mandating consideration of the environment before any major federal action is taken.

The first Earth Day is celebrated, heightening public awareness of environmental issues.

The Clean Air Act of 1970 establishes nondegradation of existing clean air as a principle and, for the first time, requires the states to attain air quality of specified standards within a specified time.

At Cornell University, Professor Tom Cade begins a program to breed peregrine falcons in captivity, subsequently to return them to the wild.

1972   The Federal Water Pollution Control Act of 1972 becomes law, establishing regulatory programs.

DDT is banned within the United States.

1973   The Endangered Species Act becomes law, requiring both protection of listed species and recovery programs.

1974   Annie Dillard's *Pilgrim at Tinker Creek* is published.

The first scientific paper theorizing on the migration of chloro-fluorocarbons into the stratosphere, where they would deplete the protective ozone layer, is published.

The nesting site of the seagoing marbled murrelet, high in trees of old-growth forest in the Pacific Northwest, is discovered.

1977   Wendell Berry's *The Unsettling of America* is published.

1978   *Of Wolves and Men*, by Barry Lopez, is published.

Peter Matthiessen's *The Snow Leopard* is published.

1980   Paul Brooks publishes *Speaking for Nature.*

The Alaska National Interest Lands Conservation Act becomes law, increasing by nearly four times the size of the National Wilderness Preservation system and more than doubling the size of the National Park and National Wildlife Refuge systems.

First natural reproduction of peregrine falcons east of the Mississippi in twenty years is carried off successfully.

The population of the United States is 226,504,825.

1981   Antarctic experiments show loss of stratospheric ozone. For the first time in history, human activity is shown to have substantially altered Earth's atmospheric chemistry.

1982   Paul Shepard's *Nature and Madness* is published.

1984   The National Academy of Sciences reports that approximately 53,500 synthetic chemicals are in use in the United States. Fourteen percent of these have been tested sufficiently to allow a partial hazard assessment.

1985   In *An Environmental Agenda for the Future,* the chief executive officers of the ten largest American environmental organizations write, "Continued economic growth is essential."

In the Southwest, groundwater withdrawals exceed natural replenishment by 21 billion gallons per day.

1986   *Arctic Dreams,* by Barry Lopez, is published.

Nonpoint pollution (from such diffuse sources as agricultural runoff and not regulated by the Clean Water Act) is found to affect nearly one in every four miles of U.S. rivers and one in every five lakes.

1987   Over President Reagan's veto, Congress commits to fighting nonpoint pollution.

As part of a captive breeding program, the last wild California condor is captured and taken to the San Diego Zoo.

The last known dusky seaside sparrow dies, the species a victim of habitat development and contamination in its limited Florida range.

A record 867 million tons of coal is mined in the U.S.

John Hay's *The Immortal Wilderness* is published.

1988   In a season of severe drought, North Dakota's Red River valley reports topsoil losses of greater than 15 tons per acre.

Wildfires ravage 4 million acres in seven western states and Alaska.

1989   The *Exxon Valdez* runs aground in Prince William Sound, Alaska, spilling 11 million gallons (35 thousand tons) of crude oil.

1990   *The Norton Book of Nature Writing,* edited by Robert Finch and John Elder, is published.

The northern spotted owl, a species living in old-growth forests of the Northwest, is listed as an endangered species. Four days later, loopholes are written into the listing, to allow more logging.

The Worldwatch Institute estimates annual U.S. topsoil loss at 1 billion tons.

United States population is reckoned at 248,709,873. The figure is widely regarded as lower than the actual population.

Douglas Peacock's *Grizzly Years* is published.

Gary Snyder's *The Practice of the Wild* is published.

1991   Terry Tempest Williams's *Refuge* is published.

Conservation tillage, leaving one-third of a field's plant residues intact, is used in more than 28 percent of the 281 million planted acres in the U.S.

Marcia Bonta's *Women In the Field* is published.

1992   The first captive-bred California condors are released into the wild.

1994   The Environmental Protection Agency lists 1,286 hazardous waste sites in the U.S.

The U.S. Fish and Wildlife Service reports that of the 1,524 endangered and threatened species listed, recovery plans have been prepared for 513. By 1997, the corresponding figures are 1,651 and 652.

The California Desert Protection Act puts 7 million acres into various categories of preservation.

1995   Wolves are returned to Yellowstone National Park.

1996   *American Nature Writers,* edited by John Elder, is published in two volumes, with in-depth coverage of seventy writers and more than a dozen special topics.

Grand Canyon National Park receives 4,537,703 visitors.

President Clinton establishes Grand Staircase-Escalante National Monument in Utah.

Keith H. Basso's *Wisdom Sits in Places* is published.

1997   The Environmental Protection Agency lists the ten worst states in pollution releases: Texas, Louisiana, Ohio, Pennsylvania, Indiana, Illinois, Tennessee, Alabama, Michigan, and North Carolina.

River, by Colin Fletcher, is published.

Hannah Hinchman's *A Trail Through Leaves* is published.

1998   Ian Marshall's *Storyline: Exploring the Literature of the Appalachian Trail* is published.

1999   NASA reports that "two cubic miles of ice per year have been melting away from Greenland since 1993 due to increased global temperatures."

Ellen Meloy's *The Last Cheater's Waltz* is published.

Waiting for Aphrodite, by Sue Hubbell, is published.

The Salt House, by Cynthia Huntington, is published.

2000   Carolyn Servid's *Of Landscape and Longing* is published.

Bradley P. Dean's edition of Thoreau's *Wild Fruits* is published.

The world population is estimated at over 6 billion.

In the heaviest fire season since 1910, some 6.7 million western acres burned.

David Brower, "archdruid" of the modern environmental movement, dies.

A TAXONOMY OF NATURE WRITING

"... this incomperable lande"
—JEAN RIBAUT, *The Whole & True Discouerye of Terra Florida*
(London, 1563)

IF WE FIRST DESCRIBE nature writing in quasi-taxonomic terms, we can see in a general way what is important about the genre and how its themes are developed. I must sound a cautionary note, though, before laying out a proposed classification scheme of American nature literature: the types I have listed tend to intergrade, and with great frequency. This may be somewhat irritating to lovers of neatness who would like their categories to be immutable, but nature writing is not, in truth, a neat and orderly field. Nevertheless, we can make a few sound and, I hope, helpful generalizations. First and most fundamentally, the literature of nature has three main dimensions to it: natural history information, personal responses to nature, and philosophical interpretation of nature. The relative weight or interplay of these three aspects determines all the permutations and categories within the field. If conveying information is almost the whole intention, for example (see the left-most column of the spectrum on p. 22), the writing in question is likely to be a professional paper or a field guide or a handbook, most of which are only intermittently personal or philosophical or literary. A good example is Roger Tory Peterson's *A Field Guide to Western Birds* (1961). The brief description of the canyon wren's song, among other little gems in the book, immediately suggests something more than just accuracy. "Voice: A gushing cadence of clear curved notes tripping down the scale."[1] That single line may evoke the entire ambience of a shaded, slickrock canyon somewhere in the Southwest on a June morning. But few people would expect a field guide to be a literary effort.

When expository descriptions of nature, still the dominant aspect of a book, are fitted into a literary design so that the facts then give rise to some sort of meaning or interpretation, then we have the basic conditions for the natural history essay. The themes that make natural history information into a coherent, literary whole may be stated by the author in the first person, as in John Hay's *Spirit of Survival* (1974), where Hay found in the life histories of terns wonderfully cogent statements of the beauty and vulnerability of life itself, the life we share with these birds; or the themes may emerge from the facts as related in a third-person, objective fashion. This latter way was Rachel Carson's choice in *The Sea Around Us* (1950); she arranged the facts of oceanography and marine biology tellingly, so that the drama and interplay of forces pointed inescapably toward a holistic, ecological view of nature.

The defining characteristic of the natural history essay is that whatever the method chosen for presentation, the main burden of the writing is to convey pointed instruction in the facts of nature. As we move toward the right on the spectrum, the role and relative importance of the author loom a bit larger: experience in nature—the feel of being outdoors, the pleasure of looking closely, and the sense of revelation in small things closely attended to—takes an equal, or almost equal, place with the facts themselves. In the ramble, a classic American nature writing form, natural history and the author's presence are more or less perfectly balanced. The author goes forth into nature, usually on a short excursion near home, and records the walk as observer-participant. Almost the entire work of John Burroughs, to take a prominent example, fits into the category of the ramble, including his earliest published bird walks in *Wake-Robin* (1871). Burroughs's own personality and way of responding to the natural scene were very much a part of his writing and were important to his popular success. His intense feeling for the woods

WRITING ABOUT NATURE: A SPECTRUM

FIELD GUIDES AND PROFESSIONAL PAPERS	NATURAL HISTORY ESSAYS	RAMBLES	SOLITUDE AND BACKCOUNTRY LIVING	TRAVEL AND ADVENTURE	FARM LIFE	MAN'S ROLE IN NATURE
Clarence King, *Systematic Geology* (1878)	John Muir, *Studies in the Sierra* (1874–1875)	John D. Godman, *Rambles of a Naturalist* (1828)	Henry David Thoreau, *Walden* (1854)	William Bartram, *Travels* (1791)	Hector St. John de Crèvecoeur, *Letters from an American Farmer* (1782)	John Burroughs, *Accepting the Universe* (1920)
Olaus Murie, *A Field Guide to Animal Tracks* (1954)	Rachel Carson, *The Sea Around Us* (1950)	John Burroughs, *Wake-Robin* (1871)	Henry Beston, *The Outermost House* (1928)	Henry David Thoreau, *The Maine Woods* (1865)	Liberty Hyde Bailey, *The Harvest of the Year to the Tiller of the Soil* (1927)	Joseph Wood Krutch, *The Great Chain of Life* (1956)
Roger Tory Peterson, *A Field Guide to Western Birds* (1961)	Ann Zwinger and Beatrice Willard, *The Land Above the Trees* (1972)	John K. Terres, *From Laurel Hill to Siler's Bog* (1969)	Sigurd F. Olson, *Listening Point* (1958)	Charles Sheldon, *The Wilderness of the Upper Yukon* (1911)	Wendell Berry, *A Continuous Harmony* (1972)	John Hay, *In Defense of Nature* (1969)
Roland H. Wauer, *Birds of Zion National Park and Vicinity* (1997)	John Hay, *Spirit of Survival* (1974)	Annie Dillard, *Pilgrim at Tinker Creek* (1974)	Edward Abbey, *Desert Solitaire* (1968)	Edward Hoagland, *Notes from the Century Before* (1969)	Michael Pollan, *Second Nature* (1991)	Dolores LaChapelle, *Sacred Land Sacred Sex* (1988)
	Ron Lanner, *The Piñon Pine* (1981)	Richard K. Nelson, *The Island Within* (1989)	Anne LaBastille, *Woodswoman* (1976)	Barry Lopez, *Arctic Dreams* (1986)		Bill McKibben, *The End of Nature* (1989)
	Kathryn Phillips, *Tracking the Vanishing Frogs* (1994)	Terry Tempest Williams, *Refuge* (1991)	Jack Turner, *Teewinot* (2000)	Ann Linnea, *Deep Water Passage* (1995)		Stephanie Mills, *In Service of the Wild* (1995)
	Bernd Heinrich, *Mind of the Raven* (1999)					

and fields of his home ground—there may never have been such a homebody in all of American literature as Burroughs—is also a distinguishing mark of the ramble-type of nature writing. Burroughs became identified with the patchwork of farms and woods in the vicinity of the Catskill Mountains in New York. The writer of rambles usually does not travel far from home ground, and seldom to wilderness; he or she is primarily interested in a loving study of the near and, often, the pastoral. To say that the ramble is local, however, or that it often takes place on worked-over ground, is not to imply that it is in any way superficial. As Annie Dillard showed in *Pilgrim at Tinker Creek* (1974), deep familiarity with the most ordinary landscapes can blossom into immense themes.

Continuing rightward on the spectrum, we begin to move away from the primacy of natural history facts to a forthright emphasis on the writer's experience. In essays of experience, the author's firsthand contact with nature is the frame for the writing: putting up a cabin in the wilderness as Richard Proenneke did in *One Man's Wilderness* (1973); canoeing down a clear, wild river (John McPhee, *Coming into the Country,* 1977); walking the beach at night (Henry Beston, *The Outermost House,* 1928); rebuilding the soil of a rundown farm (Louis Bromfield, *Malabar Farm,* 1948); or contemplating a desert sunset (Edward Abbey, *Desert Solitaire,* 1968). And much else. Instruction in natural history is often present in the nature experience essay, but it is not what structures the book. We are placed behind the writer's eyes here, looking out on this interesting and vital world and moving through it with the protagonist.

Within the broad category of the nature experience essay, there are three fairly well-defined subtypes, each with a distinctive avenue for philosophical reflection. Essays of solitude or escape from the city, as might be expected, work much with the contrast between conventional existence and the more intense, more wakeful life in contact with nature. This subtype, like the ramble, is a classic American form, but it tends to be much more critical and radical—compare Thoreau at Walden, anathematizing the false economy of society, and Abbey in the desert, waiting until the engineers drive away in their jeep, then pulling up and throwing away the stakes they had pounded into the ground to mark the location for a new, paved road.

Accounts of travel and adventure (which usually have a strong element of solitude in them) often present the same sort of contrast between the too-safe, habituated existence left behind and the vivid life of discovery. The travel and adventure writer often seems like a ramble writer gone wild; there is less emphasis on natural history and more on movement, solitude, and wildness. Often, the account is framed on the great mythic pattern of departure, initiation, and return,[2] and always the account gains meaning from the basic American circumstance that wilderness, where the traveler and adventurer are usually found, has always in our history been considered a realm apart. It is true that some travelers, such as William Bartram, have been deeply interested in the natural history of the new territories they have explored: for example, in *Travels* (1791), Bartram made extensive lists of the species he encountered. Nonetheless, the exhilaration of release from civilization, the sense of self-contained and self-reliant movement, and above all, the thrill of the new are the prominent qualities.

The farm essay, with its rooted and consistent emphasis on stewardship and work (rather than study, solitude, or discovery), may seem at first to be unrelated to the nature essay. It might be argued, too, that since farming is only about ten thousand years old, whereas our connections with wilderness are unimaginably deeper, the entire sensibility may be different. The sublime, so important to the aesthetic of the traveler, and even to the rambler, seems somehow foreign to the farmer. But we should be alert to blendings. In practice, American farm writers from Hector St. John de Crèvecoeur in the late eighteenth century to Wendell Berry in the present day have paid close attention to the wildlife on and around their places and have conveyed the deep, poetic pull of nature on the spirit. Berry, for example, describes how observing some birds at his family's land in Kentucky became instrumental in his development of a place-based point of view. Stewardship, so prominent in farm literature, also has ecological ramifications; the common understanding of American farm writers is that fitting into natural patterns, rather than imposing some sort of abstract order upon them, is the farmer's proper role. In this ethical commitment, nature writers with an agrarian point of view join with the mainstream philosophy of American nature writing.

On the right-hand edge of the spectrum are the analytic and comprehensive works on humans and nature. In these works, interpretation predominates, and the natural history facts or the personal experiences are decidedly secondary. They are illustrations for the argument. Here, philosophy is all. The actual points that are made, typically, are not different from those made in natural history essays or in personal experience essays, but the mode of presentation tends to be more abstract and scholarly.

I need to add here that the usual terminology covering all of the forms of nature writing tends to lump them together. They have all, at one time or another, been called natural history essays or nature essays interchangeably. I see no real problem in this state of affairs, nor much practical benefit in any attempt to promote an academically rigorous classification. Nature writing itself, in any case, would not rest easily in any static system, prizing as it does vitality and variety, the virtues of its subject. The categories offered here are meant simply to show the breadth of the spectrum and to help indicate some of the special powers each type within the genre may possess.

Whatever the artistic means chosen, and whatever the type of essay we may choose to call a certain piece of nature writing, the fundamental goal of the genre is to turn our attention outward to the activity of nature. This is so, across the spectrum. Time and again, the literary record displays the claim that there is a lifting and a clarifying of perception inherent in this refocusing, which opens up something like a new world. The sense of wonder conveyed is perhaps very much in the American grain. It may eventually be seen as a more important discovery than the finding of new lands.

THE AMERICAN SETTING

THE FIRST AND GREATEST influence on nature writing, of course, is the land itself. The major temperate ecosystems are represented beautifully in America, and the sheer variety is staggering. Just to name a few of the places that have inspired excellent nature writing is to get the sense of an amazing range of possibilities for experience: Cape Cod, that spare and vivid arm of land crooking out into the North Atlantic; the richly mulched eastern deciduous forest, pealing with the songs of thrushes; the bright green of the Florida peninsula, where William Bartram derived a vision of paradise unspoiled; the plains and prairies, over which massed and rumbled one of the world's primary symbols of wild abundance, the bison; the wide, still deserts of the Southwest, with their daunting and exhilarating space; sublime, sacred Yosemite; and the Grand Canyon, of which so much has been written, although almost every writer at last has declared in despair the inadequacy of words.

What seems to have made the deepest—indeed, an indelible—impression on both explorers and settlers in the beginning was simply the morning freshness of the continent. The New World, as they called it, was ecologically intact and exuded the beauty of health. We did not come to an abused land. The fact that a continent, occupied for thousands of years, appeared to European eyes as the quintessence of virgin nature is a tribute of the highest order to America's native inhabitants; even so, the point, for our literature and for our whole American sense of the world, *was* that wild freshness. What it offered to us was a chance for renewal.

The French Huguenot sailor Jean Ribaut, looking over coastal South

Carolina in 1562 with a colony for dissenters in mind, responded to the unspoiled landscape so strongly that his account, written almost a year afterward and not in his native tongue, still sings:

> . . . on the other side, [we] enterd and veued the cuntry therabowte, which is the fairest, frutefullest and plesantest of all the worlde, habonding in honney, veneson, wildfoule, forrests, woodes of all sortes, palme trees, cipers, ceders, bayes, the hiest, greatest and fairest vynes in all the wourld with grapes accordingly, which naturally and without mans helpe and tryming growe to the top of the okes and other trees that be of a wonderfull greatnes and height. And the sight of the faire medowes is a pleasure not able to be expressed with tonge, full of herons, corleux, bitters, mallardes, egertes, woodkockes, and of all other kinde of smale birdes with hartes, hyndes, buckes, wild swyne, and sondery other wild beastes as we perceved well bothe then by there foteing there and also afterwardes in other places by ther crye and brayeng which we herde in the night tyme. Also there be cunys, hares, guynia cockes in mervelus numbre, a great dele fairer and better then be oures, silke wormes, and to be shorte it is a thinge inspeakable, the comodities that be sene there and shal be founde more and more in this incomperable lande, never as yet broken with plowe irons, bringing fourthe all thinges according to his first nature, whereof the eternall God endued yt.[1]

The discoverer's note of rejuvenation sounds again and again in American nature literature, even to the present day when the official wilderness area is a remnant that has to stand for the world in its once and former wholeness. Coming upon an abundance of wild animals or birds or a sweep of undiminished rugged country—experiences described in the works of Robert Marshall and Barry Lopez, to name just two representative figures from recent times—may bring a shock of recognition, a sense of reentering a world greater and older than anything dominated by humans. The mind, as if suddenly given back its accustomed scope, becomes alert to the moment.

But the history we have created here as a culture quite obviously does not reflect this inner, new life as anything more than a minority response. We have not, in the main, been so alive to the country. No doubt there are many reasons for our comparative numbness; in what follows I propose just one speculation, attempting to focus on what it might be that distances and dulls perception so pervasively that in order to see the world as new and living we have to be hit over the head, as it were, with pure wilderness.

The great traditions of Western civilization that stand behind our history, identified succinctly by Matthew Arnold as Hebraism and Hellenism, are traditions of a powerfully dualistic cast, both philosophically and psychologically, tending to enforce the separation of mind from matter, self from surroundings, and humanity from nature.

Both the Christian and rationalist influences deriving from Hebraism and Hellenism promote a centralized, isolated sense of identity for the individual and for humanity in general. The Christian concept of humanity as a special creation and the Aristotelian concept of reason as the best and distinguishing part of humanity alike foster egoism and its collective form, anthropocentrism. This is not to "blame" Christianity and the Greek inheritance; no doubt they merely embody human predispositions of much earlier origin. The sense of self as a separate and distinct entity, that sense that seems to place nature at a distance, may indeed trace all the way back to one of the innate features of human consciousness: the ability to perceive objects in a one-at-a-time, sequential fashion. This ability may give rise to a certain logic: if there is a world of separate and distinct objects out there, then in here, behind these eyes, there must be a likewise distinct entity—a subject. Every moment of perception on the one-at-a-time basis generates anew the consciousness of "I," or ego. The other givens of human consciousness, especially the sense of the world that Freud referred to (rather scornfully) as the "oceanic," seem to decline in use before the persuasiveness of the egoistic vision. Again, to state the obvious, there should be no particular fault or blame declared here—clearly, the universe grew the human ego just as naturally as it grew columbines and wood thrushes.

It seems equally clear from the historical record, however, that the Mediterranean and European culture known to the world as Western civilization has put a sharp point, in effect, on the egoistic sense of life. The perceived distinctiveness of the individual self, and humanity's separateness from the rest of the world, were given what amounted to cosmic sanction in Christianity's theology of special creation. As success reinforced the Western mentality, particularly during the great period of European expansion from the sixteenth through the nineteenth centuries, a certain heedlessness also became characteristic.

There are two consequences of the dominant Western worldview that have had particular impact on the American context, both on the land itself and on the intellectual and moral climate of this country. One is that egoism tends to inspire the expansionist behavior associated with "the frontier." The logic in this case seems to be that from a perceived position of isolation, the ego, or identity, needs to secure itself, but that each success at creating security only enlarges the zone needing security. The other consequence is that the one-at-a-time mind does not see context and relation very well, and thus it tends not to notice the side effects of its activities, overlooking information that could urge self-restraint. The frontier mind does not perceive things as an ecological whole. Working from the commanding need to secure itself, a task that has a strong, innate tendency to grow and keep growing, the frontier mind becomes preoccupied with use. From this narrowed outlook, nature consists merely of natural resources. The focus on utility not only seems to hinder perception of basic, practical relations—between forest clearing and the drying up of springs, for example—but also to limit the possibility of empathy. In America, the cutting and burning of the largest deciduous forest on earth proceeded rapidly and without notable hindrance on either practical or ethical grounds. The expropriation and, indeed, extirpation of the native inhabitants over much of their territory was accomplished with few serious objections; the extermination of the most magnificent assemblage of birds, the passenger pigeons, and the near extinction of the most astounding assemblage of large herbivores, the bison, were, records seem to show, largely matters to which most Americans were ethically indifferent. What happened, in essence, was that a people with a strong tradition of righteousness carried off an invasion of the frontier with remarkable success and little apparent reflection.

Within such a history, naturalists and nature writers make up a distinctly nonconforming, even heretical, minority. The principal cultural heresy expressed in American nature writing is the refocusing of vision outward from the individual self, and from the corporate self, our species. A radical proposal follows on the widened vision: that the environment, nature, is the ground of a positive and sufficient human joy. Nature writers and naturalists do not appear to have conceptualized America as "a vast body of wealth without proprietors," in the phrase of one student of the frontier period;[2] on the contrary, they very often recognized the priority of the Indians' claims and sympathized with them. John Lawson (who, ironically, was killed by Indians), William Bartram, Henry David Thoreau, Mary Austin, and Bob Marshall are a few of those who shared this concern. Though some naturalists, to be sure, pursued the morally anomalous practice of "collecting"—that is, of killing animals for specimens—well into the twentieth century, no one in this group took part in the casual slaughter of wildlife.

It is probably not coincidental that the nature essay developed as a distinct genre only toward the close of the eighteenth century, after the romantic movement in philosophy and literature had helped give the individual nature experience, in all its intuitive and emotional vagueness yet penetrating insight, some credibility and standing. Many of the values seen in nature writing are shared with romanticism: affirmation of the world as congenial to humans, in essence; skepticism toward purely rationalistic (that is, logical and sequential, as opposed to intuitive) thought; scorn for materialism; love for what is spontaneous, fecund, and life-giving; and a predilection for the simple and primitive.

But nature writing is not simply romantic; it also owes much to science, both in its use of the empirical findings of scientists and in its incorporation, over more than two hundred years, of scientific theories. Edgar Allan Poe, who perhaps is representative of many romantic thinkers, complained of science's demystification of the world, but Henry David Thoreau stated clearly the accommodating attitude of most nature essayists: "Let us not underrate the value of a fact," he wrote; "it will one day flower in a truth."[3] Nature writers have been inveterate and important synthesizers, from the time of the early Argument from Design (the proof of God's wisdom and beneficence as shown by the intricate workings of nature) through the Darwinian revolution, seeking always to express the possible meanings and implications of new data. John Muir, for example, working in the very early years of the science of glaciology, made painstaking studies of moraines and striations and erratic boulders in the Sierra Nevada, discovered sixty-odd small, active glaciers high in the range, placed stakes in some of them to measure their movement, and organized all of his findings into a narrative of the mountains' glacial history. Then he went the crucial step further and described the work of the glaciers as only one element in a grand evolutionary process, a process that, for Muir, expressed the divine activity. For Muir, there was no conflict between science and religion in the highest, nonsectarian sense; any new scientific finding simply filled in the sacred pattern a little more completely.

Muir's synthesis may be instructive. It happens that some of the most important scientific discoveries of the last two centuries, the evidence for ecological relationship and evolutionary change (as opposed to the old theories of immutable entities—species—walking across stagelike settings) are remarkably consonant with the intuitive and experiential theory of holism espoused by many romantics and transcendentalists. The romantic listens to the heart and hears that it beats in profound cooperation with all else; the follower of the scientific method sees in nature undeniable evidence of relationships and symbioses, patterns strongly suggesting the inadequacy of any theory based upon separate entities. There is a true convergence here. But of course not all nature writers share John Muir's ultimate confidence in the divine pattern or see pattern as necessarily divine. The important point demonstrated in the literature of nature since late in the eighteenth century is that the experience of and the detailed study of nature may both lead toward an ecological understanding of the world.

In the eighteenth century and through much of the nineteenth, the enlarged scope of scientific attention retained a theistic or deistic premise. What science was building then, as many thought, was a conclusive Argument from Design; it was on just such a basis that science had entered mainstream Christian culture, showing that the marvels of nature—the circulation of blood, the movements of planets, the incredibly intricate lives of social insects—were further evidence of the omniscience of the Deity, making Him, in our awakening eyes, all the more worthy of awe and worship. William Bartram's view was typical of this period: "Perhaps there is not any part of creation, within the reach of our observations, which exhibits a more glorious display of the Almighty hand, than the vegetable world. . . . The animal creation also, excites our admiration, and equally manifests the almighty power, wisdom and beneficence of the Supreme Creator and Sovereign Lord of the universe."[4]

The ability to see pattern, and thus, for many, to see the "Almighty hand" as William Bartram did, was considerably enhanced in the eighteenth century by the development of a logical system of classification for the world's flora and fauna. The major figure in this endeavor was the Swedish systematist Linnaeus, whose arrangement of class, order, genus, and species, with the species itself to be known by just two Latin names, not only made a disciplined approach to nature study possible (and possible even for the layperson, an important point), but also focused attention on likenesses and pattern in nature. Plants and animals began to sort out into recognizable groupings and possible lines of descent—though the mechanism for any such descent was as yet undiscovered. The logical categorization of nature increased the likelihood of seeing relationships of all kinds, and it is no exaggeration to say that Darwin, and indeed all subsequent investigators into evolution, stood on the shoulders of Linnaeus. The debt remained even though Linnaeus's particular arrangement was later supplanted.

With the Darwinian revolution in the mid- and late nineteenth century, the theistic or deistic premise of science began to be replaced by a naturalistic approach, of which Muir can be seen as a transitional figure. Writing in the late nineteenth and early twentieth centuries, Muir used the term "God" freely, but with a more diffuse reference, apparently, than William Bartram intended when he spoke of his "Supreme Creator." Muir accepted much of the theory of evolution and natural selection, though he balked at the "struggle for existence." He preferred to see the elements of the world as a partnership, with God representing more of a divine principle synonymous with the whole rather than a separate, transcendent Creator.

Most nature writers in the twentieth century have been rather quiet on the subject of deity, according well with the temper of the time, perhaps, but they have without exception maintained a reverential attitude toward nature. Oneness with nature, awe, and the spiritually potent deepening of consciousness beyond the egoistic level brought about by intimacy with an environment remain prominent. So strong are these elements, and so closely linked with the emotion of joy, that nature writing, unlike other genres, did not decline into pessimism or determinism with the so-called death of God or with the ominous development of the modern urban-industrial state. Instead, nature writers have simply become more militant critics of urbanization and industrialization while maintaining, in the great majority, a consistently affirmative vision.

Besides incorporating great intellectual currents, nature writing in America has also responded to actual historical conditions, in particular the decline of environmental quality as the country was settled and relentlessly developed. The nation's fall from pristine wholeness burned itself into the minds of nature writers, so resplendent had been the original sightings and reports. John Josselyn, an early student of natural history, noted that between 1638 and 1663, wild turkeys, formerly abundant, had been virtually eliminated from seaboard Massachusetts, and the Swedish visitor Peter Kalm, in the mid-eighteenth century, was alarmed at the profligacy with which Americans treated valuable woodlands. A century later, Henry David Thoreau lamented that the environment he and his generation had been bequeathed was like a book with pages missing, and Wilson Flagg, a near contemporary of Thoreau, looked with sorrow upon the importation of modern, citified tastes and modern farming methods into the rural landscape of New England; he made a plea for a modified kind of wilderness preservation as at least a partial corrective to the rush of progress. In the twentieth and now the twenty-first century, as an already large American population continues to grow and to make use of an extraordinary energy subsidy from fossil fuels, to the detriment of the environment, contemporary nature writers continue to take pained note of losses, and more than a few have expressed denunciation. From about the time of World War II, nature writers have mounted detailed critiques and proposed specific corrective measures for environmental outrages: John Graves's portion of *The Water Hustlers* (1971); Edward Abbey's fiery "The Second Rape of the West" in *The Journey Home* (1977); Barry Lopez's somber account of the American campaigns against wolves in *Of Wolves and Men* (1978); and Charles E. Little's *The Dying of the Trees* (1995) are good examples. Perhaps the most effective critique in the modern era has been Rachel Carson's *Silent Spring* (1962), a careful, understated thesis against the careless and excessive use of chemical pesticides and herbicides. *Silent Spring* declared, as Paul Brooks writes in *Speaking for Nature* (1980), "the basic responsibility of an industrialized, technological society toward the natural world."[5] Its influence on the environmental awakening of the 1960s and 1970s, and upon public policy to some degree, is unquestioned.

In almost every practical aspect, we today live in a world that would perhaps dishearten someone as close to us in time as Henry David Thoreau. We have lost a great deal in just the time since he compared the natural America he inherited to a damaged volume: many rivers, formerly free-flowing; many valuable wetlands;[6] many old-growth forests; and much plain, open space and possibility. We have set in motion trains of cause and effect—notably those arising from the broadscale use of toxic chemicals and the burning of coal and oil—whose consequences may be enormous and are almost certain to be negative. In addition to having wrought deep changes in our surroundings, we have used our advantage to construct, in the century or so of the oil-powered industrial age, a radically more insulated life than was possible in Thoreau's time. It is highly interesting, perhaps a mark of the true complexity of the American character, that natural history study and nature writing persist and possibly even gain in influence.

Our literature of nature owes a great deal of its content and development, and its currency now, to the major contributions of romanticism and science. It has always been morally alive to the circumstances of its environmental moment. But in the end, the deepest influence, the inner life of the nature essay, is still the writer's response to the land itself. In the face of all that has happened, in a modern nation where pavement is now said to occupy as much territory as protected wilderness, the setting that F. Scott Fitzgerald described so memorably as the "fresh green breast of the new world" continues in mythic potency to generate profound allegiance and durable affirmation.

BEGINNINGS

THE MODERN PERSONAL ESSAY began with Michel de Montaigne's *Essais* in 1580, but more than two centuries would pass before the nature essay emerged as a literary form. When the two great eighteenth-century revolutions in natural philosophy had progressed far enough that both the response of an individual to nature and the role of nature in revealing God were legitimized, the preconditions for nature writing were in place. There also had to be sufficient knowledge of natural history, of course, and this was being provided by the tremendous growth in field observation taking place during the Enlightenment period. The first signs that the times were ripe for nature writing were, in England, Reverend Gilbert White's *A Natural History of Selborne* (1789), a text much read in America, and, in this country, the writings by Thomas Jefferson and Hector St. John de Crèvecoeur in the 1780s. When William Bartram published his *Travels* in 1791, he became the first American nature essayist.

But though there were no formally or philosophically realized essays before the late Revolutionary period, there were attempts at cataloging American nature and frequent responses to its pristine beauty. These remain interesting in their own right and often presage a great deal. Early travelers to the New World and some colonists had the incomparable fortune to see America in its aboriginal state. Their accounts, naive and sometimes relatively innocent of scientific knowledge, and even, at times, looking over the shoulder of the country toward some other goal, have the undeniable strength of priority.

The earliest visitors to North America, by and large, were preoccupied with gold seeking, market seeking, European power politics, or simply survival, but they often made interesting observations, some of which have proved useful to later ecological historians. Giovanni da Verrazzano's description of Rhode Island in 1524, for example, mentions "champaigns [meadows] twenty-five to thirty leagues [seventy-five to ninety miles] in extent . . . without any . . . trees," and this has helped to challenge the image of the tangled eastern forest.[1] Even explorers who were caught up in more pressing concerns made appreciative remarks. Christopher Columbus, for example, wrote in his journal for October 15, 1492, "These islands are very green and fertile and the breezes are very soft, and it is possible that there are in them many things, of which I do not know, because I did not wish to delay in finding gold, by discovering and going about many islands." Six days later the commander wrote wistfully, "The singing of little birds is such that it seems that a man could never wish to leave this place."[2] (Leave he did, though.)

In the sixteenth century, we have Jacques Cartier's pleased amazement at the multitudes of seabirds frequenting the islands in the Gulf of St. Lawrence (1534); Alvar Nuñez Cabeza de Vaca's rather vague account of bison, seen during his eight-year struggle to cross the Southwest (1528–1536), which was the first description of this animal to reach Europe; and Coronado's sighting of huge herds of bison in 1540, probably somewhere in modern Kansas. Often in the early accounts the authentic note of freshness is heard—for instance, the innocent vagueness in Thomas Heriot's description of the outer-banks and near-shore wildlife of North Carolina. Though Heriot was known as a man of wide learning in natural history, a scientist in his time, his report of 1585 is revealingly brief and poised at the very moment of discovery: "I have the names of eight and twenty severall sorts of beasts, which I have heard of to be here and there dispersed in the countrey, especially in the maine: of which there are only twelve kinds that we have yet discovered; and of those that be good meat we know only them before mentioned."[3]

The first extended descriptions of North American nature come out of New England in the 1630s. The two most valuable early accounts, Thomas Morton's *New English Canaan* (1637) and William Wood's *New England's Prospect* (1634), showed a lively interest in wildlife, the environment in general, and Indians. (It seemed natural for Europeans, at one time, to describe Indians under the heading of natural history.) In the case of Morton, whom we remember now for "Merrymount," the interest in wildlife seems to have been mainly gustatory. With an apparent pleasure reminiscent of the Elizabethan tone, he was sure to note in his lists of birds and animals which ones tasted best: "Teales, there are of two sorts greene winged and blew winged: but a dainty bird. I have bin much delighted with a rost of these for a second course."[4] The wild turkeys likewise pleased this gentleman's palate, being "by mainy degrees sweeter than the tame Turkies of England, feede them how you can."[5] The word "commodity" appears regularly in Morton's account (it seems to have been the seventeenth-century equivalent of our term "resources"), but he also took an aesthetic satisfaction in much of what he saw. Sparrow hawks (kestrels), for example, were beautiful to him, "the fairest, and best, shaped birds that I have ever beheld of that kinde."[6]

William Wood was much more thorough than Morton, perhaps because he was not inclined to notice the Puritans, much less to castigate them for page after page, as Morton did. The focus in Wood's *Prospect* falls much more steadily on the natural world. There are apt and reliable descriptions in this book. Henry David Thoreau, reading Wood's account in 1855, liked it for its gusto and wrote that Wood was "not to be caught napping by the wonders of Nature in a new country."[7] Wood wrote a clear, concrete prose that supports his claim of purely "experimentall" (experience-derived) description. He declared that the aim of his stay in New England (from 1629 to 1633) had been observation pure and simple, which is certainly unusual, if not unique, among the first waves of Europeans coming to these shores. His description of a flight of passenger pigeons, one of the earliest on record, is a good example of Wood's engaging and image-filled style: "I have seen them fly as if the airy regiment had been pigeons, seeing neither beginning nor ending, length or breadth of these millions of millions."[8] His natural history catalog, as might be expected and forgiven, is incomplete—he lists only two species of owl, for instance, apparently the screech owl and the great horned owl—but his obvious feeling for animals and his care in describing them mark him as having something of the poetic-scientific temperament of many later, more accomplished nature writers. He notes the migration of birds and the hibernation of snakes with accuracy, something that not every observer of his time was able to do. He does say that wolves have no joints in their bodies, an odd blunder that Thoreau later noted, and worse, he falls into the ancient and common error of supposing predation by wolves to be an unmitigated evil for nature—"the greatest inconveniency the country hath."[9] It is less easy to fault Wood for this particular opinion if we remember that it was well into the twentieth century before a better understanding of predation, and particularly predation by wolves, became widespread.

What develops out of such early accounts as Morton's and Wood's is a valuable picture of New England before European activity had drastically modified it. As William Cronon has shown in his ecological history of New England, *Changes in The Land* (1983), a remarkable diversity in vegetation patterns flourished at the beginning of the settlement period, with much open meadowland, particularly in the southern portions of the region. There was a great deal of "edge," the fruitful zone where different types of natural communities meet. Edges have more niches, and this is why New England's "mosaic of tree stands with widely varying compositions,"[10] in Cronon's words, supported a superlative abundance of wildlife. As Cronon also points out, the diversity was in part created and maintained by the Indians' biannual undergrowth burnings, so that over large areas of New England, the image of the "forest primeval" as a dark tangle had little basis in fact. It was to a degree a managed landscape, but the nature of the management was subtle enough, or (more likely) different enough from patterns the Europeans were accustomed to, that most of the settlers perceived the country as unmanaged, that is, as a wilderness. This image had a practical effect, helping to justify the expropriation of land and conversion of it to European patterns of ownership and use. The result of settlement, overall, was a simplification of plant and animal communities. The fur trade, lumbering, road building, and especially grazing and plowing had a major impact on ecosystems. Overgrazing became a problem even in Governor William Bradford's time, in the first generation of colonists; so rapid was the transformation of the land and the accompanying decimation of wildlife that as early as 1718, Massachusetts was forced to declare a three-year moratorium on deer hunting.[11]

One of the earliest observers to note the importation of new species (weeds, specifically) and the decline in native wildlife was John Josselyn, who made two extended trips to New England, the first in 1638 and the second in 1663. Josselyn has been described as "the first Englishman to write of the New England flora with any degree of scientific interest."[12] His *New England's Rarities Discovered* (1672) includes as one of its major divisions of the flora "such plants as have sprung up since the English planted and kept cattle in New England,"[13] and describes under the heading twenty-two weeds. Two years later, in his second book, *An Account of Two Voyages to New-England, Made During the Years 1638, 1663* (1674), he points out that the first cattle in New England had been brought to New Plymouth in 1624, some fourteen years before his own first arrival, so his weed list must have involved a certain amount of reconstruction and inference on his part, as well as a historian's motivation. Indeed, he appears to have been quite conscious of his role as a recorder of momentous things, for a chronology that he appends to *Two Voyages* runs from 265 B.C. to 1674! Apparently no great friend of the Puritan rule of Massachusetts,[14] and thus no apologist for the changes that were befalling the country, Josselyn was forthright in noting the precipitous decline of turkeys, once one of the distinctively abundant birds of the Bay Colony area. In *Rarities*, after describing how he had once seen "three-score broods of young turkies on the side of a marsh, sunning of themselves in a morning betimes," he quickly adds, "but this was thirty years since; the English and the Indians having now destroyed the breed, so that 'tis very rare to meet with a wild turkie in the woods."[15] (Josselyn makes no further remark on the subject of Indian complicity, but other evidence shows that the Indians were rather quickly absorbed into the European style of resource extraction and contributed to the decline of wildlife as their dependence on the new economy of the land deepened.[16])

Besides making an early statement of loss, Josselyn's writings anticipate other aspects of later nature literature. He wrote in a rather quirky, jumpy manner, never staying with an idea long enough to develop it into a finished essay, but he did venture both nature-experience narratives and philosophical commentaries based on natural history. In *Two Voyages*, he describes tracking and shooting at a wolf that had taken one of his brother's goats on a farm in the "Province of Main," and he also presents a lively account of an Indian moose hunt, presumably in the same region. When the hunters have run down and lanced the moose, "the poor Creature groans, and walks on heavily, for a space, then sinks and falls down like a ruined building."[17] Upon certain other occasions in *Two Voyages*, Josselyn departs from narrative to make interpretive comments on the ways of nature. One of these is a capsule statement of the Argument from Design, but one attributing more to the Design than mere mechanical ingenuity. Josselyn's Design has heart. "There are certain transcendentia in every Creature, which are the indelible Characters of God, and which discover God. . . ."[18] Shortly after this apparent ascription of soul to animals, Josselyn makes what is probably the first interpretive ecological statement in American literature. Describing the moose, he suddenly inserts an italicized passage:

> *Some particular living Creatures cannot live in every particular place or region, especially with the same joy or felicity as it did where it was first bred, for the certain agreement of nature that is between the place and the*

thing bred in that place: As appeareth by Elephants, *which being trans-*
lated and brought out of the Second or Third Climate, though they may
live, yet will they never ingender or bring forth young. So for plants,
Birds, &c.[19]

This wide-ranging author also appreciated Indians rather unbiasedly.
"I have seen half a hundred of their *Wigwams* together in a piece of
ground and they shew prettily. . . ."[20]

What we see in Josselyn's interesting work is many of the materials
of the American nature essay assembling loosely, in effect, ahead of their
time. Those materials would begin to jell as parts of a recognized view
of the world, and as a literary possibility, about a century after Josselyn.
In that period, both in Europe and America, there grew up widespread
acceptance of the idea that studying nature in detail, even as a life work,
and caring deeply for animals and plants, were appropriate things for a
member of Christian society to do. A movement toward such a new attitude began to be evident in England in the seventeenth century, and
gained momentum in the early decades of the eighteenth, partly as a result of the immensely popular work of John Ray, who was both a clergy-
man and a naturalist. Ray's major work, *The Wisdom of God Manifested
in the Works of the Creation* (1691), summarized the Argument from
Design with authority. Just as significantly, it drew from the Design a
major inference, the disenthronement of humanity from its accustomed, self-described position as the centerpiece of creation. Ray was
quite clear on this point:

> It is a generally received Opinion, that all this visible World was created
> for Man; that Man is the End of the Creation; as if there were no other
> End of any Creature, but some way or other to be serviceable to Man.
>   . . . But tho' this be vulgarly receiv'd, yet wise Men now-a-days
> think otherwise.
>   . . . For my part, I cannot believe that all Things in the World were
> so made for Man, that they have no other Use.[21]

In this nonutilitarian view of nature, which grants spiritual standing to the "Things in the World," we see what one scholar of Ray's period calls the beginnings of the "modern sensibility."[22] The effect of the new doctrine was to give a great push forward to natural history. In America, John Banister and John Lawson, two British colonists in Virginia and Carolina, respectively, indicated some of the scope of the new thinking, and the general interest in nature now in the air, by their plans to write comprehensive natural histories of their areas. Both men made important botanical collections, and Lawson actually completed a valuable book, *A New Voyage to Carolina* (1709), deriving from a 550-mile, two-month surveying trip into the interior of the colony. But both men were killed in the wilderness, Banister in a hunting accident in 1692 and Lawson by Indians in 1712, before bringing their natural history ambitions to fruition. Drawing upon his 1700–1701 winter expedition into the backcountry, Lawson had infused the "Natural History of Carolina" section of *A New Voyage* with vivid details and personal responses to sights and sounds, giving indication that, had he lived, he might have written truly significant nature literature. His writing shows not only a ready responsiveness to the scenes before him but also a certain flair, a recognition of some of the responsibilities of authorship to tell a story and present information in unified fashion. *A New Voyage* has some shape to it, in short, which was lacking in Josselyn's work, for instance. Banister, who first came to Virginia in 1678 and who was probably, as his modern editors write, "America's first resident naturalist"[23] (or at least university-trained naturalist), also had a sharp eye. His drawings of plants are detailed and lifelike and could only have been produced by someone passionately interested in what was before him. His writing, as Joseph Kastner notes in *A Species of Eternity* (1977), was bright with the delight he took in nature.[24]

The first attempt at a comprehensive natural history of the colonies to reach something like its hoped-for completeness was that of another Englishman, Mark Catesby. Catesby invested his life work, *The Natural*

History of Carolina, Florida, and the Bahama Islands (two volumes, 1731–1743), with enough detail (some of it borrowed from Lawson, to be sure) and artistic skill that it lasted as an authority on its subject for close to a century. Supported by a modest inheritance from his father's estate, Catesby was able to make two extended visits to America, the first from 1712 to 1719 and apparently consisting mainly of leisurely stays at plantations in the South (including William Byrd's Westover in Virginia), and the second from 1722 to 1726, when he got down to the serious business of compiling a full-scale natural history. Although he did not, apparently, have university training,[25] he seems to have been acquainted with John Ray and, perhaps through Ray's influence, to have been fired with a profound interest in the natural world. He dedicated his life to producing as complete a natural history of the Southeast as he could and even taught himself engraving, so that his illustrations might reflect as accurately as possible what he had observed.

During his second stay in America, Catesby undertook long journeys on foot, collecting, taking extensive notes, and making drawings. Many of these drawings were from live specimens, a practice that, in the case of birds in particular, sets Catesby apart from the great majority of subsequent students and artists. After four intensive years he returned to England and began his book. He would put very nearly the rest of his life into it: the first volume, devoted to birds, was published in 1731; the second, covering fish, snakes, and plants, in 1743; and an appendix was completed in 1747, two years before the author's death.

The stature of the work derives from its attempted exhaustiveness, its impressive detail and accuracy in many of the descriptions, and its 220 evocative plates. Catesby listed 113 species of birds, and his documentation of these was authoritative enough for so careful a student as Thomas Jefferson, whose own list of birds in *Notes on the State of Virginia* (1785) was basically Catesby's plus 33 of his own observation.[26] Catesby also tried to cover all of the snakes in authoritative fashion: "Of serpents, very few, I believe, have escaped me, for upon showing my designs of them to several of the most intelligent persons, many of them confessed that they had not seen them all, and none of them pretended to have seen any other kinds."[27] (One could hardly ask for a comment more revealing of this naturalist's pioneering position.)

Besides listing and describing species, Catesby also attempted a broad-gauge ecological overview by dividing Carolina into four main zones, each denoted by a dominant vegetation type: rice country, oak and hickory country, pine barrens, and scrub oak land. This is one of the earliest attempts to describe an ecotype by means of key species. Catesby's *Natural History* also makes a good guess, for its time, about bird migration: "The Place to which they retire is probably in the same Latitude of the southern Hemisphere, or where they may enjoy the like Temperature of Air, as in the Country from whence they came. . . ."[28]

Catesby could be fooled, as in his account of the "Hog-nose Snake," which he believed to be "of the venomous Tribe,"[29] and some of his plates and descriptions are not very precise (his "Little Thrush," for example, could be any one of several species in the thrush family), but on the whole his care shines through. He is not an essayist in the Montaigne-Bacon-Addison tradition—that is, he does not develop formed essays from a distinctive personal point of view—but many of his descriptions, if not literary in the traditional sense, are vivid and do suggest the experience of nature. The "Regulus Cristatus" (ruby-crowned kinglet), he wrote, can often be found with other winter species "ranging the woods together, from tree to tree, as if they were all of one brood, running up and down the bark of lofty oaks, from the crevices of which they collect their food, which are Insects lodged in their Winter-dormitories, in a torpid state."[30]

In the end, probably, it will be Catesby's art that ensures his being remembered. His rendering of the blue jay, to take an example of particular excellence, will stand well beside any subsequent representations of that bird. The vivacity and activity captured in that engraving show clearly that at this point in the mid-eighteenth century, it was possible to look very closely at even "useless" wildlife and to see there the material of art.

The first European thoroughly trained in Enlightenment science to come to America was the Swede Peter Kalm, who had been a student of Linnaeus at the University of Uppsala. Kalm arrived in the colonies in the fall of 1748, sent by the Swedish Royal Academy to look for useful plants that might do well in the cold climate of Sweden. From his home base at the Swedish settlement of Raccoon (now Swedesboro, New Jersey), Kalm traveled for two and a half years in the middle Atlantic region and made journeys as far north as Lake Champlain and Canada and as far west as Niagara Falls, all the while keeping a remarkably detailed journal. This record, *Travels in North America* (first published in English in 1770), is a kind of early, undeveloped "de Tocqueville" on American habits and offers a great deal of useful commentary on the state of the American environment in the mid-eighteenth century. It is a travel journal and thus inevitably fragmentary, but it contains three of what would become standard themes in later and more finished American nature writing: the decline of abundance caused by carelessness and greed; the agrarian dream of life in a decentralized, rural situation; and the adventure to the edges of the wilderness—the sublime.

Kalm's training in descriptive science appears to have helped make him a judicious observer and interviewer. His account of the depreciation of the American environment was necessarily secondhand. "All the old Swedes and Englishmen born in America whom I ever questioned asserted that there were not nearly so many edible birds at present as there used to be when they were children, and that their decrease was visible. They even said that they had heard the same complaint from their fathers...."[31] But he followed up this sort of report with personal observations. Writing of the Philadelphia area, he stated that "people are here (and in many other places) in regard to wood, bent only upon their own present advantage, utterly regardless of posterity. By these means many swamps are already quite destitute of cedars...."[32] Cedars were being used for shingles in the growing city of Philadelphia, but no attempt was being made to plant replacement trees. The same sort of disregard for the future appeared in the exploitation of wildlife and aroused Kalm to one of his strongest comments on America. He wrote of the yearly assault on vulnerable waterfowl, "In spring the people still steal eggs, mothers and young indifferently, because no regulations are made to the contrary. And if any had been made, the spirit of freedom which prevails in the country would not suffer them to be obeyed."[33]

Kalm was attracted, however, to the agrarian life led by most Americans at this time. He criticized careless farming practices, particularly the widespread habit of letting livestock run loose over the land, but some of his accounts of the yeoman-farmer existence suggest a kind of paradise:

> As we went on in the forest we continually saw at moderate distances little fields which had been cleared of the wood. Each one of these was a farm. These farms were commonly very pretty, and a walk of trees frequently led from them to the highroad. The houses were all built of brick or of the stone which is found here everywhere. Every countryman, even the poorest peasant, had an orchard with apples, peaches, chestnuts, walnuts, cherries, quinces and such fruits, and sometimes we saw vines climbing in them. The valleys were frequently blessed with little brooks of crystal-clear water.[34]

At Niagara Falls, Kalm's placid prose took on some new life: "It is enough to make the hair stand on end of any observer who may be sitting or standing close by, and who attentively watches such a large amount of water falling vertically over a ledge from such a height. The effect is awful, tremendous!"[35] In the manner of the writer of adventures, Kalm dramatized his feelings by introducing into the narrative some "Indian lads" who "walked right out to the very edge of the cataract . . . and looked down. . . . I was chilled inside, when I saw it, and called to them; but they only smiled, and still stood a while on the outermost brink."[36] This depiction of Niagara is one of the early descriptions of American nature in the vein of the "sublime," an aesthetic category that would, in later times, elevate the literary respectability of wilderness considerably.

The first literarily coherent American works based in some significant portion on nature experience or natural history were Hector St. John de Crèvecoeur's *Letters from an American Farmer,* published in London in 1782, and Thomas Jefferson's *Notes on the State of Virginia,* published in Paris in 1785. Crèvecoeur's *Letters* is the more consciously literary of the two. The ideas in *Letters,* and in Crèvecoeur's *Sketches of Eighteenth Century America* (essays that were not published together until 1925 but were all written between 1770 and 1778), flow from the distinctive personality and responses of the narrator-participant. Crèvecoeur's sympathetic temperament and his very good eye for the telling detail give his work an identifiable tone, a literary personality. The very first paragraph of "A Snow Storm as It Affects the American Farmer," an essay that the author translated into French and included in the 1784 Paris edition, *Lettres d'un Cultivateur Americain,* evinces a command of theme and a strong emotional presence.

> No man of the least degree of sensibility can journey through any number of years in whatever climate without often being compelled to make many useful observations on the different phenomena of Nature which surround him; and without involuntarily being struck either with awe or admiration in beholding some of the elementary conflicts in the midst of which he lives. A great thunderstorm; an extensive flood; a desolating hurricane; a sudden and intense frost; an overwhelming snow-storm; a sultry day—each of these different scenes exhibits singular beauties even in spite of the damage they cause. Often whilst the heart laments the loss to the citizen, the enlightened mind, seeking for the natural causes, and astonished at the effects, awakes itself to surprise and wonder.[37]

Crèvecoeur then narrates a snowstorm, such as undoubtedly he experienced at Pine Hill, his farm in Orange County, New York, sometime during his happy tenure there from 1769 to 1778. "The wind, which is a great regulator of the weather, shifts to the northeast; the air becomes bleak and then intensely cold; the light of the sun becomes dimmed as if an eclipse had happened; a general night seems coming on."[38] As the storm develops, Crèvecoeur describes in detail the preparations the careful farmer has made and narrates the farm family's activity within the snug safety of their home. The American agrarian point of view is explicit: "Finally they go to bed, not to that bed of slavery or sorrow as is the case in Europe with people of their class, but on the substantial collection of honest feathers picked and provided by the industrious wife."[39]

D. H. Lawrence may have had just such a sentimental passage in mind when he termed Crèvecoeur the emotional prototype of the American,[40] but it is not true that the American farmer was entirely swept up in agrarian dreaming. In "Reflections on the Manners of the Americans," another essay he translated into French for the 1784 *Lettres,* Crèvecoeur gave very particular details on the financial process of acquiring a farm (farms did not simply materialize as part of the boon of all Americans; by Crèvecoeur's time most of the good land on the eastern seaboard was in fact owned by someone), and he went further to show that economic realities may shape a farmer into something quite unlike the honest yeoman of agrarian mythology. He wrote that the farmer may become shrewd, litigious, even deceitful. "Fearful of fraud in all his dealings and transactions, he arms himself, therefore, with it. Strict integrity is not much wanted. . . ."[41] As further evidence of Crèvecoeur's realistic streak, he criticized the deforestation that could accompany the establishment of an agrarian society. In "Thoughts of an American Farmer on Various Rural Subjects," Crèvecoeur anticipated the work of George Perkins Marsh (author of *Man and Nature,* 1864) and other critics of watershed abuse:

> I could show you in this county the ruins of eleven grist-mills which
> twenty years ago had plenty of water, but now stand on the dry ground,

with no other marks of running water about them than the ancient bed of the creek, on the shores of which they had been erected. This effect does not surprise me. Our ancient woods kept the earth moist and damp, and the sun could evaporate none of the waters contained within their shades. Who knows how far these effects may extend?[42]

This last sentence is a somber echo to Crèvecoeur's upbeat (and better-known) rhetorical question, "Who can tell how far it [North America] extends?" in the much-anthologized essay, "What Is an American?" This farmer, like the great majority of agrarian essayists to come after him, was well aware of the changes abroad in the land. Crèvecoeur also paid close attention to the birds, wasps, bees, and other less obviously utile inhabitants of his farm. He did more than pay attention—he delighted in them and viewed them as coinhabitants. In "On Snakes; And on the Humming Bird," one of his *Letters from an American Farmer,* he praised the ruby-throated hummingbird:

> On this little bird nature has profusely lavished her most splendid colors.... The richest pallet of the most luxuriant painter, could never invent any thing to be compared to the variegated tints, with which this insect bird is arrayed.... When fatigued, it has often perched within a few feet of me, and on such favourable opportunities I have surveyed it with the most minute attention. Its little eyes appear like diamonds, reflecting light on every side: most elegantly finished in all parts it is a miniature work of our great parent; who seems to have formed it the smallest, and at the same time the most beautiful of the winged species.[43]

Thomas Jefferson's *Notes on the State of Virginia* is noteworthy for its demonstration of the importance of nature to the just-forming American national identity. It catalogs various life forms, much in the fashion of earlier lists, and at one point makes use of dramatic personal narrative to convey the awesomeness of a local geological formation (the Virginia Natural Bridge), both techniques integral to much nature writing. But perhaps the American identity of *Notes* is most clearly manifested in its author's attack on a curious idea promoted by the French encyclopedist George Louis Leclerc, Comte de Buffon, that New World animals were smaller, weaker, degenerate versions of similar European species. This supposition had been put forth in Buffon's monumental *Histoire Naturelle, Générale, et Particuliere* (1749–1788), where it was presented as simple truth. Using logic, citation of his own observations, and scholarly references to Catesby, Kalm, and the work of his Pennsylvania friend John Bartram (who was America's first native-born naturalist of stature), Jefferson proceeded to demolish the mythical comparison, proving that American animals were actually quite robust. He also defended the American Indian against Buffon's assertion that "the savage is feeble, and has small organs of generation ... and no ardor whatever for his female" by merely adding, "An afflicting picture indeed, which, for the honor of human nature, I am glad to believe has no original."[44]

John Bartram, a friend also of Crèvecoeur, was a farmer whose land lay on the west bank of the Schuylkill River just a few miles from Philadelphia. Besides running a farm, he was a far-journeying collector of plants for his English sponsor, the London cloth merchant Peter Collinson, and a self-taught naturalist of real stature. Linnaeus himself described Bartram as "the greatest natural botanist in the world."[45] Crèvecoeur, who praised him in *Letters from an American Farmer,* saw the Pennsylvanian as proof of the goodness of the simple life—close to nature and at the same time rational. Beginning as a plant collector in 1734 at the age of thirty-five, in four decades Bartram increased the European catalog of New World plants by some 150 species, and in the process came to know in person or by correspondence most of the world's leading naturalists. He was not a writer, either by intention or accomplishment, but he did leave succinct journal accounts of some of his wilderness travels, in which a modern reader can learn, for example, that there were wolves in Florida in 1766 or that the Catskill Mountains held a remarkable diversity of rare trees and shrubs. Bartram's journals and letters also demonstrate the eighteenth-century opening of thought. His experience in nature convinced him that sentience was not limited to human beings. "I also am of the opinion that the creatures commonly called brutes possess higher qualifications, and more exalted ideas, than our traditional mystery-mongers are willing to allow them," he wrote.[46] He saw the hand of God in the natural world, a common enough view in his time, but when his deistic leanings brought him to deny the divinity of Jesus, he let his ideas be known, and there was a falling-out with his Quaker meeting. A man who during the course of his life had built four stone houses, provided for a large family, taught himself the new natural science, and traveled thousands of wilderness miles in search of plants, Bartram was unaffected by the meeting's show of disapproval and continued on his own, independent way.

One of John Bartram's sons, William, grew up practically at the center of the American Enlightenment and enjoyed some second-generation advantages. In contrast to his father, "Billy" had a very good education; he showed artistic inclinations quite early, as well as ability in natural history, and was encouraged in these areas. He accompanied his father on a collecting trip to the wild Catskills in 1753, at the age of fourteen, and was apparently introduced there to what became, the evidence seems to show, the supreme pleasure of his life: a kind of wandering botanizing, done in an exploratory, discovering, goalless frame of mind, so that the forest world, as he walked slowly through it, became a garden of delight and revelation. New plants, unusually large trees, the manner in which sandhill cranes take off and gain altitude, the elegance of fish seen swimming in clear springs, just about everything that he came upon in his life of travels except alligators and thunderstorms (and these moved him to awe, another sort of delight) touched William Bartram's aesthetic sense and brought him joy. His praise for others was framed in terms of their sensibility, to use his word, and it is clear that his own was high and refined. As a teenager he was apprenticed to a Philadelphia merchant, and he later tried business on his own, setting up a store at Cape Fear on the Carolina coast. But he did not take to business, and his ventures failed.

By the middle 1760s he was at loose enough ends that he could accompany his father on another botanizing trip, this one to Florida. He was again immersed in the beautiful wilderness and, it is fair to suppose, confirmed in his fundamental desires. In 1772, he received the sponsorship of a British physician and amateur botanist, John Fothergill. One year later, bolstered by a salary of fifty pounds per year, he went back over the river routes through Florida that he and his father had taken in the previous decade and then pressed on into new country farther inland. He spent the better part of the years 1773 through 1777 happily rambling through the backcountry of the Southeast on a loose itinerary that may be surmised in passages like the following from his record of the trip: "On my return to the store on St. Juan's the trading schooner was there, but as she was not to return to Georgia until the autumn, I found I had time to pursue my travels in Florida, and might at leisure plan my excursions to collect seeds and roots in boxes, &c."[47]

Bartram's account of these four blithe years, published in 1791 under the title *Travels Through North and South Carolina, Georgia, East and West Florida, the Cherokee Country, the Extensive Territories of the Muscogulges, or Creek Confederacy, and the Country of the Choctaws*, and for good reason known usually as Bartram's *Travels*, is rambling, diverse, florid, oddly put together in places, sketchy on dates and distances traveled, clogged in places with long lists of Latin names of plants, and probably more than a little repetitive. But it is also the first fully developed nature essay in this country; it is a brilliant evocation of a mind and vision and of the land that inspired them. Perhaps the greatest single impression is of the author's receptivity and the fluid ease with which his mind followed the hints that nature provided. At one point in his journeying along the east coast of Florida, Bartram had gone out to botanize. While he was admiring some agaves and myrtles, he found his attention attracted to some butterflies, then suddenly to a large spider in the process of stalking a bumblebee. He described the spider in detail, drawing himself into the drama by noting that the predator kept an eye on him while conducting the attack. The scene is vivid and reinforces the author's theme at this point in the narrative, which is that the animal creation "offers manifest examples of premeditation, perseverance, resolution, and consummate artifice," a theme that further illustrates the overall idea of the continuity of humanity and other forms of life. Bartram's ready impressionability to whatever he happened upon, and his mind's quickness to recognize not only relationships but also the possibility that he himself might be included in them in some fashion, create his ecological style. He saw a grand, systematic patterning, all revealing the "Almighty hand," so that whatever a person of sensibility and training looked well upon became meaningful. Simply walking through the woods or catching an unexpected view of the ocean could evoke from this sensitive man a spiritual excitement. "O thou Creator supreme, almighty! how infinite and incomprehensible thy works! most perfect, and every way astonishing!"[48]

Inevitably, both as a man of the Enlightenment who at home had doubtless heard many philosophical discussions and as one who had, on his own travels, many times crossed the meaningful border between civilization and the wilderness, Bartram reflected upon human nature and human society. Describing a camp in the wilderness of backcountry Georgia, where he had ventured with a few companions, he wrote, "How supremely blessed were our hours at this time! Plenty of delicious and healthful food, our stomachs keen, with contented minds; under no control, but what reason and ordinate passions dictated, far removed from the seats of strife."[49] He continued interpretively, "Our situation was like that of the primitive state of man, peaceable, contented, and sociable. The simple and necessary calls of nature being satisfied, we were altogether as brethren of one family, strangers to envy, malice, and rapine."[50] That Bartram was not a primitivist, however, is shown by his admiration for well-kept plantations and his musing, at times, upon the possible commercial advantages a particularly fruitful site, still in a wild state, might someday have. It was 1791, after all, and the horse-drawn nation's first census had just counted fewer than four million inhabitants. It would be another forty-odd years before there came a serious call for the preservation of large areas of American wilderness—a call embodying the suspicion, perhaps, that progress might in truth be insatiable.

Just three years after Bartram's *Travels* appeared, the Reverend Samuel Williams of Rutland, Vermont, published a most interesting survey of his state, *The Natural and Civil History of Vermont* (1794). Unlike Bartram's book, this book was not framed on personal experience, but on statistics and observations of a more dispassionate nature. Williams, a man of wide interests who had for eight years lectured at Harvard on mathematics and astronomy, was conscious that Vermont in his time was "rapidly changing from a vast tract of uncultivated wilderness, to numerous and extensive settlements."[51] Perhaps moved by this awareness, he recorded facts such as that there was still a good Atlantic salmon run in the Connecticut River, all the way to its highest branches; that there were still cougars in Vermont; and that the "most aged" white pine tree in the state was between 350 and 400 years old, with a diameter of 6 feet and a height of 247 feet.[52] *The Natural and Civil History of Vermont* used a straightforward encyclopedic style to describe exactly where the state stood, in space as well as in time. Williams's organization would today be called bioregional: the first six chapters are "Situation," "Mountains," "Rivers and Lakes," "Climate," "Vegetable Productions," and "Native Animals." Only then are the Indians discussed, and finally the white man's political history. Williams's promotion of a wider ethical outlook toward animals was also modern. While he described wolves as "noxious" (in common with most writers of his time and much later), he nevertheless criticized certain other manifestations of anthropocentric arrogance:

> To the tribes of reptiles and insects, we have affixed the idea of something, unpleasant, diminutive, or odious. The designs, the wisdom, and

the power of the Creator, are not to be estimated by such feelings, fears, and prejudices.[53]

Just why wolves were excluded from the Creator's wise planning, Williams did not say. Here indeed was a species that provided a difficult final examination in ecological consciousness, not just for Williams but for many American naturalists down to very recent times.

Williams's book presented Vermont in transition, virginity gone. For a glimpse of the pristine, a modern reader can do no better than to consult the journals of the Lewis and Clark expedition, written a little more than a decade after the Vermont history. The record of the outward trek in particular is impressive in its evocation of the immensity and quiet of the country and the spectacular abundance of wildlife. The High Plains region was perhaps the most vast wilderness of all; going westward from the Mandan villages in 1805, the expedition's members did not see even a single Indian for some four months. Meriwether Lewis, perhaps more than the rest, seemed to respond to the utter wildness:

> The whole face of the country was covered with herds of Buffaloe, Elk & Antelopes; deer are also abundant, but keep themselves more concealed in the woodland. The buffaloe Elk and Antelope are so gentle that we pass near them while feeding, without appearing to excite any alarm among them; and when we attract their attention, they frequently approach us more nearly to discover what we are, and in some instances pursue us a considerable distance apparently with that view.[54]

Lewis frequently went off by himself to contemplate long views, and he wrote quite often of the romantic appearance, to use his phrase, of scenes like the "Missouri Breaks." He had projected a three-volume history of the expedition in 1807, just a year after the company's return; the third volume would deal with natural history.[55] In this third volume, we might have seen Meriwether Lewis emerge as a significant American nature writer. Few men, literally, had seen more of the country, and there is no doubting his sensitivity to it, nor his natural history knowledge. But Lewis died in 1809 under mysterious circumstances; the journals of the expedition remain just that, in the literary sense—they were never shaped into the history Lewis had envisioned. Even so, they evoke the untamed dimension of the American wilderness as nothing else can. They give a sense of the original, by which all that followed can be measured.

William Bartram was invited to accompany Lewis and Clark but declined on account of his age. From 1777 until his death forty-six years later, Bartram lived quietly in Philadelphia. His travels were confined mainly within the eight-acre botanical garden his father had established (the first such garden in North America, apparently). He kept records of bird migration, helped care for the garden, wrote his great book, maintained close contact with the American scientific community (which at that time was centered in Philadelphia, where both the American Philosophical Society and the Academy of Natural Sciences had their headquarters), and in the first decades of the nineteenth century found himself becoming a mentor to a new generation of naturalists. He was particularly helpful to two young immigrants who came to the garden, one from Scotland and one from England, both of whom became giants in American natural history. Alexander Wilson and Thomas Nuttall revered Bartram for his knowledge and generous spirit. Wilson, who had met the older naturalist in 1802, lived at the Bartram garden for a time. Nuttall, who first visited Bartram within weeks of his arrival in this country in 1808, also had a room reserved for him at Bartram's. Both Wilson and Nuttall profited greatly from Bartram's fund of knowledge won from the field, and from his position as elder statesman of natural history, for through him they were able to make contacts crucial to their own enterprises.

Wilson's is one of the most compelling stories from the early period of American nature study—a time not lacking in interesting characters. Born in Scotland in 1766, he had been "put" to a weaver as a bound apprentice in 1779, had achieved journeyman weaver status, and had eventually become a peddler, going on foot from village to village in the Scottish countryside, carrying a large pack of cloth goods. His journals and letters from these early days indicate a sensitive, aspiring man who suffered periods of despondency. Inspired by his countryman Robert Burns, Wilson wrote poetry, some of it quite good (in fact, one of his efforts, published anonymously, was widely believed to have been written by Burns), and when he had enough poems for a volume he peddled subscriptions to his book right along with his cloth. In 1794, after being accused of libel and spending some time in jail for writing a radical poem in which he had satirized a local capitalist, Wilson emigrated to the United States, where he supported himself at first by weaving and later by teaching school. At some point during his first years in this country he became deeply interested in the birds of his adopted land, and after he met Bartram the interest became a passion. Within a year of their meeting he had declared, "I AM NOW ABOUT TO MAKE A COLLECTION OF ALL OUR FINEST BIRDS."[56]

Over the remaining ten years of Wilson's life, this collection would become *American Ornithology; or, the Natural History of the Birds of the United States* (published 1808–1814, in nine volumes), the first comprehensive description of American birds and thus a monument in science, and a book whose clear, precise prose and heartfelt enthusiasm make it a significant work in the literature of nature. To gather data for the descriptions, and to secure the birds themselves for his paintings, which illustrated the text, and finally to sell subscriptions for the work, Wilson traveled some fifteen thousand miles in America, most of it on foot. He drew from life, he said, and furthermore scorned those he called "closet-naturalists and sedentary travellers."[57] ("Closet" as a term of utter derision turns up again and again in the writings of the early American field naturalists.) Almost entirely self-taught both in science and art (though he must have benefited from Bartram in both areas), Wilson seemed undaunted by the magnitude of his undertaking and saw eight volumes through the press before his death from dysentery in 1813. The ninth and final volume was published the next year.

Wilson's love of fieldwork, together with his poet's eye for the focal image, helped give his writing concreteness and a dramatic sense of behavior in context. Even the expository, nonnarrative accounts of species—for example, Wilson's description of the ivory-billed woodpecker—are likely to convey the energy he felt in nature. The miles and years in the woods came most obviously to bear in narrative vignettes of behavior, as in this meeting with a nesting yellow-billed cuckoo:

> While the female is sitting the male is generally not far distant, and gives the alarm by his notes, when any person is approaching. The female sits so close that you may almost reach her with your hand, and then precipitates herself to the ground, feigning lameness to draw you away from the spot, fluttering, trailing her wings, and tumbling over, in the manner of the Partridge, Woodcock, and many other species.[58]

Wilson's efforts toward an emotionally resonant yet empirically accurate prose, a style that would in effect poeticize science, represent an improved synthesis over Bartram's style. Wilson's writing is an improvement over that of every American naturalist who had gone before him on this central point of the linking of science and art, with full expression of both dimensions. Where Catesby had written of his "Little Thrush" that "it never sings, having only a single note,"[59] Wilson made a very considerable advance by describing several species of the thrush family, carefully noting their various songs and calls, and then, in the descriptions of the birds' typical habitats, giving a strong sense of the ambience of these places through poetically charged images and emotional responses of his own. He seemed to realize that he was engaged in a great leap beyond what had gone before, and not only in literary and scientific terms; this would be the first national bird book as well. Wilson worked hard to find travelers' accounts so that his range of descriptions would be complete. He cited Meriwether Lewis, whom he knew, Zebulon Pike, and others, looking always for the authentic field person's word. There seemed to be almost the joy of possession in his search, a looking with high expectancy to all the far reaches of the land. He came to know his adopted country, and in the end, his ten-year book amounted to a hymn of love to American nature. It should be regarded as an important American document.

Thomas Nuttall, who also enjoyed the mentorship of William Bartram, had an aesthetic sense for natural history much resembling Wilson's, as well as a similar dedication, but in the course of a long career he was able to amass far greater scientific knowledge. Indeed, he may have been the most knowledgeable of the all-purpose naturalists of the early period in this country. He was also a writer who conveyed more adequately than anyone before him, that is, with more scientific precision, the complexity of the relationships between species and their habitats. In its description of these tightly woven relationships, Nuttall's introduction to his *Manual of the Ornithology of the United States and Canada* (1832) is one of the important natural history essays of its time.

Nuttall came to America in 1808, specifically to study nature. Within weeks of his arrival in Philadelphia he had been hired as a field researcher for Benjamin Smith Barton, a botanist and professor at the University of Pennsylvania. With his first excursions, botanical errands for Barton into Delaware, Pennsylvania, and New York, Nuttall began one of the most energetic field careers in American science. He would spend a total of thirty-three years in this country, a surprising proportion of that time in the field. He made several extended journeys into the wilderness, often traveling solo. In 1810 he crossed the "Old Northwest," mostly on foot, and was with the Astorians at the Mandan villages in 1811. After descending the Missouri and Mississippi to New Orleans and then waiting out the War of 1812 in England, Nuttall came back to America and spent almost two years botanizing in the Southeast. From 1818 to 1820 he was out on the prairies, following the Arkansas River westward. In 1830, doing research for his *Manual of Ornithology*, he walked some twelve hundred miles in the southeastern states. In 1834, after resigning his curatorship at the Botanic Garden at Harvard (where he had also been a lecturer since 1822), he journeyed overland to the Pacific with the Cambridge entrepreneur Nathaniel Wyeth, eventually sailing on to the Sandwich Islands and then, in 1835, back to the California coast, where, thousands of miles from Massachusetts, he met up with former Harvard student Richard Henry Dana, a meeting later described in *Two Years Before the Mast*. On the way back to Boston, Nuttall wanted to be put ashore at the stormy tip of South America to botanize, but the ship's captain demurred. Finally, following the proviso of a will that kept him in England for six months of every year (he had inherited a small estate), he lived out the rest of his life rather placidly in the country of his birth, making a last visit to the United States from 1847 to 1848.[60]

Some of his remarkable life in the American outdoors found expression in Nuttall's written work. *The Genera of North American Plants* (1818), the *Manual of Ornithology* (1832), and the final two volumes of *The North American Sylva* (1841), covering western trees (the first three volumes were the work of Francois Andre Michaux), are his major contributions to science, with the latter two works having some literary interest as well. The two journals he kept of his expeditions ("travels" does not seem to be the right word in Nuttall's case), only one of which was published in his lifetime, are interesting for their presentation of the author's character, which was stoic about hardship, illness, and loneliness, and mostly ecstatic about nature. They also comment on frontier life in America with some acerbity. The daily diary of Nuttall's 1810 trip to Michilimackinac from Pennsylvania (not published until the mid-twentieth century) is not high-grade literary ore, although its understatement of the author's sufferings from malaria has a poignant quality.[61] By 1820 he had a more mature command of his materials, and the *Journal of Travels into the Arkansa Territory, During the Year*

1819 (first published in 1821) is framed more like an essay. Much of it describes intense experience, running the gamut from happy discovery to the alarm of a near-death situation, far in the wilderness. As he moved westward up the Arkansas River, Nuttall was energized by leaving behind the "umbrageous forest" and setting forth on the open prairies of the West. He delighted in the sweep of grassland and the innumerable flowers, describing the plains not as the Great American Desert, as other explorers had termed it, but a "magnificent garden."

Nuttall's enthusiasm for nature contrasted with his apparent view of the run of humanity on the edges of the wilderness. He made quick, cutting comments about "sharpers" and other frontier characters and spoke of the "mental darkness" in which he thought children of the frontier were being raised. Most of the time, however, he appears to have simply looked past society and humans, and much of the *Journal* has the true American Eden flavor—pure wilderness and no people. Apparently a shy man (he was said to have had a secret door by which he could exit his Cambridge lodgings when an unwanted visitor loomed), Nuttall was nonetheless not above cultivating a certain authorial identity in his published journal. The persona was that of an obsessively dedicated student of nature, naturally enough—an image corroborated, by the way, both by Dana in *Two Years Before the Mast* and Washington Irving in *Astoria*.

> In the meanest garb of the working boat-man, and unattended by a single slave, I was no doubt considered . . . one of the canaille [the lowest class], and I neither claimed nor expected attention; my thoughts centered upon other objects, and all pride of appearance I willingly sacrificed to promote with frugality and industry the objects of my mission.[62]

Among lesser naturalists from the early decades of the nineteenth century, the English traveler John Bradbury and the Philadelphian John Kirk Townsend wrote some interesting travel literature that occasionally suggests some of the subject matter of the nature essay. Neither Bradbury's *Travels in the Interior of America in the Years 1809, 1810, and 1811* (1817) nor Townsend's *Narrative of a Journey Across the Rocky Mountains* (1839), however, gets very close to its subjects or develops sustained reflections. These accounts lack the passion for nature that gives meaning and life to Nuttall's journals. For their picturesque depiction of scenes and as a record of the times, these journals do have some value. For example, Bradbury's account of the New Madrid earthquake of 1811, one of the strongest on this continent since it was settled by Europeans, and Townsend's picture of a "mountain-man" rendezvous, though drawn from both a literal and moral distance, are useful glimpses of history.

Both Bradbury and Townsend have been much reprinted. An unjustly neglected figure who, had he lived longer, might have contributed significantly to the emergence of the natural history essay as a literary form was Dr. John D. Godman of Philadelphia. Godman's major work, *American Natural History* (1826), is largely a catalog of American mammals, emphasizing anatomy, but it also contains some thoughtful essays on subjects like time and scientific truth. Godman's intellectual concerns and his careful style of reasoning indicate he probably would have been a capable participant in the great debates over evolution at mid-century and after. He was a devout Christian but exhibited a scientific turn of mind and was disposed to cut through fable and anthropomorphic folly. After noting that a good deal of folklore surrounds the life of bats, including a certain sinister imputation, Godman cleared the air with an ecologically sophisticated statement based on scientific observation:

> The fact . . . is, that the Bat is one of a large number of animals whose structure is adapted for activity and usefulness only when the light is feeble, and food is to be obtained. However amusing it may be in poetry or apouloge to consider such creatures as choosing night for their appearance from a desire concealment, it is by no means allowable for students of natural history to forget that all beings must live

in conformity to the laws of their organization, that the perfection of every species is relative to the situation in which it exists, and that our notions of beauty and deformity are neither true tests of the excellence nor importance of any inferior animal.[63]

Despite its emphasis on anatomy (Godman was an inveterate dissector of animals), *American Natural History* is in good part a philosophical text and may be seen as an important American continuation of the line established in England by John Ray. In Ray's view, science—the study of nature—promotes an expansion and naturalizing of our view of things, particularly our ethical sense. Writing of the wild cats and, by extension, of predators in general, Godman held:

> We must not rashly contend that these animals are an evil unattended by any utility or good. They are designed by nature to occupy regions where animal life is most likely to increase in undue proportion, and it is their province to keep this increase from becoming excessive.[64]

Godman's other book, *Rambles of a Naturalist* (1833), first appeared serially in *The Friend,* a Philadelphia weekly, in 1828, during a time when Godman was trying to support his family by writing and trying to stave off somehow the disease that was killing him. Before his death from tuberculosis, Godman finished twelve personal essays, most of them based on short walks close to home. These are not the great, Nuttallian expeditions into the far wilderness, but they have in them a similar sense of discovery; we might even say that Godman made as much, in literary terms, from an afternoon stroll as Nuttall did from a month's trekking. Godman writes, "One of my favourite walks was through Turner's-lane, near Philadelphia, which is about a quarter of a mile long, and not much wider than an ordinary street,"[65] and proceeds to describe mole tunnels, a small brook spangling in the sunshine, the dewdrops on a spider's web, and other sights he found extraordinary. To Godman, anything in nature, seen with a contemplative eye, witnessed the "beneficence of the great Creator"; the trick, then as now, is to go slowly and to look carefully. The essays in Godman's *Rambles* are some of the earliest in the durable subgenre of the short, instructive nature walk. They reveal a mind awake to beauty as well as to minute and interesting facts, and they confirm the suggestion that Godman's early death was a loss both to natural history and to literature. He had something to say.

John James Audubon, whose period of active field study and creative work spans the time of Wilson and Nuttall, is of course known for his expressive and beautiful paintings. In their artistry they represent a quantum leap in the painting of natural history subjects. Alexander Wilson, among others, had supplemented his works with paintings, but his aim was only accuracy. Although Audubon is much better known as a painter, he was also a writer, we may need to be reminded, and some of his prose is memorable. Like Wilson and Nuttall, Audubon had the passion; he was "fervently desirous of becoming acquainted with nature," as he wrote in his "Introductory Address" to the *Ornithological Biography* (1831–1839),[66] and, like the other two great students of birds, he demonstrated commitment by spending a great deal of time in the field. Audubon's bird biographies are often vivid with colors, shapes, and movements that could only be known firsthand. Not every observer, for instance, can have seen enough snipes and goshawks to make the following statement: "It [the goshawk] is extremely expert at catching Snipes on the wing, and so well do these birds know their insecurity, that, on his approach, they prefer squatting."[67]

That brief example shows Audubon at his most direct and concrete; often, it must be said, his prose became extravagantly literary:

It was the month of October. The autumnal tints already decorated the shores of that queen of rivers, the Ohio. Every tree was hung with long and flowing festoons of different species of vines, many loaded with clustered fruits of varied brilliancy, their rich bronzed carmine mingling beautifully with the yellow foliage, which now predominated over the yet green leaves, reflecting more lively tints from the clear stream than ever landscape painter portrayed or poet imagined.[68]

This facile side of Audubon is usually found in the sketches of American life, which he interspersed with the more sober and scientific bird biographies. But even in the sketches, some objects occasionally captured Audubon's attention so fully that he could write strong, undecorated prose. His account of the exploitation of guillemot eggs on the Labrador nesting grounds, for example, hits hard.

Audubon was saddened by the erosion of wilderness that he saw almost everywhere he traveled. By the 1820s, the clearing of the eastern forest had reached so far that swamps in remote areas offered him the best opportunities for wildlife observation. He appeared to share, however, the characteristic ambivalence of many American citizens about the march of progress; although he was sensitive on some environmental matters, he could also quite willingly take part in the killing of a cougar at one point in his travels, and of a wolf at another, and he could praise the owner of a beautiful spring in Florida for having turned it into a source of power for a sugarcane mill. This apparent variation in Audubon's viewpoint finds a parallel in his prose expression, which could move quickly from an egoism uncomfortable to read to some of the clearest devotion to the subject that ornithological literature affords, and from knowledgeable, focused anger to blithe superficiality. It could be argued that Audubon himself, whose personality is so prominent in the writing, gave his prose a certain unity and character, but the values expressed in that prose were not consistent enough to bring off the performance. A nature writing that would carry a strong sense of the author's mind but at the same time not seem limited by too much self-concern would have to wait for the next generation, the more contemplative generation of Henry David Thoreau.

THE AGE OF THOREAU,
MUIR, AND BURROUGHS

THE EARLY PURITANS, WITH their strongly dualistic worldview, conceived of wilderness as an evil opponent to Christian civilization. Breaking the wild nature of New England and setting up the City of God were thus inevitably and naturally accompanied by a certain righteousness. Little more than a century after settlement, however, both the self-congratulation and the linkage of wilderness with Satan seemed to have weakened. The woods had been pushed back, and civilization had indeed been created, but somehow the purification desired so strongly a century before had not been achieved. Ministers from the late seventeenth century and on into the eighteenth called repeatedly for renewal of the faith. Among these was Jonathan Edwards of Northampton, Massachusetts, famous for fire and brimstone. But very interestingly, Edwards's view of the wilderness was quite different from that of the earlier generations. He saw it in a positive light, as the place where an individual's renewal might begin. Describing his inward life in his *Personal Narrative* (1743), Edwards wrote that he sometimes experienced "a calm, sweet abstraction of soul from all the concerns of this world; and sometimes a kind of vision, or fixed ideas and imaginations, of being alone in the mountains, or some solitary wilderness, far from all mankind, sweetly conversing with Christ, and wrapt and swallowed up in God."[1] The level of society that had been elaborated in America, in all its success, had apparently become no more than "this world" after all; for purity, one would have to look elsewhere. Unspoiled nature was beginning to appear as a spiritual haven and would one day become popularly known as "God's country."

Also at this time, as we have seen, empirical investigation was steadily cutting into the old superstitious and anthropomorphic views of nature. By the end of the eighteenth century, science had so opened up the field of consciousness that another New England minister, Samuel Williams of Vermont, would as a scientist not only keep temperature records and measure trees, but also would question humanity's traditional, confident assignment of moral values to nature.

By the time Ralph Waldo Emerson took the pulpit of the Second Church of Boston in 1829, an intellectual climate that was amazingly liberal and open compared to that of two centuries before prevailed. The successes of the scientific method in revealing the workings of nature, the undeniable gains in standard of living, and the general psychology of a culture in a "boom" phase of growth and development all conspired to create a climate of optimism and experiment. In addition, over the preceding century, the political status of the individual had undergone changes that were literally revolutionary. Emerson, in a series of influential essays and many public lectures after leaving the ministry, spoke with great accuracy to this new state of humanity and a new sense of nature as knowable. Perhaps more persuasively than any other thinker of his time in America, Emerson made his audience feel truly modern— liberated and able to conceptualize the universe not as mystery but as something they could experience. Humanity, Emerson believed, is at home in the universe. As for tradition and authority, they were simply obstacles to our expanded, rightful consciousness of the universe; each individual could have, must have, an original relation with nature.

Emerson framed this radical proposal in homely, local terms. "In the woods," he wrote in his first book, *Nature* (1836), "we return to reason and faith."[2] The folksy, American usage, "the woods," makes a grand philosophical concept immediately available.[3] The woods is where one can transcend the limited, habitual, conforming, social self.

The experience, as Emerson described it, was expansive in the extreme (he spoke of becoming "part or parcel of God") and joyful. This was a new way of looking at the American woods.

While Emerson was entering upon the larger public scene in America, Henry David Thoreau had just been graduated from Harvard College and was looking for a suitable vocation. In the case of Thoreau, who was, as one of his later editors wrote, "constitutionally earnest,"[4] vocation meant a good deal more than the means of earning a living. Thoreau met Emerson in 1836 and probably heard Emerson's inspirational address, "The American Scholar," in August of 1837 at the Harvard commencement; if not, he certainly knew it as an essay. In the fall of 1837 Thoreau became something like a protégé to Emerson, who lived not far from Thoreau in Concord. On October 22, 1837, at Emerson's suggestion, Thoreau began keeping a journal, modeling it on Emerson's.[5] It was tempting, indeed, for many of their contemporaries to see Thoreau as an imitation Emerson (James Russell Lowell, for one, had this opinion), but it turned out that Thoreau had his own ideas and experiences and formed from them an outlook quite distinct from Emerson's. It may be pertinent that the first entry in young Thoreau's journal, after a brief bow toward Emerson, is titled "Solitude." Although Emerson had mapped so much of the new philosophical territory of nature, and humanity's connection with nature, he was never in sympathy with the intensity of Thoreau's commitment to wildness. He was unencouraging, in particular, about three of Thoreau's early, nature-centered essays, "A Natural History of Massachusetts," "A Walk to Wachusett," and "A Winter Walk."[6] It is clear that quite early in his career, Thoreau adopted a naturalistic perspective that was more radical than Emerson was willing to espouse.

This passionate allegiance to nature empowered Thoreau as a distinctive and original thinker. The note of independence, not simply from Emerson but also from much of the rest of humanity, sounded in his first published nature essay, "A Natural History of Massachusetts" (1842):

We fancy that this din of religion, literature, and philosophy, which is heard in pulpits, lyceums, and parlors, vibrates through the universe, and is as catholic a sound as the creaking of the earth's axle; but if a man sleep soundly, he will forget it all between sunset and dawn. It is the three-inch swing of a pendulum in a cupboard, which the great pulse of nature vibrates by and through each instant. When we lift our eyelids and open our ears, it disappears with smoke and rattle like the cars on a railroad.[7]

What Thoreau affirmed as absolutely instructive was his own experience of the particulars of nature:

Men tire me when I am not constantly greeted and refreshed as by the flux of sparkling streams. Surely joy is the condition of life. Think of the young fry that leap in ponds, the myriad of insects ushered into being on a summer evening, the incessant note of the hyla with which the woods ring in spring, the nonchalance of the butterfly carrying accident and change painted in a thousand hues upon its wings, or the brook minnow stoutly stemming the current, the luster of whose scales, worn bright by the attrition, is reflected upon the bank![8]

Thoreau drew, to be sure, upon the trust in individual experience that Emerson had preached, a concept that in turn reflected the confidence of their era. He also drew upon the general awakening to natural history that had been in progress for a century and a half, but the extent to which Thoreau had taken nature as his standard, the unqualified standing he proposed for such creatures as minnows and frogs, and the sure tone in which he voiced his position are his own. In this early essay, which began as a book review for the transcendentalist magazine *The Dial*, Thoreau at twenty-five upheld natural history as philosophically potent and argued that the intuitive experience of nature ("direct intercourse and sympathy") could lead to wisdom of an authentic and practical kind. Thoreau placed science and fact as helpful tools within the transcending philosophical context of experience and presented this view of the world in accomplished, even artistic, prose. It is thus fair to say that the possibilities of the nature essay as a modern literary form were outlined in Thoreau's first essay, published in July 1842.

One of the central traditions of his culture from which Thoreau declared independence was that of philosophical dualism. He posited nature, most of the time, as a realm of clarity, freedom, and innocence that the dichotomous approach to life only obscured. As early as 1841, he had become aware of the limiting effect of the ethical dualism so strong in the New England heritage:

> *Aug. 1. Sunday.* I never met a man who cast a free and healthy glance over life, but the best live in a sort of Sabbath light, a Jewish gloom. The best thought is not only without sombreness, but even without morality. The universe lies outspread in floods of white light to it. The moral aspect of nature is a jaundice reflected from man. To the innocent there are no cherubim nor angels. Occasionally we rise above the necessity of virtue into an unchangeable morning light, in which we have not to choose in a dilemma between right and wrong, but simply to live right on and breathe the circumambient air. There is no name for this life unless it be the very vitality of *vita.* Silent is the preacher about this, and silent must ever be, for he who knows it will not preach.[9]

Thoreau did not keep to this naturalistic position with perfect consistency—see the "Higher Laws" chapter of *Walden,* for instance—but there is evidence that he was deeply engaged with the problem of dualism throughout his life. His repeated dreaming of what he called "the rough and the smooth" is perhaps evidence of such a preoccupation; his love of paradox (which irritated Emerson) shows a willingness to twit the usual habits of mind. More fundamentally, some of his statements, such as his surprising deathbed utterance that it was "just as good to have a poor time as a good time," suggest that he may have reached, at the end, a profound realization.[10] For all his life, Thoreau appears to have sought above all a pure and direct experience, a nondual experience, that would transcend the usual distance between subject and object and grant participation in the wholeness of nature. The hope for this state drew forth some of his most impassioned writing:

> I heard a robin in the distance, the first I had heard for many a thousand years, methought, whose note I shall not forget for many a thousand more,—the same sweet and powerful song as of yore. O the evening robin, at the end of a New England summer day! If I could ever find the twig he sits upon! I mean *he;* I mean *the twig.*[11]

The song of the wood thrush, a common bird in the Concord area, touched Thoreau deeply, catalyzing the thought of enlightenment to nature. There are thirty-nine references to the wood thrush in his journal, almost as many as to Emerson (with those to the bird taking the honors for apparent depth of response, in any case), and it is possible to see in these references just what it was that Thoreau brought new to the American nature essay. Mark Catesby evidently did not hear the wood thrush sing, since he merely listed it as the "Little Thrush" and was not particularly attuned to birdsong in general. William Bartram did little more than list the bird. However, Wilson, Nuttall, and Audubon all testified to the beauty of its song and its power to lift the spirits, with Nuttall suggesting a mysterious, ethereal quality: "It is nearly impossible by words to convey any idea of the peculiar warble of this vocal hermit."[12] But it is from Thoreau that we learn to hear the thrush's song as the distillation of the woods itself, the essence of wildness, and thus the key to the opened self. This is an entirely new dimension.

> The wood thrush's is no opera music; it is not so much the composition as the strain, the tone,—cool bars of melody from the atmosphere of everlasting morning or evening. It is the quality of the song, not the sequence. In the peawai's note there is some sultriness, but in the thrush's, though heard at noon, there is the liquid coolness of things that are just drawn from the bottom of springs. The thrush alone declares the immortal wealth and vigor that is in the forest. Here is a bird in whose strain the story is told, though Nature waited for the science

of aesthetics to discover it to man. Whenever a man hears it, he is young, and Nature is in her spring. Wherever he hears it, it is a new world and a free country, and the gates of heaven are not shut against him. Most other birds sing from the level of my ordinary cheerful hours—a carol; but this bird never fails to speak to me out of an ether purer than that I breathe, of immortal beauty and vigor. He deepens the significance of all things seen in the light of his strain. He sings to make men take higher and truer views of things.[13]

To describe the awakening of higher consciousness in such meta-phorical but not abstract terms—to root it in nature, that is—was one of the Thoreau's major accomplishments as a writer. Such description makes "the woods" more believable as a philosophical standpoint. From the woods, Thoreau looked at his times with a wild perspective that no one before him in American life had developed so concretely or thor-oughly. He had gone beyond the Western mind's accustomed paths.

The essay "Walking," which began as a lecture more than a decade before Thoreau's death and which he revised in his last months, became his final word on the wild. He warned his readers in the opening para-graph that he would be standing apart from the "champions of civiliza-tion" in what he had to say, but the reflections that follow are not so much concerned with the differences between society and the wild as they are with the positive spark of wildness that remains and that might be redeeming. Here again, Thoreau used a familiar subject, the simple act of walking, as the base from which to develop profound metaphors for awakening and sacredness. "Walking" is an essay that asserts the wildness within the civilized self: "When we walk, we naturally go to the fields and woods"; "I believe that there is a subtle magnetism in Nature, which, if we unconsciously yield to it, will direct us aright"; "In litera-ture it is only the wild that attracts us."[14] Thus wildness is not limited to the distant wilderness but is something innate, something that might awaken one day. The nondualistic theme of the essay is further demon-strated by its emphasis on walking as a continuing process. "It is a living way, / As the Christians say," Thoreau wrote in the poem "The Old Marlborough Road," and the final sentence of the essay states that "we saunter toward the Holy Land," that is, we do not arrive there as if it were a specific locale. To think that we might arrive, if we were good enough walkers, at a discrete state of enlightenment would be to commit the same dualistic error as believing wildness is only in the wilderness. Thoreau's summary of the thrust of the essay ("what I have been preparing to say") is in this same vein: "in Wildness is the preservation of the world."[15] Not wilderness, that is, the named and the mapped, but something more inner and involving. The meaning of preservation thus suggested is not to save apart, as under glass, but to sustain creative power, that which keeps the world continually renewing. The wildness that preserves the world is the "eternal morning" that the wood thrush sings. It is what sends us out walking.

Throughout his work, Thoreau's images of nature have a palpable quality; he is not looking at scenery. Awakened consciousness, apparently, is not a separate state, a property of humans, but a partnership with real places.

> This is a delicious evening, when the whole body is one sense, and imbibes delight through every pore. I go and come with a strange liberty in Nature, a part of herself. As I walk along the stony shore of the pond in my shirt sleeves, though it is cool as well as cloudy and windy, and I see nothing special to attract me, all the elements are unusually congenial to me. The bullfrogs trump to usher in the night, and the note of the whippoorwill is borne on the rippling wind from over the water. Sympathy with the fluttering alder and poplar leaves almost takes away my breath; yet, like the lake, my serenity is rippled but not ruffled.[16]

This sense for process and involvement carried over into Thoreau's awareness of language; he once praised words like "delicious" and "avaricious" because in saying them one had to perform certain lip and jaw movements that reinforced the meaning of the words. He was profoundly aware of the physical content of thought and language, conscious that even in the most cerebral human activities the wild played an essential part. It was, as every evidence demonstrated to Thoreau, a "great pulse" preserving the world.

In contrast with the contributions made by Emerson, Thoreau, and other nineteenth-century writers to our understanding of nature, the environmental history of America in their time was marked by severe displacement and loss. Disruption of environmental patterns was nothing new, of course, having accompanied European settlement on the eastern seaboard from the earliest times. But now the new order spread rapidly across the country; with the opening of the Erie Canal in 1825, with steam navigation on the Great Lakes established by the late 1830s, and with the phenomenal increase in miles of railroad tracks beginning also in the 1830s, occupation of the interior and exploitation of its resources were greatly facilitated. By 1776, Daniel Boone had surveyed the Wilderness Road through the forests of the Cumberland Gap into the rich land of Kentucky, and the first trickle of settlers began to move across the Appalachian barrier. A mere century and a quarter later, the continental United States was trussed with a network of 197,000 miles of railroads. By the end of the nineteenth century, the herds of bison, which had in Boone's time ranged from the Great Basin to Pennsylvania and from Canada to Mexico, were virtually gone. The frontier that had beckoned Boone and others so compellingly had been declared closed in 1890. Throughout the nineteenth century, waves of immigrants, many from distressed European countries, added to the population and inevitably to its impact on the land. As the westward expansion pushed toward its conclusion, with the last "free" lands in sight, a frenzied atmosphere developed. "This restless, nervous, bustling, trivial Nineteenth Century," Thoreau had called it,[17] but he had seen nothing like what would happen after the Civil War.

The railroad network became intimately involved with the massive accumulation of capital that characterized the latter half of the century, thus facilitating the assault on the environment in two ways: mechanically, by transporting large quantities of resources that were the fruits of exploitation (crops, livestock, minerals, and lumber), and financially, by enabling the major industrial powers to become centralized. Large-scale monoculture became not only possible but profitable on land far from major markets. Centralized capital meant that environments could be affected by market forces and decisions made far from the scene; this tended to weaken any restraint, even discourage any planning for the future, that might conceivably have operated under localized control. Worse yet, the arms of the railroad "octopus," as novelist Frank Norris called it, were for several decades literally supported and fueled by wood, a fact that had significant negative impact on the size and composition of American forests. Even in Thoreau's time, during the 1850s, the railroads of the United States were using between 4 and 5 million cords of wood per year to generate steam in locomotive engines, and after the switch to coal, which itself had powerful environmental effects, the railroads still needed wood for ties. In 1910, one-fourth of the nation's total wood consumption was accounted for by this use.[18]

The factory system, and its enlargement of capacity to massive production in the decades following the Civil War, complemented the growth of the rail transportation network and the centralization of capital. In 1790, there was only one small factory in the United States, a mill in Pawtucket, Rhode Island, where cotton yarn was produced. By the dawn of the twentieth century, great factories were responsible for carrying on all of the major means of production, including the processing of agricultural products. This conclusive dominance of the economy by industry stimulated the rapid growth of large cities.

In the countryside, swamps and wet lowlands were drained and filled at almost every opportunity. Both tallgrass and shortgrass prairies, which in their pristine state had supported a stunning variety and abundance of wildlife, were converted to monocultures of corn and wheat or to pastures for domestic stock. In areas where forests were allowed to grow back, the composition of forests was often radically changed (according to a 1958 account, much of the new-growth woods in New England was "a sorry mixture of the most persistent weed trees and low-grade stump sprouts").[19] Perhaps the most striking of all changes, the hardest not to notice, was the steep decline in wildlife countrywide. This included the bison and the passenger pigeon most prominently, but also the wolf, cougar, and caribou, all of which were essentially gone from the eastern half of the country by the close of the nineteenth century. Seals, sea otters, and whales were decimated along the Pacific Coast in the same time period, and populations of shorebirds and even many songbirds were seriously reduced by market hunting. In the Rockies, elk and bighorn sheep were forced onto small islands of mountain wilderness.[20] In one century, the United States was transformed from a smallish seaboard republic, mostly agrarian, where canals and mule-drawn barges were a key link in the economy, to an urban-industrial power of some 76 million citizens.

It is well to remember, on the other hand, that it was within this same America of unrestrained growth that the first modern voices for the preservation of nature were heard. As Paul Brooks has shown in his important study, *Speaking for Nature* (1980), writers like Henry David Thoreau, John Muir, and John Burroughs, along with a number of others, reached and moved the book-reading portion of the public. Their ideas came eventually to have an effect, perhaps a significant effect, on national policy. Speaking for the wild, one might say, they helped to moderate a seemingly insatiable appetite for growth and consumption of resources.

John Muir experienced frontier America firsthand, as a child and teenager on his father's homestead in Wisconsin. The family had emigrated from Scotland in 1849, when Muir was eleven, and by the time he left home at twenty-two, they had built two farms where previously there had been a wilderness—that "glorious Wisconsin wilderness," Muir later wrote.[21] Muir spent his twenties studying at the recently established University of Wisconsin (where he was influenced deeply by both science and the philosophy of Emerson), botanizing in the countryside, working in small factories in Ontario and Indiana, and walking from southern Indiana to Florida in 1867. In his inner life, he came slowly out from under the fundamentalist Calvinism that his father had enforced upon the family. He was thirty years old when he arrived in California in 1868, and in many ways just coming to maturity.

In his journal of the southern trip, Muir had criticized the anthropocentrism of his father's religion. The journals he kept during his first winter in California, when he lived in the foothills of the Sierra Nevada, show him reaching further beyond philosophical dualism: "But out here in the free unplanted fields there is no rectilineal sectioning of times and seasons. All things flow here in indivisible, measureless currents."[22] The next summer, the baptismal and glorious summer of 1869, Muir's experiences in the mountains gave body to these concepts, leading him to an intense feeling of continuity with the wild beauty around him, simply overwhelming "petty personal hope or experience," in his words.[23] In June 1869, he had accompanied a band of some two thousand sheep into the mountains, walking slowly upward through the heat-blasted foothills into the cooler, forested portion of the Sierra proper. Starting from the sheep camp there, he was free to take long, physically demanding rambles into the high country of glacial meadows and clean gray granite. Living on simple food, surrounded for several months by only natural forms and forces, Muir stretched himself physically, learning in particular the poise and balance needed for traveling on talus slopes, as this was his initial experience of alpine country. Most of all, Muir came alive to the mountains.

> Drinking this champagne water is pure pleasure, so is breathing the living air, and every movement of the limbs is pleasure, while the whole body seems to feel beauty when exposed to it as it feels a campfire or sunshine, entering not by the eyes alone, but equally through all one's

flesh like radiant heat, making a passionate ecstatic pleasure-glow not explainable.[24]

After taking up residence in Yosemite Valley in the fall of 1869, Muir embarked on an investigation of the glacial history of the Sierra, making several extended study-journeys into the mountains over the next few years. He added to his physical and emotional "pleasure-glow" the discipline of daily practice in the scientific method. As the months and years progressed, and his knowledge of the range widened, there matured in Muir an outlook on the world that gave full scope to both the ecstatic perception of oneness with nature and the empirical discernment of its particulars. In an instructive journal entry, he outlined his own personal odyssey toward holistic understanding:

> Grand North Womb of Mount Clark Glacier
> October 7 (?), 1871

In streams of ice, of water, of minerals, of plants, of animals, the tendency is to unification. We at once find ourselves among eternities, infinitudes, and scarce know whether to be happy in the sublime simplicity of radical causes and origins or whether to be sorry on losing the beautiful fragments which we thought perfect and primary absolute units; but as we study and mingle with nature more, the pain caused by the melting of all beauties into one First Beauty disappears, because, after their first baptismal submergence in fountain God, they go again washed and clean into their individualisms, more clearly defined than ever, unified yet separate.[25]

One could hardly ask for a clearer account of the struggle to match human consciousness to the complexity of nature, or of Muir's scientific-poetic faith that all that is required, in order to transcend the usual limitations of thought, is to "study and mingle with nature more." The passage bears an uncanny resemblance to the traditional Zen Buddhist account of the passage through the "gateless gate": before one studies

Zen (that is, meditates), mountains are simply mountains; at a certain point, after the first flush of nondualistic awakening, mountains are no longer mountains; now, at last, mountains are again mountains, but in fuller realization.

In contrast with this journal entry, most of Muir's published writings, for most of his career as an author, did not focus on the inner dimension. In fact, as his biographer Linnie Marsh Wolfe pointed out, he "studied . . . to keep himself and his mystical interpretations of nature in the background,"[26] apparently believing that such matters were beyond communicating. His emphasis in writing was on what he called the "beautiful fragments": the morning light "stinging" the topmost cliffs of the Grand Canyon at sunrise; a sky full of towering, light-shot cumulus clouds building to an afternoon thunderstorm over the Sierra; the inevitably symmetrical-branching habit of the giant sequoia; and the chattering, electric energy of the Douglas squirrel. These images were not static; Muir always rendered these nouns of the world as alive and changing. His ecological consciousness was folded into his expression of the scene before him, helping to animate it. He was careful to describe nothing in isolation. Flowering plants push up through the moist earth in spring, grasses hang over stream banks and are moved by the running water, and glaciers press their weight on the land, scouring, scraping, and molding the mountains. Muir also tried to suggest, in the smooth, fluent rhythms of his sentences, the flow that was, to his mind, the primary fact of nature. His is one of the great efforts to make nature come alive on the page, and he worked hard at his writing, tapping out sentence rhythms, for example, despite his stated belief that "no amount of word-making will ever make a single soul to *know* these mountains."[27] Eventually the effort had an impact on American life. Indeed, among American nature writers, Muir's effectiveness is one of the easiest to quantify, from his ideas for a watershed-encompassing boundary for Yosemite National Park to his direct influence on President Theodore Roosevelt in the matter of forest and park preservation and his role in inspiring the important Lacey Antiquities Act of 1906.

Muir's contribution to the developing American nature essay was threefold: he enlarged it to include wild-country adventures while essentially continuing Thoreau's philosophy of wildness; he deepened its evolutionary and ecological content with his emphasis on flow and harmony; and he added a strong new note of militancy in response to the dramatic environmental conditions of his time. As is often pointed out, Henry David Thoreau may have been at least momentarily disquieted when he scrambled alone onto the summit plateau of Mount Katahdin in 1846, only to find himself in the midst of blowing cloud. He described his state there in the wild elements as "more lone than you can imagine."[28] Muir, though, never admitted to being daunted, at least for long, whatever the circumstances—a free solo climb of Mount Ritter in the Sierra; a forced bivouac in a storm, near the summit of Mount Shasta; or a dangerous traverse of a deeply crevassed glacier in Alaska. Any experience in the wilderness seemed to be proof for his theme that the mountains were "home." In Muir's view, the wild universe gave birth to us and was not to be feared. At the start of the Inyo earthquake of 1872, a shock that toppled hundreds of tons of rock from the cliffs of Yosemite and sent inhabitants of the valley fleeing out of the mountains, Muir emerged from his cabin calling out (so he wrote to the Boston Society of Natural History), "A noble earthquake!"[29] He described the earthquake, one of the strongest recorded in United States history, as "Mother Earth . . . trotting us on her knee."[30]

Muir's transmutation of the fear of death into a hymn of praise, a motif often repeated in his work, is closely related to his concept of wilderness as familiar. To Muir, wilderness was not any sort of "other," much less a threat, but simply the most obvious manifestation of the total patterning of things—not chaos but a complete, unified order that included humans. His best statement of this point was in "Wild Wool," an 1875 essay later reprinted in *Steep Trails* (1918), in which he held that all creatures are "killing and being killed, eating and being eaten," and that this constant predation results only in harmony and rightness: "And it is right that we should thus reciprocally make use of one another, rob, cook, and consume, to the utmost of our healthy abilities and desires."[31] All would be well in this naturalistic universe except that humanity, thinking itself special, has interfered with the evolutionary integrity of other beings in the pattern and bent them to its exclusive use. Taming apples, roses, and sheep, we proceed to build up not only an economy of separateness, but also a mentality of separateness, and we lose sight of the beautiful fitness of things.

> No dogma taught by the present civilization seems to form so insu-perable an obstacle in the way of a right understanding of the relations which culture sustains to wildness, as that which declares that the world was made especially for the uses of men. Every animal, plant, and crystal controverts it in the plainest terms. Yet it *is* taught from century to century as something ever new and precious, and in the re-sulting darkness the enormous conceit is allowed to go unchallenged.[32]

The glacier study had awakened Muir's sense of both geologic time and the many subtle interweavings of causes and effects that had evolved into the present state of things. His sense of evolutionary time strength-ened his interpretation of the world as congenial. Humanity, he wrote, had "flowed down" through other forms of life, incorporating parts of them and becoming in the process "most richly terrestrial."[33] "Terres-trial" for Muir meant "sacred," so in effect his evolutionary view kept spirituality, reverence, and other sacred matters alive but rooted in Darwinian realities.

Though he did not have the command of history and cultural refer-ence of Thoreau, Muir could comment forcefully on his times, usually in the manner of the Old Testament prophets, by holding up the sordid against the clear beauty of the wilderness. As might be expected, given his rearing, he had a strong feel for damnation and salvation, though his definitions of these states became roughly opposite those of his culture, and his vituperation of the thoughtless or selfish had thunder in it. When he described how herds of sheep had been driven into a once-beautiful Sierra meadow, it was in terms of Biblical desecration: "The money changers were in the temple."[34] In the great battle of his life, the struggle to save the Hetch Hetchy Valley of Yosemite from dam builders, Muir's outrage was again cast in language reflecting his religious upbringing: "Dam Hetch Hetchy! As well dam for water-tanks the people's cathedrals and churches, for no holier temple has ever been consecrated by the heart of man."[35] He also defended nature on scientific and practical terms, arguing consistently as early as 1875 that forest preservation simply made good sense for watershed health.[36] But his major thrust was philosophical and moral: "The battle for conservation will go on endlessly," he once wrote. "It is part of the universal warfare between right and wrong."[37]

Muir's militant criticism of modern society may not have been as broad or as deep as Thoreau's, but it was topically to the point, and it was pitched accurately to his times. His ideas, his rhetorical strategies, and his whole style as a man spoke effectively to an age in philosophical transition. He alerted people to the moral dimension of the attack on wild nature, and he demonstrated the qualities of heart and mind that would be needed for a post–frontier civilization to come into being. In his acceptance of evolution yet retention of an essentially religious view of the world, he demonstrated that "studying and mingling more" with nature could help a Christian culture enter the new philosophical era.

That new era, of course, centered on the work of Charles Darwin. Darwin himself, as is well known, had studied for the ministry and had begun the famous voyage on HMS *Beagle* as a believer in Genesis. Five years of fieldwork, another twenty or more of scholarly pondering, and Darwin had come to a different view. The world, in all its intricate relational complexity, was still wonderful, but it had become that way, and was continuing onward to who knows what state, through an entirely natural process that included, integrally and importantly, a good deal of accident. With the publication of *On the Origin of Species* in November 1859, the traditional and rather placid view of the world as divinely ordained began to come apart. The great work of natural philosophy since that time has been to explore the naturalistic universe, where relativity and change are the basic laws, and where chance is completely pervasive, to see if there might exist anything solid upon which to base the conduct of human life. In short, evolution and natural selection, coming out of somewhat obscure researches in natural history, have laid waste absolutist and revealed theories and have thrown the philosophical door wide open.

Among naturalists and nature writers, however, the impact of Darwinism was not devastating or even, apparently, terribly shocking. Nature literature since Darwin does not reflect any sense of terror at being adrift in a blankly materialistic universe. As we have seen, American nature writers for some time had been criticizing anthropocentrism and anthropomorphism and had been promoting wider views based upon empirical evidence. In a sense, Darwin merely took this same theme further. Evolutionary theories had circulated for decades; his contribution was to explain its heretofore unseen mechanism. This was no small thing, for understanding the mechanism—natural selection—involved a revolution in Western thought. The point is that Darwin's great work should be seen as part of an expansion of knowledge and perspective that had been under way among students of natural history for more than two centuries.

Henry David Thoreau read *On the Origin of Species* a few weeks after its publication and took several pages of notes, but he was not revolutionized. Perhaps one reason for his interested but mild reaction was that he was accustomed already to a relational view of the world. Mutable species did not seem to shock him. "Am I not partly leaves and vegetable mould myself?" he had asked in *Walden*,[38] having already found his own answer.

The most common stance in American nature literature, after Darwin had thrown open the great questions of existence and meaning, was to grant science the realm of the finite, preserving the divine as an

infinite but indwelling mystery—a principle rather than a familiar anthropomorphism. This was essentially the position of Muir and of John
Burroughs, the two most important American nature writers in the
time of the Darwinian controversy. This position stops short of pure
mechanism—the view that all phenomena in nature can be explained in
terms of mechanical principles and material causes—and leaves room
for the mysterious, ecstatic feeling of intense connectedness with the
world that is, for many nature writers, the root of and the justification
for right conduct. Most of American nature literature since Darwin has
simply incorporated evolution and natural selection into its perception
of the web of life, without any particular hitch. Many writers have not
emphasized these subjects at all. But there was a time, extending roughly
from 1860 to 1920, when the new theories and the resulting need for
grand-scale philosophizing and interpretation of these views necessarily
occupied center stage. In that time, John Burroughs was perhaps the
most congenial and effective American interpreter of the new views.

A near contemporary of Muir, Burroughs was far less of a wilderness man. He was not an activist at all in conservation matters, and his
prose had considerably less charge to it than Muir's. But he was extraordinarily popular, first as a writer of pleasant rambles, and later as
nothing less than an American country sage, a man who could make
the new universe seem an accessible, friendly place. He did this by
telling and showing people how to look. Answering the philosophical
challenge of mechanism, he set forth an approach to nature study that
preserved both empirical accuracy and the sense of wonder and enjoyment. He recommended rigor in interpreting animal behavior and was
especially scornful of the tendency to anthropomorphize. He recognized that nature is ruled mostly by evolutionary patterning and instinct and felt that we needed to be clear about this. But at the same
time, he believed there is an ineffable dimension to life—our own experience of deep agreement with nature, of being at home in it, and
then the great and mysterious pattern of the whole—and this must

simply remain ineffable. "We cannot find God by thinking," Burroughs wrote.[39]

From his earliest works, Burroughs had charmed his readers with relaxed, realistic accounts of fields and woods. Reading his books, the novelist and critic William Dean Howells said, was like taking a summer vacation. Typically, the author went on short walks out into the country, where he saw and heard everything with remarkable receptivity, and where he was refreshed and made reflective and appreciative by the experience. Burroughs was a companionable guide who spoke confidingly to his readers, instructing them genially in the ways of nature and providing a model for a reasonable and fitting emotional response. As a nature writer he was less testing than Thoreau and less heroic than Muir, but his middling way nevertheless presented nature in some experiential depth.

Much of the emotional resonance in Burroughs's descriptions derives from his powerful attachment to his home ground, the Catskill Mountains of New York and the surrounding farm country. He was born and raised on a farm there, came back to the area in adulthood as soon as he was financially able to settle, and eventually purchased the old family property. His friend William Sloane Kennedy wrote in *The Real John Burroughs* (1924) that "the *idee fixe* of John o' the Catskills is that there is no place like his home locality, and there are no birds, anywhere in the world equal to those of his native hills."[40] It may even be true that Burroughs's often expressed sense of the universe as home, as in, "the universe is good, and . . . it is our rare good fortune to form a part of it,"[41] originated in those softly rolling hills and pleasingly varied rural landscapes.

Burroughs's mature idea of the scheme of things, in the large sense, probably owed much to the influence of the poet Walt Whitman. In 1863, at twenty-six, young Burroughs had gone to Washington, D.C., to seek employment. He had been thinking of himself as a writer for some time and had published an essay of Emersonian tone in the *Atlantic*

Monthly, but he had been unable to support his wife of six years. At this crucial time he met Whitman, who was working as a government clerk while tending sick and wounded Civil War soldiers in Washington hospitals, and the poet heartened the younger man by the sheer force of his charismatic and nurturing personality. Burroughs, demonstrating the character he later described as "very yielding, and very quick to receive an impression,"[42] took on some of Whitman's cosmic confidence. He became a writer with more of his own voice (though at first there were strong overtones of Whitman's in it, certainly), and, just as importantly, he began to develop a concept of nature that went beyond scenery-oriented romanticism. In his first book, *Notes on Walt Whitman, As Poet and Person* (1867), Burroughs described the poet's idea of nature and said that he understood it:

> The word Nature, now, to most readers, suggests only some flower bank, or summer cloud, or pretty scene that appeals to the sentiments. None of this is in Walt Whitman. And it is because he corrects this false, artificial Nature, and shows me the real article, that I hail his appearance as the most important literary event of our time.[43]

Whitman remained a friend and an influence. Burroughs closed his literary career almost as he had begun it: the final chapter of *Accepting the Universe* (1920), which was the last book published during his lifetime, was entitled "The Poet of the Cosmos" and was a tribute to Whitman's scope and seriousness.

Burroughs's reaction to Darwin, whom he first read in 1883, was much like his response to Whitman. He saw the naturalist as the bringer of a whole new vision. "Everything about Darwin indicates the master. In reading him you breathe the air of the largest and most serene mind," Burroughs wrote in his journal. "[His theory] is as ample as the earth, and as deep as time."[44] To Burroughs, the largest minds saw beyond the usual categories of good and evil, predator and prey, life and death, and perceived that all terms that seemed to be polar opposites were essentially complementary, as was the great system that gave birth to them. This penetration is what "accepting the universe" means. Typically, Burroughs framed his exposition of this truth in very specific, natural history terms:

> The conflicting interests in Nature sooner or later adjust them-
> selves; her checks and balances bring about her equilibrium. In vegeta-
> tion rivalries and antagonisms bring about adaptations. The mosses
> and the ferns and the tender wood plants grow beneath the oaks and
> the pines and are favored by the shade and protection which the latter
> afford them. The farmer's seeding of grass and clover takes better under
> the shade of the oaks than it would upon the naked ground. In Africa
> some species of flesh-eaters live upon the leavings of larger and stronger
> species, and in the tropics certain birds become benefactors of the cattle
> by preying upon the insects that pester them. Fabre tells of certain
> insect hosts that blindly favor the parasites that destroy them. The
> scheme has worked itself out that way and Nature is satisfied. Victim
> or victor, host or parasite, it is all one to her. Life goes on, and all forms
> of it are hers.[45]

With this breadth of acceptance, Burroughs demonstrated that he had come a long philosophical way in the half century since his first nature book, *Wake-Robin* (1871), in which he had written quite forthrightly of killing a black snake for the crime of eating a catbird, and of removing a baby cowbird from the nest of a Canada warbler and dropping the cow-bird chick into a nearby creek.

Burroughs once described himself in comparison to Thoreau as "soft, flexible, and adaptive,"[46] but it is doubtful that the victims of his lash in the "nature-faker" controversy would have agreed. In the March 1903 issue of the *Atlantic Monthly,* Burroughs attacked a school of na-ture writing (specifically, two popular writers, Ernest Thompson Seton and the Reverend William J. Long) for spicing their narratives of nature by attributing humanlike reason and emotion to animals, and for de-scribing as perfectly factual certain improbable happenings. The article stung, and a sometimes rancorous exchange of open letters and articles ensued, drawing into the heated controversy even the president, Theodore Roosevelt (on Burroughs's side). The overall effect, however, was undoubtedly healthful for nature writing. Burroughs had reinforced in the public mind the scientific content of the genre and helped to establish standards of credibility for the interpretation of animal behavior. The controversy also brought out nature writing's potential for insight into the human condition in nature, for in defining the minds of the other animals, one necessarily tries to deal with what might make humanity distinctive. Burroughs himself demonstrated some of the good effects of the discussion in a fair-minded and reflective book, *Ways of Nature* (1905). In this study, he carefully differentiated instinct from judgment, and the ability to communicate feeling from language. He found, in the end, that although "the line that divides man from the lower orders . . . has many breaks and curves and deep indentations,"[47] it is a line nevertheless. He described sentimentality (excessive line crossing) as simply anthropomorphism, a distraction hurtful to clear understanding.

But Burroughs did not want science to completely demystify or mechanize our response to nature. Experience, for him, always stood equal in importance with knowledge.

> I have taken persons to hear the hermit thrush, and I have fancied that they were all the time saying to themselves, "Is that all?" But should one hear the bird in his walk, when the mind is attuned to simple things and is open and receptive, when expectation is not aroused and the song comes as a surprise out of the dusky silence of the woods, then one feels that it merits all the fine things that can be said of it.[48]

The genteel tradition, which helped set the tone for many literary works of the later nineteenth century, was well represented in the nature essay. Indeed, nature writing may seem made to order for gentility. On the surface, at least, all is well and upright in the world of nature. It is pleasurable, harmless, and uplifting to walk out and hear the birds. But even in some of the most obviously genteel nature writers, deeper issues involving humanity and its relationship with the environment have a way of coming to the surface. The work of Wilson Flagg, an insurance agent and clerk at the Boston customs house as well as an inveterate walker, is illustrative.

When Thoreau read Flagg's *Studies in the Field and Forest* (1857), he wrote to a friend that Flagg "wants stirring up with a pole," and could gain a little vigor, which his sentences seemed to need, by "turning a series of somersets rapidly."[49] Flagg's own description of his purposes as a writer, set forth in 1872, was mild enough—he would try to "inspire [his] readers with a love of nature and a simplicity of life, confident that the great fallacy of the present age is that of mistaking the increase of national wealth for the advancement of civilization."[50] There was little energy, much less Muirian denunciation, in such a statement. But in his long walks on what he called "by-ways," the meandering roads and paths that had served the New England of an earlier day, Flagg came to a clear idea of what he thought was right for the land. When he considered the spread of "model farming," which, in the name of efficiency and order, was plowing every square rod of land, leaving no edge for wildlife, and creating an artificial landscape around farmhouses, he became aroused. He realized that he was witnessing the death of the old ways, with their pleasing variety, and the model of the new age disturbed him. "We may distinguish the possessions of these model farmers by observing, as we pass by, their singular blankness, such as you observe in the face of an overfed idiot."[51]

Flagg's ideal landscape was the old American middle ground, the pastoral zone, but he recognized that wilderness, rather near by, was fundamentally necessary to the existence of that favorite environment. "Woods and their undergrowth are indeed the only barriers against frequent and sudden inundations, and the only means in the economy of nature for preserving an equal fullness of streams during all seasons of the year"; furthermore, "civilization has never, in any country, long survived, the destruction of its forests."[52] Accordingly, he proposed what he called "Forest Conservatories." These would amount to "three or four square miles each, in the ratio of one such tract to every square degree of latitude and longitude." Within these special areas, there would be no hunting, trapping, or landscaping, and the walking paths would be only a few feet wide (thus barring carriages). There would be a little farming allowed, but not for profit (Flagg thus implies a government entity over-seeing the land, or a beneficent landlord, or philosophically minded farmers), because, as he thought, "rustic tillage would be needful for the subsistence of the birds and animals."[53] Flagg did not develop many of the possible implications of his proposal, nor did he ever describe the practical steps that would be needed to institute it, but the idea remains suggestive. (It is somewhat similar to Thoreau's better-known proposi-tion that each village should have a wilderness woods adjacent to it.) Suggestion, indeed, was Flagg's method as a writer; he had a light touch. "Studies" were his chief mode:

> I never believe so much in the immortality of the soul as when, at sun-set, I look through a long vista of luminous clouds, far down into that mystic region of light in which, we are fain to imagine, are deposited the secrets of the universe. I cannot believe that all this panorama of unimaginable loveliness, which is spread out over earth, sea, and sky, is without some moral signification. The blue heavens are the page whereon nature has revealed some pleasant intimations of the myster-ies of a more spiritual existence; and no charming vision of heaven or immortality entered the human soul, but the Deity responded to it upon the firmament, in letters of gold, ruby, and sapphire.[54]

The undeveloped portions of the desert Southwest had special at-tractiveness for nature- and wilderness-minded people at the close of the frontier era, because here the freshness of unspoiled land persisted. There were great stretches of uninhabited country, along with silence and isolation, and where there was culture, it tended to have a native, authentic stamp of the country on it. Most of this is gone now, of course, as another kind of life blossoms in the Sun Belt, but less than a century ago the desert corner of this country was largely wilderness. Even as recently as the 1930s, the forester Robert Marshall found some 18 million acres of pristine land in Utah in a survey of government holdings in that state. Wild country on a scale like that speaks, to some, of powerful and illuminative experience.

Thus the meanings that writers attached to the Southwest, from the late nineteenth century onward, have been consistently transcendental and spiritual. There is a strong mystique of place, even today. On a slightly less elevated level, the flora and fauna of the area, in their remarkable adaptations to the environment, fairly shout the lessons of ecology. So it is for substantial environmental reasons, at heart, that the desert has been predominant in the nature literature of the West, down to the present.

From the start, describers of this dry quarter have insisted that pastoral and romantic conventions of scenery appreciation do not apply here; they frame perception, when what is needed is a wilder way of seeing, some way to open the mind to the bright light and the raw-looking, naked, and rocky landscape. You cannot call the Grand Canyon charming. The first appeal for a new perception was made by a United States Government surveyor, Clarence Dutton, who spent parts of several years doing geological surveys of northern Arizona and southern Utah. In his *Tertiary History of the Grand Cañon District* (1882), Dutton repeatedly urged the abandonment of tradition: "Forms so new to the culture of civilized races and so strongly contrasted with those which have been the ideals of thirty generations of white men cannot indeed be appreciated after the study of a single hour or day," he wrote, recommending lengthy immersion. He also recommended a respectful realism: "There is no need, as we look upon them [the Vermilion Cliffs], of fancy to heighten the picture, nor of metaphor to present it. The simple truth is quite enough."[55]

John Charles Van Dyke, a librarian and a professor of art history at

Rutgers College who spent most of three years on long, difficult solo treks in the deserts of California and Arizona and who wrote from that experience one of the most highly regarded xeric texts, *The Desert* (1901), must have felt the same aesthetic challenge keenly. Already well-known as an expert on art before he entered the desert in 1898 for the first of his journeys, Van Dyke had been deeply influenced by the work of the British critic John Ruskin, and he was particularly like Ruskin in his acute awareness of his own aesthetic responses. His perceptions in *The Desert* are given in painstaking, step-by-step fashion, with attention to form, color, perspective, and all other possible ingredients of a view. Perhaps the desert has had no better-trained pair of eyes look on it. Indeed, there may be no more detailed parsing-out of scenes anywhere in American nature writing.

But Van Dyke's attention was not fragmented. He had a moral passion for the desert, an overwhelming love that kept him traveling in it despite some serious health problems, and his perceptions unified around that master feeling. His consciousness of the land was fundamentally participative, not remote.

> The long line of dunes at the north are just as desolate, yet they are wonderfully beautiful. The desert sand is finer than snow, and its curves and arches, as it builds its succession of drifts out and over an arroyo, are as graceful as the lines of running water. The dunes are always rhythmical and flowing in their forms; and for color the desert has nothing that surpasses them. In the early morning, before the sun is up, they are air-blue, reflecting the sky overhead; at noon they are pale lines of dazzling orange-colored light, waving and undulating in the heated air; at sunset they are often flooded with a rose or mauve color; under a blue moonlight they shine white as icebergs in the northern seas.[56]

Passion unified Van Dyke's sensibility, and it also inspired him to want to tell only the truth about the desert and its wildlife. The truth of the struggle for life under hard conditions, the simple realism of it, existed beyond traditional, human categories of judgment. "Nature neither rejoices in the life nor sorrows in the death. She is neither good nor evil; she is only a great law of change that passeth understanding."[57]

Like Ruskin, Van Dyke scorned the utilitarian view of nature; the desert was not, he wrote, a "livable place," and it should never be reclaimed. Its virtue, a kind of partnership with a finer, liberated human awareness, was on an entirely higher plane. If we could only perceive nature with clarity, Van Dyke argued, we would know better than to turn the earth to account with blunt instruments. Seeing an appropriate human role on the earth is partly a matter of taste, one could judge from Van Dyke's writings, but not a taste that can be cultivated indoors. One needs to go out—way out, to where the earth is still wild enough to manifest its beautiful power clearly. "I was never over-fond of park and garden nature-study," Van Dyke wrote in his preface to *The Desert*. "If we would know the great truths we must seek them at the source."[58]

This sense of the power of experience beyond the fences is also prominent in the work of Mary Hunter Austin, who, like Van Dyke, saw wildness and all of its soul-stirring meanings come to their sharpest focus in the desert. She had come to southern California in 1888 at the age of twenty, accompanying her brother and her widowed mother to a homestead near Bakersfield. The difficult environment could hardly have been less like that of the family's home in Carlinville, Illinois, and during their first year in the West, Mary was undernourished and ill a good part of the time. But she had a strong curiosity, particularly about natural history (she had majored in science at Blackburn College in Illinois), and she walked and rode out into the hills as often as possible, attempting to learn something of the new land. During one of these outings on an April morning as she led her horse down an arroyo, she suddenly and quite unexpectedly perceived with extraordinary intensity the flame-colored poppies she was walking among and was moved to feel, as she wrote later, "the warm pervasive sweetness of ultimate reality."[59] The experience affirmed for Mary Hunter something she had been holding on to, a memory of a similar experience at age six: her identity as "I-Mary," a level of being much more profound and whole than the social self; or "Mary-by-herself."[60] I-Mary was alert to nature, highly intuitive, and able to see into the way entities that seem separate actually interpenetrate each other. This was Mary Hunter's mystical center, and when she became Mary Austin, it sustained her through a difficult marriage, gave her confidence in her ideas and in her writing, and, directly relevant to her study of nature, kept her awake to the relational aspect, the ecological patterning of the fabric of life. A sense for pattern became one of her strongest faculties.[61]

In the dry hills and mesas surrounding the Owens Valley in eastern California, where she went with her husband, Stafford Austin, in 1892, young Mary resumed her outdoor study. Emotionally abandoned by her husband, as she said, and deeply tried by the birth of her hopelessly retarded daughter, Austin was thrown back upon the resources of her deeper self. As often as she could, she walked out into the dramatic landscape of rocky canyons and sun-blasted foothills, looking and absorbing, waiting for the "transaction," as she later named it, between her "spirit and the spirit of the land."[62] In later years, after she had written many books, she spoke with great assurance of her ability to renew the connection:

> ... Let me loose in the desert with the necessity for discovering
> truth about any creative process of the human mind, and I can pick
> up the thread from the movement of quail, from the shards of a broken
> bottle in the grass, from anything of beauty which comes my way.[63]

But it is clear that the thirteen years she spent in the California deserts were a difficult and lonely apprenticeship. Though she was helped, in her understanding of the "transaction" between herself and the land, by some members of a local Indian tribe, and though she was aided toward publication by the southwestern-culture aficionado Charles Fletcher Lummis, she was on her own in the task of making a whole expression out of her observations.[64]

The sustained freshness and artistic unity of her first book, *The Land of Little Rain* (1903), are thus marks of a coming through. Each of her sharp images in some way expressed the ecological coherence of the desert. Vultures perched themselves in a row on fenceposts, drooping in the heat and glare, and thirsty mules made "hideous, maimed noises";[65] where there was water, the aliveness of the favored place and its visitors seemed naturally expressed in metaphors of liquidity and flow:

> The crested quail that troop in the Ceriso are the happiest frequenters of the water trails. There is no furtiveness about their morning drink. About the time the burrowers and all that feed upon them are addressing themselves to sleep, great flocks pour down the trails with that peculiar melting motion of moving quail, twittering, shoving, and shouldering. They splatter into the shallows, drink daintily, shake out small showers over their perfect coats, and melt away again into the scrub, preening and pranking, with soft contented noises.[66]

The ecological sense of place is also strong in three other books by Mary Austin that can be considered under the nature writing heading: *The Flock* (1906), a tribute to outdoor folklife centered on sheep raising; *California, the Land of the Sun* (1914, reprinted in 1927 as *The Lands of the Sun*), which contains fairly specific instruction on how to come into deep and creative contact with a landscape; and *The Land of Journeys' Ending* (1924), an account of Austin's return to the Southwest from the literary world of New York. The last of these three books was also (as she called it) a "book of prophecy" about how the American desert lands could, and would, give rise to "the *next* great and fructifying world culture."[67] But as Austin gained wider acceptance in the cultural world, leaving Owens Valley for the Carmel artists' colony in 1905 and later moving on to New York and Europe, her literary treatment of the environment, understandably perhaps, tended to become less sharp. She began to favor broad, sweeping statements and appeared to enjoy the oracular persona she presented to the world: I-Mary of the desert. Thus the return she describes in *The Land of Journeys' Ending* is rather like that of a prodigal. Although the book makes enigmatic, grand-scale remarks about the power of the desert to shape history and the mind of humanity, the writing also presents, here and there, the illuminated detail that seems to have come with fresh experience—in a vivid description of the blooming and fruiting of the giant saguaro or a close-focus account of the way a common tree may suddenly strike an observer as a thing entirely new and alive. It appears that on Austin's motor trip across the Southwest, as she was doing fieldwork for her projected book of homecoming, she went below the drama of the occasion and found the desert again, the place of her authentic inspiration. It was again a country where at any moment there could occur between writer and landscape the "flash of mutual awareness."[68]

Mary Austin's death in 1934 came at the close of a great transitional era. Only a century before, when Henry Thoreau was a seventeen-year-old college student, the railroads were in their infancy, little more than experimental, and crossing the continent, as Thomas Nuttall did in that year of 1834, was a serious expeditionary undertaking. Huge stretches of the country were still wild, and there were many Indian tribes in the West still living in the old way. Now, in 1934, the United States had consolidated as a modern technological state. The frontier had been closed for almost half a century, and the remaining wilderness, outside Alaska, had been reduced to fragments. Even in the early 1920s, Mary Austin in her homecoming had traveled over Arizona and New Mexico by automobile, rather comfortably. The wild bloom was gone, in fact, from a good deal of the desert, where the reclamation that John Van Dyke had said should never be imposed on what he called the "breathing-spaces" of the West was well under way. Hoover Dam (which Austin had opposed) had been completed in the early 1930s, inaugurating an intense, decades-long period of reservoir building that would alter the face of much of the western landscape. Most Americans' daily lives took place within a built, managed environment. The overriding concern in the country, in the Depression year of 1934, was how to get the economic system back to the health it had enjoyed in the long boom. What room would there be, in an increasingly artificial, dollars-and-cents world, for nature and the "flash of mutual awareness"?

THE TWENTIETH CENTURY

THE AMERICAN LITERATURE OF nature may seem, on first acquaintance, to have undergone little development, as if it had somehow resis-
ted, at the core, the realities of changing times. From the age of Bartram
to the present, the main outlines of the genre—presentation of instructive natural history information, description of personal experience in
nature, and commentary on our relationship with the wild world—
have not changed an iota. The great question, "How shall we live?" is
the same today as when William Bartram described his paradise of a
wilderness campsite in Georgia, comparing it to the strife-filled civilization he had temporarily left behind.

But the twentieth century has required of nature writers a depth of
response that is fundamentally new. In the brief survey that follows, I
have chosen a few representative writers to illustrate how the capacities
of nature literature have been stretched by modern conditions. First
and most obviously, writers about nature have had to keep up with a
tremendous increase in natural history knowledge. For example, it is
probably fair to say that John McPhee (as shown in *Basin and Range*,
1980, and *Rising from the Plains*, 1986) has had to learn more geology
than John Muir, who first made a reputation with a study of Sierran
glacial history, ever knew, in order to describe landforms in their true
depth. When Muir died in 1914, plate tectonics, a major reference for
McPhee, was not yet even a hypothesis, though there had been intuitions
about continental drift. It can be argued that Muir, with his limited factual knowledge, saw as deeply into the implications of geology as McPhee
does, and thus made as much of his materials, however primitive. But to

write precisely about nature now simply takes more study than it did a century ago. There have also been great advances in marine biology, so that if Rachel Carson were alive today to update once more *The Sea Around Us* (first published in 1950, revised in 1951 and 1961), she would be faced with an enormous new body of research data to incorporate. Equally far-reaching advances have been made in cellular biology, where Lewis Thomas has made a literary breakthrough; in ethology, the study of animal behavior, out of which insights into our own lives leap regularly; and in evolutionary biology and ecology, which provide a literally endless array of evidence on the interdependence of life forms and their environments. New knowledge has invigorated nature writing with a fresh infusion of subjects for wonder and has increased the importance of the genre's status as an interpretive literature. Today, in an age of specialization and overspecialization, it is commonly the nature essayist who ponders the human and cultural implications as new facts come to light.

Nonetheless, individuals probably continue to experience the environment in much the same way as in preindustrial times; not enough time has passed in the impoverished, indoor situation for there to have been alterations in the ways of the brain and mind. Indeed, the essay of experience in nature continues to celebrate widened perception and the numinous moment of connection. But there have been sweeping changes in the human ecology of America that have to be taken into account. The brute fact is that urban industrialism is now pervasive and totally dominant. There are no more blank places on the map—those wild realms that Thoreau in the nineteenth century and Aldo Leopold in the twentieth, with many of their countrymen, thought to be a necessity of life. The Wilderness Act of 1964, an admirable piece of protective legislation, nevertheless could only safeguard remnants. The science of island biogeography, first described in a technical paper in the 1950s, has shown that most present wilderness areas, even large ones, cannot sustain populations of all species. Furthermore, even in the most remote wilderness area the sights and sounds of the modern apparatus may prove inescapable: jet planes pass overhead, making noise and leaving trails across the sky, and at night the satellites (of which there are now several thousand) cross and recross—reminders, if we need reminding, that the environment is virtually saturated with message-bearing long waves, medium waves, shortwaves, and microwaves.

The specter of a tamed world has haunted many American nature essayists. In "Walking," Thoreau asked, "What would become of us, if we walked only in a garden or a mall?" but in his day the question could be only conjectural. The situation had become more ominous by 1969, when John Hay wrote, "As we diminish our environment, both physically and in terms of our attitude toward it, so we diminish our range of attention. Half the beauties of the world are no longer seen. What will we be when left to nothing but our own devices!"[1] But as the truly wild places in the natural world have been cut back, many modern nature writers, while militantly decrying this process, have at the same time recognized their own membership in the dominant modern pattern. This is a crucial realization, granting authenticity to their observations and allowing the nature essay to reach toward a new psychological comprehensiveness. One could choose to write only of the "green" side of oneself, but the insights would be unpenetrating. The best of the modern writers reveals much more. In *The Undiscovered Country* (1981), a book that makes a strong argument for living settled in one place, John Hay begins with a statement of his own sense of displacement after World War II. Hay describes watching a sunset on Cape Cod, which is where he came to rest, "with no sense that having moved to this place I was really planted anywhere."[2] Edward Abbey, with his typical knowing sense of humor, declares his preference for refrigerated beer, even (or especially) in the hot desert, and describes himself driving a "safe and sane" eighty-five miles an hour down a two-lane road in Utah. Edward Hoagland demonstrates his membership in our complex human scene by writing of wolves, bears, mountain lions, and wilderness with an ardent lover's tone and yet somehow with a city person's edge of realism, coolly assessing the chance for survival of the nonhuman among the human. Barry Lopez sees the ironies in being transported by airplane to the wild Arctic and describes with evident fellow-feeling the oil-rig workers whose job, in effect, is to undo the wilderness he honors. These writers, and many others today, respond to the national gestalt from a position both in and out of it. The vision they present seems unmistakably modern and more comprehending than the simple ambivalence that prevailed in the day of Audubon.

Modern nature writing has acquired another level of intellectual complexity from the discovery in the past century of a vast amount of new knowledge about humanity's past. We know a great deal more about our ragged course on earth than our eighteenth- and nineteenth-century counterparts could have. Through such disciplines as archaeology, anthropology, paleontology, and paleobotany, we have learned, for example, that agriculture emerged only some ten or twelve thousand years ago, that the first cities are only half that age, and that the very establishment of agriculture, long regarded as integral to progress, may in fact have involved some serious, perhaps irreparable, negatives. A different perspective is latent in findings such as these, and we have become self-conscious as a species in much the same fashion as we have on the individual level. Not only do we know that we have become a major force on the earth, but we also know in fairly good detail how we got that way.

The writings of two influential twentieth-century nature essayists, Aldo Leopold and Joseph Wood Krutch, incorporate much of the modern perspective. Both men had an acute interest, quite scholarly in Krutch's case, in Western humanity's ecophilosophical history, and both were conscious of having made, in their own lives, a significant intellectual turn. As they moved from the traditional, dualistic outlook on the world to an ecological view, each writer left a clearly marked trail of his journey and, in the process, helped shape the great change in our outlook on the environment.

Aldo Leopold, a graduate of the School of Forestry at Yale University, went to the Southwest in 1909 as a ranger in the brand-new United States Forest Service. At that time, he apparently agreed with the emphasis on production that has colored the philosophy of the Forest Service from its founding in 1906, and, in addition, joined with a will the Service's public relations campaign to gain favor with local stockmen. To that end, Leopold became a leader in the war on predators in Arizona and New Mexico. The idea behind this program of elimination was that fewer wolves and mountain lions would mean more deer for hunters and more safety for cattle and sheep. "In those days we had never heard of passing up a chance to kill a wolf," Leopold later wrote.[3] From his official position, Leopold exhorted southwesterners to kill, in his words, "varmints" and "vermin"—that is, predatory animals. However, this crusade did not subsume all of Leopold's attitudes toward nature. He was also aesthetically sensitive to wild country, particularly the mountainous southwestern corner of New Mexico and the nearby ranges of eastern Arizona, and as a hunter he enjoyed backcountry pack trips greatly. He proposed to his superiors in the Forest Service the preservation of "representative portions of some forests" for recreation as the highest use.[4] As early as 1922, he argued for wilderness classification for over a million acres of land in the Gila Mountains of New Mexico, and in 1924 the Gila Primitive Area was created as the first such protected wilderness on Forest Service land.

Despite this signal accomplishment, Leopold's major emphasis during his southwestern years was on production-oriented resource management. He searched for the keys to the increase of trees, cattle, sheep, wild turkeys, and deer. Over the years, as his career took him to Wisconsin and specialization in game management, and as he found repeatedly that manipulations of the environment based upon linear cause-and-effect theory did not work as planned, Leopold gradually came to believe that nature was more complex, mystifyingly more complex, than the traditional, managerial outlook could understand. His ecological research into population fluctuations of white-tailed deer showed that deer numbers were more sensitive to habitat health and climatic factors than to hunting regulations; humanity, Leopold found, could not turn on and turn off wildlife populations like so many faucets. More and more, he came to see productivity as a function of the overall health of the habitat.

In 1936, Leopold made a trip to the mountains of Chihuahua, Mexico, and there had an experience that seemed to focus his uneasiness with the simple, linear, resource-management outlook. It was in Chihuahua that he "first clearly realized that land is an organism, that all my life I had seen only sick land, whereas here was a biota still in perfect aboriginal health. The term 'unspoiled wilderness' took on a new meaning."[5] The frustratingly complicated world of game management, and then this sudden vision of wild integrity, together appeared to have catalyzed Leopold's philosophical awareness. Clearly, when humanity attempted to manage nature on simplistic lines (almost always for selfish reasons, to boot), it was acting out of both ignorance and arrogance. Ecology was showing an infinitely more complex world than had heretofore even been suspected, and humanity's ethical sense should somehow expand to match the new knowledge.

In *A Sand County Almanac* (1949), Leopold brought his humbling scientific research, his illuminative experience of the Mexican wilderness, and an admission of his complicity in predator elimination together into a daring, elegantly phrased ethical formula:

> A thing is right when it tends to preserve the integrity, stability, and beauty of the biotic community. It is wrong when it tends otherwise.[6]

These two sentences have become a rallying point for biocentrist thinking in the decades since their publication. They represent perhaps the clearest statement we have that moral content may be found in the science of ecology and in the experience of wild beauty. The intellectual, aesthetic, and ethical understanding is here founded in biological reality, and that fusion may amount to one of the few genuinely new philosophical statements of the twentieth century.

Joseph Wood Krutch's intellectual journey was a bit different, since he had never been a forest ranger nor killed a predator, but in essence it maps the same critical watershed of thought. As a professor of literature and a well-known drama critic living in New York City, Krutch in the 1920s and 1930s was in touch with the main intellectual currents of his time and place. In an influential book, *The Modern Temper* (1929), he expressed what seemed to him the thinking person's only logical response to the naturalistic universe that science had revealed: pessimism. But Krutch's pessimism had a heroic tinge: "Ours is a lost cause and there is no place for us in the natural universe, but we are not, for all that, sorry to be human. We should rather die as men than live as animals."[7] One could hardly ask for a neater, more ringing summary of the dualistic and specist view of life. Krutch's position here was similar to Sigmund Freud's, voiced in 1930 in *Civilization and Its Discontents,* especially in its concept of humanity and its tragic-heroic separateness. It may be taken as representative of a predominant theme in urban Western thought. "Humanism" and "Nature," Krutch declared, "are fundamentally antithetical."[8]

But Krutch apparently was not as dogmatic as his book's conclusion would indicate. Perhaps influenced by Thoreau, whom he first read in 1930 and about whom he wrote an insightful biography in 1948, and perhaps also influenced by the surroundings of his country home in Connecticut, he began sometime in the late 1930s to move away from the alienated position of *The Modern Temper.* By 1950, as demonstrated in his prologue to *Great American Nature Writing,* Krutch had become doubtful that the assertion of human separateness was true to the facts. In that essay he leaned strongly toward the countertradition of empathy with nature. A sabbatical year in the Arizona desert seems to have been decisive in his philosophical turn, for in 1952 Krutch moved to Arizona and commenced an intensive, devoted study of the desert flora and fauna. In the next several years, he wrote some of the most important nature essays of the post–World War II era, essays in which the great theme was human intelligence coming awake to its essential continuity with nature. This was, of course, his own story. In *The Voice of the Desert* (1954), he quietly rejected the dualistic model of human consciousness, a major step.

> Perhaps the mind is not merely a blank slate upon which anything may be written. Perhaps it reaches out spontaneously toward what can nourish either intelligence or imagination. Perhaps it is part of nature and, without being taught, shares nature's intentions.[9]

Living in the desert, studying its well-adapted life forms, opening up to what he wittily called the "xeric profundities" of the Southwest, Krutch seemed to come alive to nonseparatist possibilities. When birds sing, he wondered, why shouldn't they be expressing joy as well as marking their nesting territories? He scorned the Cartesian, mechanistic description of animals' lives and looked for lines of connection between them and humanity. As he learned more about ecological patterns, and then experienced wilderness firsthand in the Grand Canyon and in Baja California, he began to consider the possibility of wildness as an overarching concept. His books became wilder and wilder. Perhaps, as Thoreau had said, wildness was the sustaining, creative principle of the world—its preservation. As such, it would of course be far greater than our powers of intellect and thus might suggest to us a wholeness beyond alienation. In one of his last essays, Krutch affirmed the possibility of a healing, spiritual allegiance to the wild:

> Faith in wildness, or in nature as a creative force, has the deeper, possibly the deepest, significance for our future. It is a philosophy, a faith; it is even, if you like, a religion. It puts our ultimate trust, not in human intelligence, but in whatever it is that created human intelligence and is, in the long run, more likely than we to solve our problems.[10]

However clearly writers like Leopold and Krutch were affirming this new view, actual practice in industrial America through the 1940s and 1950s continued virtually undisturbed by the implications of ecology. World War II accelerated the development of certain technologies like the bulldozer, airplane, and helicopter and enlarged the arsenal of chemicals used against insects and weeds. In the economically prosperous 1950s, as the nation resumed the boom psychology it had not enjoyed for over twenty years, all of these instruments and more were used on the American environment, to great effect.

Not many questions were asked. When Rachel Carson, an editor and writer who had gained fame as an essayist on the sea, finally marshaled a body of evidence against the careless use of pesticides and herbicides in *Silent Spring* (1962), so outraged was the chemical establishment at this unaccustomed criticism that the author herself became a center of controversy and an object of attack from industrial and bureaucratic quarters. But Carson had earned her standing as an ecologist, and her work stood firm. Using a large number of case histories, she demonstrated that the chemical warfare against certain insects and weeds, which had begun only in the mid-1940s, had by 1962 already worked an incalculable negative effect on the biotic community and on humanity itself. It came as a shock to many readers of *Silent Spring* to learn that our capacity for environmental mischief was now, with the new power to affect life on the cellular and genetic levels, much more serious than mere mischief. The very character of our influence on the earth had changed, becoming both more penetrating and more universal. In this new situation, where over-the-counter consumer products were damaging biological communities hundreds and even thousands of miles distant, nothing less than an ecologically conscious public would be required.

Carson was well prepared for this challenge. She was the first female editor in chief for the United States Fish and Wildlife Service and had written three substantial and well-researched books on the ocean and the littoral zone: *Under the Sea-Wind* (1941); *The Sea Around Us* (1950), which became one of the best-sellers of its time and which has subsequently been translated into some forty languages;[11] and *The Edge of the Sea* (1955), also much honored. In these books, in a deceptively simple style, Carson structured remarkable quantities of data, bringing the facts of oceanography and marine biology to life by stressing their interrelationships. She also conveyed the poetry and sublimity of her subjects, though keeping narrative accounts of her own responses to a minimum, by a precise combination of dramatic language, well-considered rhythms, and the concrete terminology of science. Thus, the sudden drop from the continental shelf to the abyssal plain shows, in her words, the "grandeur of slope topography." Combining aesthetic and scientific language in this manner allowed Carson to describe vast and complex natural systems with impressive economy: in *The Sea Around Us*, for example, her account of the formation of the planet, the possible origin of the moon, the gathering of the oceans, the establishment of continents, and the history of life on earth—in outline, to be sure—comes to only a little over twelve pages of text, yet it is so well controlled in shape and pace, so vivid in its images and accurate in its choice of verbs, and so careful and scholarly in its attributions, that it persuades conclusively.

The key to the economy of her writing and her ability to evoke the full sense of life is her concentration on relationships. In *The Sea Around Us*, Carson describes each element in the complex food chains of the ocean, from the salts that wash from the land to the herrings that swarm in certain good locations, making sure that her readers perceive the linkages that make abundance possible. The diverse wind patterns, the differences in salinity of the various oceans, even the varying sea levels all create different, immensely ramifying ecological conditions; thus each ecosystem has a unique complement of flora and fauna. Carson's genius was to portray relationship not as some sort of structural juxtaposition but as the living quick of things.

The fundamental responsibility to facts, and then the artistic control of a complex, interactive scene, are what give *Silent Spring* its authority.

It was absolutely necessary to the book's success that its readers understand living relationships. Carson directed her strengths as a writer to
that end. But that was not all, for after understanding there must come
action. To the ecological lecture, she added sharp, plainspoken criticism,
designed to arouse her readers. A careful description of the complexity
and aliveness of soil, for example, is followed by "the plain truth is that
this critically important subject of the ecology of the soil has been largely
neglected even by scientists and almost completely ignored by control
men."[12] A similarly detailed account of the fire ant, a recent import into
the Southeast that had aroused great alarm in some quarters, is rounded
out by a concise denunciation of the chemical campaign against it:

> Never has any pesticide program been so thoroughly and deservedly
> damned by practically everyone except the beneficiaries of this "sales
> bonanza." It is an outstanding example of an ill-conceived, badly exe-
> cuted, and thoroughly detrimental experiment in the mass control of
> insects, an experiment so expensive in dollars, in destruction of animal
> life, and in loss of public confidence in the Agriculture Department that
> it is incomprehensible that any funds should still be devoted to it.[13]

Silent Spring became a force in American life. There had been solid
books about our abuse of the environment well before its time, of
course, notably George Perkins Marsh's pioneering *Man and Nature*
(1864), and Fairfield Osborn's *Our Plundered Planet* (1948) in Carson's
own day, but none had rested on so wide a knowledge of ecological
processes, and none had aroused such a strong response. Carson's work
has been a basic text for the ecological awakening of the past almost
forty years because it told clearly what can happen when intricate natural systems are, in effect, bludgeoned. It brought right down to earth, to
daily life, the need for ecological consciousness.

The expanding technosphere, some of whose consequences were described so cogently by Rachel Carson, has also had an inevitable effect
upon the literature of solitude. In the modern era, being alone in nature

may still refresh the spirit, but the literary record indicates there now may be, quite often, a certain shadowed quality to the experience. Henry Beston, for one, felt the historical moment keenly, as he makes clear in his poetic record of a year on the Great Beach of Cape Cod, *The Outermost House* (1928). He does not give his personal reasons for wanting to spend a year alone, facing out to the ocean not far from the pounding surf on the forearm of the Cape, but he does describe the insulation and malaise of modern humanity: "The world to-day is sick to its thin blood for lack of elemental things, for fire before the hands, for water welling from the earth, for air, for the dear earth itself underfoot."[14] Solitude, then, is a recovery, quite consciously undertaken. Beston's writing conveys a tactile sense of the sandy footing and the scouring, dune-shaping wind, a clear awareness of the stars at night and the look of the rocking waves offshore. These things bring a restoration of health. On the Great Beach, where the outlines of one's world are simpler than in most places, each element and each perception seem to register deeply. The world appears charged with meaning. A flock of shorebirds wheels in the bright air, their sudden changes of direction mysterious, absorbing: "Does some current flow through them and between them as they fly?"[15]

Good evidence for the healing effect of Beston's year on the beach may be indicated by his positive, natural-seeming attitude toward other people. He describes his nearest neighbors, the young men of a Coast Guard station some miles up the beach, with interest and care, sharing a comradeship of night and storm with them on several occasions. The great natural context of the beach grants humankind here what Beston's contemporary, the poet Robinson Jeffers, called the "dignity of rareness." In an incident that occurs near the end of his record, one carrying a certain summary emphasis perhaps, Beston comes upon a young man swimming in the surf. He sets forth a description of this swimmer with the same well-knit phrasing and clear imagery that he has used to express his reverence for birds, or for deer seen playing on the beach, or for the breaking surf itself.

It was all a beautiful thing to see: the surf thundering across the great
natural world, the beautiful and compact body in its naked strength
and symmetry, the astounding plunge across the air, arms extended
ahead, legs and feet together, the emerging stroke of the flat hands, and
the alternate rhythms of the sunburned and powerful shoulders.[16]

The Outermost House closes with earnest exhortations, as if marking
a far traveler's return to the world of humanity: "Whatever attitude to
human existence you fashion for yourself, know that it is valid only if
it be the shadow of an attitude to Nature. . . . Do no dishonour to the
earth lest you dishonour the spirit of man. . . . Touch the earth, love the
earth, honour the earth, her plains, her valleys, her hills, and her seas;
rest your spirit in her solitary places."[17]

It was forty years before another talismanic book of solitude in
American nature appeared. Those forty years included the Great Depression, World War II, the invention and use of the atomic bomb, the
rise and flourishing of a sophisticated, existential outlook that deeply
undercut our ability and willingness to make confident statements on
the meanings of things, and, in the developed countries, perhaps especially in the United States, the ascendancy of consumerism, which is to
say, the tendency to trivialize all items by seeing them as commodities.
The world that developed in those forty years inspired urgency by its hec-
tic and worsening political and environmental conditions; at the same
time, the intellectual climate tended toward super self-consciousness
and thus a certain ironic attitude toward any human motivation. In this
modern time it is difficult to be wholehearted, even about nature; we
have that orientation, after all, pigeonholed as "romanticism."

By the time of the publication of *Desert Solitaire* in 1968, Edward
Abbey seems to have digested the implications, at least as they applied
to writing about experience in nature, of this modern complexity.
He had developed a style that spoke idiomatically to his audience—
Americans who believed almost as a genetic article of faith that there
was still a wilderness somewhere, where perhaps purification was still

possible, but who also had purchased enough shoddy goods in their lifetimes to be profoundly skeptical people. In *Desert Solitaire* and other works, Abbey has reproduced this mixed consciousness perfectly, preserving the authenticity of his deepest commitment, which is to wilderness, honoring it in its essential mystery above all else, and yet at the same time speaking knowingly, with an edge of black humor, as a realist firmly in touch with his time.

The seriousness of *Desert Solitaire* is paradoxically well served by its bantering, self-deprecating, yet often hyperbolic prose. The style is loose, able to move about in the world, so to speak, not constricted too much by righteousness or self-importance. Using this style, Abbey is able to breathe life into some of the hoariest dilemmas of philosophy, such as the ancient conflict in epistemology between realism and idealism, and he is able to present his own search for meaning in the desert (a quest that must transcend that old perceptual dilemma, among other obstacles) in personal, accessible terms.

The scene of *Desert Solitaire* is the deeply dissected Colorado Plateau country of southern Utah, mainly the area in and around Arches National Monument (now Arches National Park), where Abbey was a seasonal ranger for some years. The plot, loosely, is separation into solitude, attempted initiation, and return: classic. The central quest, although Abbey probably would not call it that, is to come into contact with the desert, to know the desert if possible, to learn there something about life in general—"what it had to teach," as Thoreau said in *Walden*.

Noon is the crucial hour: the desert reveals itself nakedly and cruelly, with no meaning but its own existence.

My lone juniper stands half-alive, half-dead, the silvery wind-rubbed claw of wood projected stiffly at the sun. A single cloud floats in the sky to the northeast, motionless, a magical coalescence of vapor where a few minutes before there was nothing visible but the hot, deep, black-grained blueness of infinity.

Life has come to a standstill, at least for the hour. In this forgotten place the tree and I wait on the shore of time, temporarily free from the force of motion and process and the surge toward—what? Something called the *future?* I am free, I am compelled, to contemplate the world which underlies life, struggle, thought, ideas, the human labyrinth of hope and despair.[18]

Looking to know that world better in action, Abbey hikes into the Grand Canyon, climbs to the summit of a thirteen thousand-foot mountain, and descends into "terra incognita," a maze of canyons, among other journeys, tests, and inquiries. In the end, what he reports back as real and undeniable are, in his word, "surfaces": "the sunlight on rock and leaves, the feel of music, the bark of a tree, the abrasion of granite and sand, the plunge of clear water into a pool, the face of the wind—what else is there? What else do we need?"[19]

Apparently, some of us believe we need much more, and in illustration of the society of surfeit Abbey presents "industrial tourism." The object of this consumerist mode of travel is to go to as many certified destinations as possible, as swiftly as possible, in maximum comfort. In Abbey's satiric but somewhat compassionate depiction, however, the industrial tourist, for all possessions and seeming command of time and space, is a victim, forced to cover enormous mileages by car, to endure fatigue, and to face heavy and dangerous traffic, in order to have only a quick look at a famous scene. What the industrial tourist ought to do, if the spark of revolution were to touch, is escape the machine. "In the first place you can't see *anything* from a car; you've got to get out of the goddamned contraption and walk, better yet crawl, on hands and knees, over the sandstone and through the thornbush and cactus."[20] But the victim remains immured, a poignant case, last seen making "the long drive home at night in a stream of racing cars against the lights of another stream racing in the opposite direction, passing now and then the obscure tangle, the shattered glass, the patrolman's lurid blinker light, of one more wreck."[21]

Like the journey into solitude, the theme of commitment to a piece of land as a steward derives from an old and honored American circumstance. In the twentieth century, though, in response to radically changed conditions, writing based on farm life has matured significantly, growing in its range of comment well beyond the emotional core of agrarianism. As we have seen, even Crèvecoeur in the late eighteenth century depicted the dark side of the farmer's existence, but it is doubtful that he could have imagined what would be demanded of a farm essayist in the age of agribusiness.

The prominent American attitude toward the small family farm, which might be termed the "Currier and Ives" view, remains alive in the urban-industrial era but is rendered sentimental and more or less irrelevant by demographics: the number of people on farms, which amounted to 90 percent of the United States population in 1800, had slipped to only slightly more than 30 percent by 1920. By 1950, only 15 percent of Americans lived on farms, and by 1982 the figure had eroded further to just 3 percent. In less than two hundred years, capitalism and industrialism had fully transformed American agriculture, consolidating farmland into the paying proposition of large-scale monoculture, a revolution greatly facilitated by the change in farming's energy base from human and animal labor to fossil fuels. The often-cited independence of the American farmer, a trait that to Thomas Jefferson had seemed a fundamental ingredient of democracy, had had its economic base severely undercut. The trend was evident early in the nineteenth century; by the time of *Walden* (1854), Thoreau lamented the "fall from the farmer to the operative" as a fact of New England life. Between 1820 and 1860, writes Jan Wojcik, a modern agricultural historian, American farming changed from "many self-sufficient enterprises to fewer commercial enterprises growing cheap food for good profits."[22] Centralization proceeded even during the homestead era, and continues at present.

What all this has meant for the writer is that the farm has become a battleground between two great value systems. Hamlin Garland, in fiction, depicted the takeover of land by the absentee power of capitalism; Liberty Hyde Bailey, one of the important essayists of farm life in the early twentieth century, saw the displacement of the farm population as the work of the city, which he described as a "parasite, running out its roots into the open country and draining it of its substance."[23] Wendell Berry, in our own time, sees the farm "problem" as essentially the moral and spiritual problem of our civilization at large—we want food and fiber, and much else, but we do not want to work or take responsibility for these things. We want our needs to be supplied by industrial magic.

These writers see the farm as emblematic. For Bailey, for example, agriculture was not a problem that could perhaps be solved, or at least tinkered with, in the way a positivist society approaches its difficulties. What was required for a healthy agriculture was no less than a revolution in a people's entire concept of the world. In *The Holy Earth* (1915), Bailey wrote that American agriculture could not be restored to health, and thus to its full, necessary role in civilization, by "instructing the young" or by "any movement merely to have gardens, or to own farms." Nor would "rhapsodies on the beauties of nature" help much. A deep change, the adoption of what he called the "brotherhood relation," was needed, so that in our view of things, "the creation, and not man, is the norm."[24] Here, in this sample of what might be termed the "higher agrarianism" of the modern era, Bailey illustrated the essential continuity of the farm essay and the nature essay. He was proposing the same ecological and ethical outlook as John Burroughs, for example, or Aldo Leopold. Leopold, in fact, acknowledged Bailey as an influence.[25]

The emphasis on proportion and rightness that marks the moral essays of Wendell Berry appears to derive in large part from his working a small farm in Kentucky. A home place that had been in his family for generations, he returned to it in the 1960s after a foray into the national (which is to say, largely urban) literary world. The homecoming, as Berry described it in *The Long-Legged House* (1969), grew into a kind of revelation:

> I began to think of myself as living within rather than upon the life of the place. I began to think of my life as one among many, and one kind

among many kinds. I began to see how little of the beauty and the richness of the world is of human origin, and, how superficial and crude
and destructive—even self-destructive—is man's conception of himself
as the owner of the land and the master of nature and the center of the
universe.[26]

In the succeeding thirty-odd years, Berry's writing has elaborated
upon that moral insight. He farmed the ancestral acres, dealing with
inherited problems of erosion and trying to build up the health of the
soil; while doing this work, he wrote, after *The Long-Legged House*, *A
Continuous Harmony* (1972), *The Unsettling of America* (1977), and *The
Gift of Good Land* (1981), and these books form an interesting progression. After the return and the dawning of commitment, *A Continuous
Harmony* describes the work of restoration:

> At home the great delight is to see the clover and grass now grow-
> ing on places that were bare when we came. These small healings of the
> ground are my model accomplishment—everything else I do must as-
> pire to that. While I was at that work the world gained with every move
> I made, and I harmed nothing.[27]

The Unsettling of America applies the lessons learned to the larger
scale of American agribusiness. The crisis in industrial agriculture connects to the crisis in the environment in general, and to the physical diseases, social problems, and moral malaise that bedevil our time. "No
longer does human life rise from the earth like a pyramid, broadly and
considerately founded upon its sources. Now it scatters itself out in a
reckless horizontal sprawl, like a disorderly city whose suburbs and pave-
ments destroy the fields."[28] *The Gift of Good Land* continues at wide focus
by examining traditional (small-scale, labor-intensive) farming in a
couple of places where it still survives and by looking again at the religious and philosophical roots of our culture to see if there might be a
directive toward stewardship there, one that we could revive. The effect
of juxtaposing the practical and philosophical inquiries is to imply a

complete reconsideration of our way of life. Berry presents his heresy of humble stewardship with workaday calmness; all that is new in it is actually quite old, he implies, and well tested. The working base of the needed modern revolution, pointing toward the enlightened fitting together of humanity and nature, may turn out to be nothing more radical than "an excellent homestead." Berry describes a farm he visited:

> Everywhere you look you see the signs of care. You are in what appears to be a little cove, a wedge of flat land tucked in against a wooded hill. The natural character of the place has been respected, and yet it has been made to accommodate gracefully the various necessities of a family's life and work.[29]

The American nature essay based on travel obviously has a different bent from the agrarian essay; its charge of interest comes from the excitement of crossing the frontier between civilization and wilderness. In the modern time such a crossing is still potent, but now commonly involves a more complex awareness on the part of the traveler, who is a member of a world-dominant technological society and who is likely to realize that wilderness exists today only if human society wants it to exist. A certain balance has been tipped. Thus a modern traveler into the wild will be sensitive to his or her own perceptions and values, with regard to the wilderness, in ways that would not have been possible for someone of earlier times.

Two good examples of this present-day heightening of consciousness are furnished by the writings of Edward Hoagland and Barry Lopez. Hoagland, who describes himself as living half the year in New York City and the other half in Vermont, unblinkingly registers the actual state of the environment (the very small amount of true wilderness in New England, for instance) while letting his heart go out to its fated beauty. He hears the wilderness singing, but it is, in his words, a "swan song." He gravitates toward old-timers and field students who can perhaps convey what it was like to touch the former world. In *Notes from the Century Before: A Journal from British Columbia* (1969), Hoagland's most developed travel essay, he describes a journey into a realm of health and variety and interest that may even now be as remote as any fictional Shangri-la. In the summer of 1966, Hoagland left New York and in a few days, traveling by airplane, train, and boat, reached the tiny hamlet of Telegraph Creek, on the Stikine River in northwestern British Columbia. "To me it [Telegraph Creek] was a crossroads . . . where I could step back to the Snake River of 1885, hearing stories which hadn't worn threadbare with handling."[30] As the summer bloomed, he walked, boated, drove on primitive roads, and flew by bush plane over a magnificent wild area the size of two Ohios, as he says, reveling in the greenness. In the shadow of helicopters, almost literally, and just ahead of the bulldozers, he managed to interview some eighty people, from ancient Indians and holdover prospectors to the very young on their way up, growing up with the country, as the frontier phrase has it. He moved swiftly from one discovery to the next, exhilarated both by the country and the people. An undertone of elegy was provided by the trembling fragility of some of the old-timers and by the always ominous presence of helicopters—there had been a copper strike nearby. But Hoagland didn't stall on nostalgia; he was busy making a record.

The spirit of the summer was set with the author's first sight of Telegraph Creek. A young pilot, himself a newcomer and nervous about flying to Telegraph Creek for the first time, ferried the writer from lower on the Stikine in a two-seat Cessna floatplane:

> We fly over an old clearing, with its sole horse and its laborious log houses close enough to the bank for a fishing line to be run out the window. Telegraph Creek is a scatter of buildings, fantastic after coming so far. Both relieved, we land on the lake behind and unload the groceries. Nobody meets us except a curlew that does a curlew. I take it to be a good omen. The sky is clearing. The boy roars into the air, and I walk the two miles to town. The brush is full of birds cheeping and whistling. There's an elaborate system of flumes and trestles which

carries spring water, and I follow them down. The town is wonderfully sprinkled out on a half-dozen terraces, high levels and low. People wave and smile. I can scarcely remember ever being any happier.[31]

By the end of summer, Hoagland was tired from the sheer abundance of it, but he concluded his explorations ringingly, interviewing two of the old heroic surveyors, Frank Swannell in Victoria and E. C. Lamarque in Vancouver. These men had made prodigious journeys into the wilderness in a time when the wild was not recreation ground. As Hoagland put it, referring to Swannell's case, "These walks were just about the last go-round—the last exploration of the continent by foot that we'll ever have."[32] Hoagland described one of Lamarque's treks in terms suggesting what his own experiences that summer had meant: "It was that airy, aerial moment in time when a man is in country which nobody has ever set eyes on before, feeling blithe and surrounded by the sublime, yet constantly moving, as though to stop would be to founder and fall like a trapeze artist."[33] In Vancouver and at the airport before flying back to New York, plunged suddenly back into the "relentless, metronome scurry around," Hoagland sensed the true significance of the flight ahead of him:

It wasn't like coming home from one of the ancient cities of Europe or a month's isolation in one of the second-growth forests of Maine. This was a return to man himself from the previous existence, about to be sealed off and stoppered. I was alarmed by the crush.[34]

Barry Lopez has also gone north to see the remnant wilderness world, and has also witnessed the dismaying suddenness with which its ecosystems can be unraveled. In *Arctic Dreams* (1986) he has recorded his quests, and those of several others who preceded him, into the difficult and fragile Far North, and he has attempted to go beyond recording events and observations into an investigation of the mentality of seeking itself. *Arctic Dreams*, therefore, is a highly self-conscious book. But

Lopez's consciousness of self and nature is meant to be representative, and what develops is an exposition of two paths, two ways of seeing. We can approach the wild world (which is to say, the world) with designs on it, projections and preconceptions, or we can try to simply perceive it, to let it be whatever it is. Lopez's exposition becomes then a contemporary statement, almost a précis, of what may be the major ethical motif in American nature literature, the choice between domination and democratic membership. The alternatives frame the great question of how we should live.

What helps make this question fresh, when asked in the Arctic, is that the environment there is strange to us. Its extremes of light, its simplicity of contour, and of course its climate, taken together, make a perceptual field that people from the temperate zone are not accustomed to; it is, in some true sense, a "new world." For all our technological powers to make ourselves comfortable in the Arctic, and they are considerable, in the ways of the mind we have been placed again in a position somewhat like that of sixteenth-century Europeans confronting the lower latitudes of America. The Arctic has given us a chance to see the world anew. What most have done so far, as Lopez makes clear, is replay the heroic-tragic explorations (the search for the Northwest Passage, for example) and then the careless, gutting exploitation that has marked our settlement of the temperate zone. But there have been occasional quiet spirits who responded to the North on its own terms, not caring to convert it into something else but wanting positively to go to it as a student, in particular to learn the ways in which its native inhabitants lived, and possibly to see there some relevance for humanity in general. With a time lag of a century or two, and perhaps with a new historical awareness that opens up possibilities for ethical behavior, we have come again (very late, though, and with the world behind us pushing) to the wilderness in its innocence. The choice that defines us is before us once again. "Like other landscapes that initially appear barren, arctic tundra can open suddenly, like the corolla of a flower, when any intimacy with it is sought."[35]

In a brief magazine note, Barry Lopez ventured the rather daring idea that nature writing "will not only one day produce a major and lasting body of American literature, but that it might also provide the foundation for a reorganization of American political thought."[36] In a sense, I think, this has already happened; the foundation is in place, if we understand political thought to mean fundamentally the understanding of relationships. William Bartram, Henry Thoreau, John Muir, John Burroughs, Mary Austin, Aldo Leopold, Wendell Berry, Marcia Bonta, and many others have set forth a vision of the world that is fully and authentically political, and democratic. Politics, properly understood, is not simply human affairs; it involves the standing of each and every element making up the one world, the biosphere we partake of. Democracy properly understood gives the vote to trees—they *should* have standing, as Justice William O. Douglas argued in a pathfinding dissent—and to hawks, worms, aquifers, coal seams, wolves, bats, and the life-sustaining atmosphere. Democracy, as American nature literature has presented it, widens and fulfills the American premise. It is not the portioning out of power strictly within human society, but a much deeper movement of mind and heart, an opening of the self in recognition and gratitude to an all-including greater self.

As we record another twelve years since the first edition of this book, we must stand in awe of the faithfulness of nature writers and the stability of their subject. There has been nothing in this decade or so to change the nature essay in its fundamentals, but there has been an explosion of output and a suddenness of critical attention by the academy. Two hundred years (1790–1990) had produced 500 books, more or less. Ten years (1990–2000), 175—and still counting.

The two chief reasons for the new wave are the rapid decline of the environment—caused mainly by population growth—and the rise of feminism. Other, more specifically critical movements, such as deconstruction, have also received attention, but haven't had much effect on nature literature.

In 1987, world population stood for a moment at about 5 billion; in

1999 it was 6 billion. In just twelve years, we added to the world one hundred Los Angeleses. In doing so, we subtracted a great deal from the planet. The population bomb is real, and it is the underlying cause of the problems in pollution and loss of ecological integrity. Daily newspapers bring more headlines, and we are stunned, perhaps, into silence. Now of course American nature writers can do little about this but write. But write they certainly have.

To understand the effect of broad movements such as feminism, which has operated in the field of nature writing as it has in every other genre, it is necessary to look at the actual output. Feminism has had an amazing impact, resulting in many more female writers and, with that, an invigorated genre. In the last five years or so, there have been as many women authors as men, quantitatively, and, qualitatively, there is no difference.

Lorraine Anderson's *Sisters of the Earth: Women's Prose and Poetry about Nature* (1991) and Marcia Bonta's *Women in the Field* (1991), two critical anthologies, signaled the opening of the field for women. Both featured women who had been neglected, and both in effect argued for female equality. Bonta followed with *American Women Afield* in 1995, a collection of writings featuring female naturalists that was used as a textbook, and nowadays anthologies of nature writing are certain to include women. Nature writing takes full part in the general, healthful trend sponsored by feminism.

Irene Diamond and Gloria Feman Orenstein printed most of the papers from a 1987 conference in *Reweaving the World: The Emergence of Ecofeminism* in 1990; it would be hard to find a clearer statement. (Of Rachel Carson, the editors write, "Although Carson was not an avowed feminist, many would argue that it was not coincidental that a woman was the first to respond both emotionally and scientifically to the wanton human domination of the natural world."[37]) Despite such an introduction, however, it would take a sharp-eyed critic indeed to find nature writing with an ecofeminist slant. The writing seems to

have been done in the traditional manner, that is, without overtly feminist ideology.

To see the effect of feminism, we need to step back a little. We need
to look at the mere existence of a book—for example, Janisse Ray's
Ecology of a Cracker Childhood (1999). We can't know absolutely, absent
the feminist movement, whether this book would have been written.
But the themes of the book, the writing style, the courage of the author,
do exist, and we are the richer for it. Ray writes early in the book:

> As soon as I learned to walk, I would wander into the beyond,
> where the junk began, touching the pint-sized redbud my mother had
> planted or the hymn of chinaberry that dropped wrinkled and poison-
> ous drupes into the grass. When my mother called, I would crouch in
> the dirt behind the water pump, perfectly still and quiet, making her
> search for me. It wasn't a game.
> "Half-wild," she'd murmur. She had to tie bells on my shoes, silver
> jingle bells that gave away my whereabouts and led her to me.[38]

Ray's voice leads readers to her just as insistently. We haven't any choice
in the matter. We are going to learn about the junkyard in which the
house sits, and about the family, and the grandparents, and finally the
great lost pine forests of Georgia. Once the life of the girl growing up
and the fate of the pine forests are integrated, nothing seems more
natural.

A deconstructive debate about wilderness would seem to be central
to nature writing, and when William Cronon fired the first round with
his essay, "The Trouble with Wilderness; or, Getting Back to the Wrong
Nature," which argued (deconstructively) that wilderness is a purely
conceptual item, it may have seemed that wild nature would never be
the same.[39] In fact, a debate of sorts resulted, with Cronon answered by
Gary Snyder and Donald Worster, among others. But looking for positive evidence of this argument in nature literature, I find profoundly
little. The writers of nature essays have focused elsewhere.

One of the themes sponsored by the new criticism is a general loosening, and a move into the new openness, by the self of the writer. One of the most interesting hikers on the Appalachian Trail, for example, is Ian Marshall, whose book, *Story Line: Exploring the Literature of the Appalachian Trail* (1998), depends upon its author's having hiked the "AT." It is a good example to look at for the impact of critical theory on nature writing; before this no critics had parlayed hiking the trail into a book. In this carefully constructed book, the author comes forward into the narrative, creating a seamlessness that works well. What you get is an authoritative look at Bartram, Dillard, Thoreau, and others, including extensive quotations from their writings, and Marshall's personal narrative criticism of authors and people along the trail—just as if you yourself were walking with him. Descriptive accounts of the trail are mixed with the critical treatment of the literature. The result is an uncommonly rich and thoughtful book.

Something similar can be said of John P. O'Grady's *Pilgrims to the Wild* (1993) and Don Scheese's *Nature Writing: The Pastoral Impulse in America* (1996), two spirited dissertations to see print in the new flood of interest in nature writing in the 1990s. O'Grady responds intensely to his subjects' desire for the wild, as he sees it, and Scheese, whose position is slightly more restrained, walks the home ground of his subjects avidly. Neither author is afraid of the personal pronoun. Such work, with its freedom from old-style graduate work and its definite authorial presence, is part of the manner of the modern dissertation.

Freedom from the traditional was in fact the trademark of criticism given to nature writing in the 1990s. Studies that were heavyweight without seeming so, such as Max Oelschlaeger's *The Idea of Wilderness* (1991), Sherman Paul's *For Love of the World* (1992), and Lawrence Buell's *The Environmental Imagination* (1995), gave solid footing to younger scholars without being overbearing. Not all the work was on paper. The founding of the Association for the Study of Literature and Environment in 1992 should be mentioned as one of the principal events of the decade. ASLE, as it is known, is the active focal point for green criticism. J. Parker Huber's journal, *Writing Nature,* began in 1990, a purely nonacademic effort that has a fine bibliography. Within the last ten years, nature writing has become a subject in several English departments at universities across the country, especially in the West. In 1987, this was a topic hardly noticed, but environmental consciousness in this country has been raised considerably.

In any general discussion of nature literature of the 1990s, we need to notice the omnipresence of the pronoun "I," the autobiographical intention. This of course is hard to limit to the nineties: after all, Thoreau, Muir, Burroughs, and others were liberal with the first person. But there is a difference. One can't know whether the basic intention is recording the self, or nature. For instance, quoting Janisse Ray again:

> In a 1995 National Biological Service assessment of biological loss, ecologist Reed Noss classified the longleaf/wiregrass community as "critically endangered." Ninety-eight percent of the presettlement longleaf pine barrens in the southeasten coastal plains were lost by 1986, he said. Natural stands—meaning not planted—have been reduced by about 99 percent.
>
> Apocalyptic.
>
> This was not a loss I knew as a child. *Longleaf* was a word I never heard. But it is a loss that as an adult shadows every step I take. I am daily aghast at how much we have taken, since it does not belong to us, and how much as a people we have suffered in consequence.
>
> Not long ago I dreamed of actually cradling a place, as if something so amorphous and vague as a region, existing mostly in imagination and idea, suddenly took form. I held its shrunken relief in my arms, a baby smelted from a plastic topography map, and when I gazed down into its face, as my father had gazed into mine, I saw the pine flatwoods of my homeland.[40]

The autobiographical impulse seems critical to most contemporary nature writing. In *Ecology of a Cracker Childhood,* the balance seems about even—which is just right for its theme. In book after book, authors try for that kind of magic.

Many of the critical studies of the nineties treat the literature as a personal account, or at least bring the self forward. Self is certainly active: look at Don Scheese, writing about Thoreau's ascent of Mt. Katahdin.

> I shall discuss the six-paragraph conclusion in a moment. First, though, some insights into "Ktaadn" based on my fieldwork. I climbed Mt. Katahdin in late July 1993, in conditions remarkably similar to those experienced by Thoreau. I, too, was whited out; clouds prohibited any expansive views. Unlike Thoreau, I did reach the true summit (along with perhaps 50 others that day). The mountain, with its plateau-like, windswept, treeless summit formed of boulders, rocks, and talus, can be quite formidable—especially when thick clouds disorient the climber. I empathized with Thoreau's sense of disembodiment.[41]

But it is self in a certain format, ego that only reveals itself to make a world. When Terry Tempest Williams or Ellen Meloy uses the word "I" to make a point, it is to take a stand that everyone can recognize. Such writing forces the conclusion that the self and the environment are one.

Felt knowledge of decline, feminism, and this "I" are enough to make a decade memorable, to account for the explosion and the sudden seriousness of academic concern.

A writer who has seen it all and still writes as if each book were her first, Ann Zwinger has continued to produce. Zwinger published two books in the 1990s that illustrate perfectly the "I" matter, from two standpoints, and which furthermore show that her work hasn't declined a bit.

Downcanyon: A Naturalist Explores the Colorado River through the Grand Canyon (1995) is a monumental study of the Canyon and its natural history. But the way it treats the self, hardly emphasizing it and yet giving it a final, overall judging role, is what draws my attention to it now. On July 19, 1934, Bus Hatch, "one of the pioneer boatmen on the river," made an interesting discovery: in Stanton's Cave he came upon "small split-twig figurines of deer and bighorn sheep." These, as it turned out, were quite old—around four thousand years—and they captured Zwinger's imagination. But several pages of park archaeologist's findings and natural history intervene, and so it is with a certain surprise that we come back to the willows. Zwinger has sat down with some willow twigs and determined to make models.

> I sit with a handful of willow withes across my knees and, anchored open by two river cobbles, the diagram of how split-twig figurines are made. With a knife I slit the first willow branch to within a few inches of the end and try fashioning a figure according to the diagram. When I bend it to a near right angle to form the back legs and back, the twig snaps. I start over. This time the proportions are better and I wrap one of the split ends around the unsplit section to form the body.[42]

The "afternoon fades gently" as Zwinger works, and we are given something very rare on a Grand Canyon trip.

> This afternoon there comes a gentleness I do not often feel on this big river because there is so much to learn, so many puzzles that gnaw, so many complex layerings, so many angles and turnings, so many thickets and so many thorns, and always, always the pressure of time, schedules to be maintained, miles to be made, promises to keep.[43]

This beautifully integrated moment could have been made only by a first-person author. Yet Zwinger has not made the self, which is the key element, any larger than it is.

The picture on the cover of *The Nearsighted Naturalist* (1998) is of Zwinger, which is a first for her. Inside, most of the essays deal with what readers would likely call autobiography, although Zwinger's tireless curiosity, leading to natural history almost inevitably, broadens the book considerably. One essay, "A Cave with a View," is charming for its portrait of the author, who seems determined to reveal herself to the readers of *Islands,* where the essay first appeared. She flies alone to Chile and then four hundred miles into the Pacific to the island on which Alexander Selkirk spent over four years (1704–1709), also alone. She stays in a cave that Selkirk had stayed in and mentions that he mounted to a ridge daily to be on the lookout for ships. She even re-reads *Robinson Crusoe* (Daniel Defoe used Selkirk as his model for Robinson) and finds the book is *"nothing* like the magical book I remember from childhood."[44]

We have an opportunity for adult-child comparison, but the moment passes. The author seems to prefer natural history curiosities, going to study maquis and zazamora, two exotic shrubs brought in since Selkirk, and chonta, a lovely palm that abounded in Selkirk's time.

When it comes time to go—"For my final day at the cave"—she walks uphill, for the view. It turns out to be beautiful.

> Wistfully, I would like to stay longer. I am loathe to part with this day. The world unfolds slowly here, holding its secrets, parceling them out one at a time. I smugly think everything is familiar, go out for a ten-minute walk, come back five hours later with an arm-long list of questions, having found still another alluring cranny to explore the next day. [45]

The point is, Zwinger's self is tied up with landscapes.

Rick Bass is a writer who has never been shy about the letter "I." But in his case the "I" is tied in so closely with the nature essays, with the very material, that it would be pointless to argue about it. The writings of Bass are of a piece, and taking one part out for criticism—the mind, for example—would be foolish. In *Brown Dog of the Yaak* (1999), he has written his finest nonfiction yet, a perfectly integrated argument for preservation of the Yaak valley (his home ground in Montana), a meditation on art and activism, and a memoir about his dog, Colter.

Colter was a dog like no other, a German shorthaired pointer who "carries a brilliance in his blood," who wanted so badly to hunt that he once chewed his way out of a camper shell on a pickup truck. He would run tirelessly, and then, after it all—after all the running—he would point flawlessly. After paying tribute to Colter, Bass turns to what he believes about the Yaak (the book is one of the Credo series of Milkweed Editions), and soon finds, as he finds in every book, that what he believes about the Yaak is tied in with what he believes about art, and that has ties to activism, and it's all threaded in his mind with Colter. So the reader is given a personal portrait of Rick Bass and knows as much about him as he knows about anyone. And yet—and this is the point—the reader has been given a complete representation of the Yaak, of the artist's art, of the peculiar energy-sapping and yet absolute necessity of activism, and finally and all through it, of a dog. The upshot is that the things of the mind are tied in with everything, and we get the first rule of ecology.

All of Bass's books share this, because it is Bass's one thing—the honest portrayal of what he is and what he knows. There are a number of items in *Brown Dog of the Yaak* that are memorable:

> We plunder—sometimes with timidity, other times with cunning, or endurance, or speed, or power—but when we come back with shining objects, it is not we who were brilliant but the places to which we traveled. Maybe there was something in our blood that hinted those places might be out there. But anyone who has ever written or made something wonderful knows intimately how much luck and grace is involved; and when people—critics—start saying how fine a reader or writer is—well, I get annoyed when a reader or writer starts believing that and forgets how damn much mystery is involved. . . .[46]
>
> I see the protection of these last little islands of untouched wilderness—there are only thirteen of them left in the valley—as a kind of gardening, as well. It's simply that what is produced from those untouched gardens is invisible, immaterial, immeasurable—though just as important, and just as nourishing.
>
> What they produce, year after year, from not being touched, not

being weighed and measured, contains the very essence of the thing we all felt stirring within us when we made the trade to come up here. . . .[47]

I think that the more wild nature is lost, the more nature writers we're going to see.[48]

Here is a nature writer who tries to leave it all on the page. In *The Book of Yaak* (1996), he prefaces remarks about connectivity and the crucial role of the Yaak, as regards conservation biology, by writing, "We need to sew the Rockies back together,"[49] and proceeds to argue, by frontal attack, indirection, subterfuge—anything—for the Yaak as indispensable connector. "Because the Yaak so strategically links north to south and west to east, it has the combined, teeming diversity of all the ecosystems of the West."[50]

Rick Bass has some of the same kind of thing going on in his head and heart; thus he is a true representative of the Yaak. He may be the most out-front of the current nature writers, but he is not alone in his sense of outrage. Among writers who realize in this new decade that what is happening is unprecedented are Dave Petersen (*Heartsblood*, 2000), Doug Peacock (*Grizzly Years*, 1990), Ellen Meloy (*Raven's Exile*, 1994, and *The Last Cheater's Waltz*, 1999), Terry Tempest Williams (*Refuge*, 1991), John Hay (*In the Company of Light*, 1998), E. O. Wilson (*The Diversity of Life*, 1992), Jack Turner (*The Abstract Wild*, 1996, and *Teewinot*, 2000), Barry Lopez (*About This Life*, 1998), and Marcia Bonta (especially *Appalachian Autumn*, 1994). Each of these writers works with urgent knowledge of the dark. But each is blessed by, call it, a memory of a fuller earth, and what has blessed them is carried to the reader.

What about African-American writers? Why are they not actively writing? A huge question, and a tough one, because it obviously calls up the racial matter. No opportunity, which is largely the responsibility of white people, has meant no tradition. Why, too, are Hispanics mostly absent from the lists? Why are Asians? The peculiar attraction that nature has had for writers of white, northern European background is a complex phenomenon and will lead us, eventually, to contemplate our entire tradition. The rise of women to something like full equality must seem a lonely battle and has to earn our unqualified praise.

At the opening of a new century, nature writing goes forward on a broader base than ever before. Though still one with certain gaps, it seems, at least to me, the most lively field of American literature. If in the future it should reveal reasons for celebration, they will bear the watermark of ancient human longings.

BIBLIOGRAPHY

THE FOLLOWING BOOKLISTS, as students of the field will recognize, are far from exhaustive. The field is indeed vast—there exists, for example, a bibliography on just one mountain range, the Adirondacks, that comes to 354 pages, and covers only materials published through 1955! (It takes a 198-page supplement to continue the Adirondack coverage just ten years further, to 1965.) So, clearly, I have made a selection here, attempting to gauge literary worth, cultural and historical significance, and intellectual challenge, along with other qualities.

PRIMARY MATERIALS

This section of the bibliography includes natural history essays; rambles; essays of travel, adventure, and solitude in nature; and accounts of farm and country living. The intent here, simply, is to list the best American nature writing.

Abbey, Edward (1927–1989). *Abbey's Road.* New York: E. P. Dutton, 1979, 1991.
The "road not taken" by most of us. The pieces collected here are defiantly anarchistic, in the best, positive, encouraging sense of the term, and also humorous, in a way that few if any nature essays have ever been. Allegiance to wild nature is the one value never satirized.

————. *Cactus Country: The American Wilderness.* New York: Time-Life Books, 1973.
The Sonoran Desert, seen through the eyes of a confirmed desert rat (one who honors above all the birthright of freedom and who likes humanity "in moderation"). There is a good deal of natural history information here, although the author states, "I am not a naturalist; what I hope to evoke through words here is the way things feel on stormy desert afternoons, the exact shade of color in shadows on the warm rock, the brightness of October, the rust and silence and echoes of human history along dusty desert roads, the fragrance of burning mesquite, and a few other simple, ordinary, inexplicable things like that."

————. *Confessions of a Barbarian: Selections from the Journals of Edward Abbey, 1951–1989.* Edited by David Petersen. Boston: Little, Brown, 1994.
Well-selected, well-edited, showing the inward Abbey. *"The cardinal values: To love and be loved*—a good wife, family, friends; good health; good work to do; intelligence, humor, sympathy, gentleness, strength, generosity; courage—without which all other virtues are useless; obvious necessities like sufficient food and shelter obtained without servitude; a beautiful home in a good place; or a humble home, any old shack, cabin, but in a free, wild, beautiful place; music, whiskey, art, poetry, sex, nature. . . ."

————. *Desert Solitaire.* New York: McGraw-Hill, 1968; Tucson: University of Arizona Press, 1988. New York: Simon and Schuster, Touchstone Books, 1990.
After the fashion of Thoreau, Abbey sharpens his narrative of solitude in nature by boiling several seasons down to one, and several years of philosophical reflection down to a few potent questions. His perception of the desert is determinedly frameless and unconventional, as is his commentary on civilization. A work steadily gaining status as a classic.

————. *Down the River.* New York: E. P. Dutton, 1982.
A gathering of articles, including a searching personal reflection on Henry David Thoreau and, in "Thus I Reply to Rene Dubos," one of the important wilderness essays of the present day.

————. *The Journey Home: Some Words in Defense of the American West.* New York: E. P. Dutton, 1977.
The energy of outrage, directed at real, on-the-ground evils; tender lyricism toward all that is innocent, wild, and threatened; the charm of a self-deprecating literary persona; and some of the most vigorous revolutionary humanism in contemporary nature writing. "The Second Rape of the West" is, in effect, all italics, and it needs to be.

Abbey, Edward and Philip Hyde. *Slickrock: The Canyon Country of Southeast Utah.* San Francisco: Sierra Club, 1971.
Southern Utah's canyon country in its vulnerable beauty, described and defended with passion. Abbey notes with wonder the obsession for paved roads and counters that poverty of outlook by demonstrating a more leisurely pace. Philip Hyde's photographs and comments do the same. A coffee-table book with heart and spirit.

Abbey, Edward and Eliot Porter. *Appalachian Wilderness: The Great Smoky Mountains*. New York: E. P. Dutton, 1970.
Intimate, almost tactile photographs by Eliot Porter and a dark, no-punches-pulled epilogue on strip mining and other abuses by Harry M. Caudill complement Abbey's descriptions of the Great Smoky Mountains.

Ackerman, Diane (1948–). *A Natural History of the Senses*. New York: Random House, 1990.
The introduction opens with, "How sense-luscious the world is." There follows an almost dizzily rich, image-filled tour through the human sensorium, with the honor of first attention given to the often-neglected sense of smell. Ackerman writes with a free, creative verve and doesn't fail to provide solid natural history information.

———. *The Rarest of the Rare: Vanishing Animals, Timeless Worlds*. New York: Random House, 1995.
The author suggests the scope of the declining state of biodiversity through elegantly written narratives of visits to endangered species and their habitats. Her point of view is that "there is a deep-down kinship among all living things, not just spiritually, or morally, or through some accident of our being neighbors, but physically, functionally, in our habits, in our hungers, in our genes." A lively call of alarm, full of visual and audible images.

Allen, Durward L. (1910–). *Wolves of Minong: Their Vital Role in a Wild Community*. Boston: Houghton Mifflin, 1979.
An illustration of how a limited ecological study—in this case of the small wolf population of Isle Royale National Park and its relationship with the moose of the island—can blossom into an ecological vision including the human perspective. Includes provocative commentary: "In degree each of us has become the hyperkinetic victim of an overpopulated range, overused living space, competition for increasingly scarce resources, and the harassment of sounds that invade every attempt to be alone."

Anderson, Edgar (1897–1969). *Landscape Papers*. Edited by Bob Callahan. Berkeley: Turtle Island Foundation, 1976.
A collection of short essays on the subject of paying attention to one's surroundings, whether they are a wildflower preserve or a crowded city. The author was not an absolutist in his views of nature or wilderness. For example, he felt we should be learning how to preserve leaf mold in urban parks as a practical

means of adapting to the world and honoring it. "If one accepts Man as a part of Nature there is always something to be found."

Anderson, Walter Inglis (1903–1965). *The Horn Island Logs of Walter Inglis Anderson.* Edited by Redding S. Sugg, Jr. Memphis, Tenn.: Memphis State University Press, 1973; Jackson: University Press of Mississippi, 1985.
The artist Walter Inglis Anderson went to Horn Island, a barrier island between the Mississippi Sound and the Gulf of Mexico, quite frequently in the years between 1944 and 1965, using it as a hermitage. Its rich life, described here in his journals, supplied his appetite for images. Editor Sugg's phrase for Anderson is "a Robinson Crusoe with the inclinations of a St. Francis."

Audubon, John James (1785–1851). *Ornithological Biography, or An Account of the Habits of the Birds of the United States of America.* 5 vols. Philadelphia: J. Dobson, 1831 (vol. 1); Boston: Hilliard, Gray and Co., 1835 (vol. 2); Edinburgh: A. and C. Black, 1835–39 (vols. 3–5).
Chatty, personal, and discursive notes on birds and the American scene, meant to accompany the great plates of *The Birds of America.* The gold under the surface here is Audubon's field knowledge. He uses the phrase "closet naturalists" for those who believe, for example, that the hen turkey doesn't have a beard. Audubon's enthusiasm and love for nature radiate from many of these pages.

———. *John James Audubon: Writings and Drawings.* Edited by Christopher Irmscher. New York: Library of America, 1999.
A splendid volume, including the Mississippi River Journal, the Missouri River Journals, sixty-four color plates, several letters, and two thorough indexes, one for birds and one for everything else. This is the best of Audubon.

Audubon, Maria R. (1843–1925). *Aubudon and His Journals.* 2 vols. New York: Charles Scribner's Sons, 1897; New York: Dover Publications, 1960, 1986.
Maria, the artist's granddaughter, included in volume 1 seventy-odd pages of biographical and autobiographical material, which (subsequent studies have shown) should be interpreted with caution. The journals are lively and marked by Audubon's quick and observant outlook, for instance, his immediate perception of a difference in song between eastern and western meadowlarks and his speculation therefrom that he might be dealing with separate species. The "Episodes" in volume 2 reprint, with one important addition ("My Style of Drawing Birds"), the sketches of American character and landscape published in the first three volumes of the *Ornithological Biography.*

Austin, Mary (1868–1934). *The Flock*. Boston: Houghton Mifflin, 1906; Reno: University of Nevada Press, 2001.

Folk life, which for Austin meant life connected to, and sensitive to, a "home place" out in the bright, clear air of the semiarid West. Following sheep across the wilderness is seen here as a healthy and fundamental activity with a mystical dimension. "There is a look about men who come from sojourning in that country, as if the sheer nakedness of the land had somehow driven the soul back upon its elemental impulses."

———. *The Land of Journeys' Ending*. New York: Century, 1924; Tucson: University of Arizona Press, 1983.

After two decades in what people call "the real world," Austin turned back toward the dry, wild spaces. She toured Arizona and New Mexico and here portrays the deep, attracting power of the desert. Her stance is oracular and generalizing, but there are strong passages of pure, and some may say awakened, perception.

———. *The Land of Little Rain*. Boston: Houghton Mifflin, 1904; Albuquerque: University of New Mexico Press, 1974; New York: Penguin USA, 1997.

This was Austin's first book, radiant with just-learned facts and truths. The title idea becomes a central ecological insight, organizing and clarifying the author's observations.

———. *The Lands of the Sun*. Boston: Houghton Mifflin, 1927; originally published as *California, the Land of the Sun*. New York: Macmillan, 1914.

A survey, almost a travelogue, but done with the Austin intensity and aura of portent. "The secret of learning the mesa life is to sit still, and to sit still, and to keep on sitting still."

Bailey, Liberty Hyde (1858–1954). *The Country-Life Movement in the United States*. New York: Macmillan, 1911.

Since the farmer is "the ultimate conservator of the resources of the earth . . . in contact with the original and raw materials," civilization has deep and permanent need of him. Bailey shows us there is more to agriculture, much more, than production of food.

———. *The Harvest of the Year to the Tiller of the Soil*. New York: Macmillan, 1927.

Part 1, "The Situation," summarizes the transformation of America from agrarian to industrial times and warns against what Bailey calls "corporationism"—what we today would call agribusiness. Part 2, "The

Incomes," consists of pithy, reflective essays on the satisfactions of farm life lived with a broader awareness of nature.

———. *The Holy Earth.* New York: Charles Scribner's Sons, 1915; New York: Christian Rural Fellowship, 1943; Ithaca: Cornell University Press, 1980.
This work conveys Bailey's reverence for the earth and for knowledge, independence, good tools, and honest work. All of these virtues, though "the days of homespun are gone," may still be combined in farm life of the higher sort.

———. *The Outlook to Nature.* New York: Macmillan, 1905.
Essays on the corrective, enlarging effect of the outward look. Bailey poetically evokes the sky and the weather and the lay of the land as basic elements of consciousness and spirituality. "Evolution: The Quest of Truth" goes beneath controversy to the issues of open-mindedness and our basic ability to correct our views and actions.

Bakker, Elna S. (1921–1995). *An Island Called California: An Ecological Introduction to Its Natural Communities.* Berkeley: University of California Press, 1971, 1984.
A well-written ecological pilot to the major biomes of the state and a guide to what the author calls "intelligent appreciation" as the foundation of conservation. Includes a useful bibliography.

Bartram, John (1699–1777). *See* William Darlington *and* Thomas Slaughter.

Bartram, William (1739–1823). *Travels through North and South Carolina, Georgia, East and West Florida, the Cherokee Country, the Extensive Territories of the Muscogulges, or Creek Confederacy, and the Country of the Choctaws.* Philadelphia: James and Johnson, 1791; New Haven: Yale University Press, 1958; Layton, Utah: Peregrine Smith, 1980; edited by Thomas P. Slaughter. New York: Library of America, 1996.
Early reviews of Bartram's *Travels* were none too favorable, and there was no American edition, after the first, for 136 years. But this book is still alive. Bartram displayed an innocent, overflowing joy in what he saw, and he noticed parallels, analogies, and relations in the natural world, and he saw the implications of these for philosophy. A primary document of American natural history and nature writing.

———. *William Bartram: Botanical and Zoological Drawings, 1756–1788.* Edited by Joseph Ewan. Philadelphia: American Philosophical Society, 1968.
Beautiful, sensitive, caring work, reproduced from the Fothergill album in the British Museum. (John Fothergill was Bartram's English patron.) William

Bartram was, as Ewan points out, "the first native-born American artist-naturalist"; his art, like his writing, deserves greater appreciation.

Bartram, John and William Bartram. *John and William Bartram's America: Selections from the Writings of the Philadelphia Naturalists.* **Edited by Helen Gere Cruickshank. New York: Devin-Adair, 1957.**
A most useful introduction and collection; certainly the most accessible gathering of John Bartram's matter-of-fact journal accounts.

Bass, Rick (1958–). *The Book of Yaak.* **Boston: Houghton Mifflin, 1996.**
A wondering, passionate, humble giving-of-thanks to the author's home valley in Montana, where there is still a full complement of species, still an amount of valley-floor wilderness (rare in America), and still a slower-paced, small-scale human world. A sharp account of the corporate attack on this remnant of wholeness, a raid abetted by land-indifferent Forest Service managers. Bass wonders if a true, nature-cognizant community can be evolved, and if it can stand up to the worshipers of the bottom line.

————. *Brown Dog of the Yaak: Essays on Art and Activism.* **Minneapolis: Milkweed Editions, 1999.**
Here the argument for the Yaak goes inside and becomes a meditation upon spirit. We realize that spirit is indomitable—that it will still be howling if there is no wilderness. But it will be different, and this is a book by one who knows it will be different.

————. *Fiber.* **Athens: University of Georgia Press, 1998.**
A brief, hard-hitting mixture of fiction and fact, leading to a plea for the Yaak Valley.

————. *The Lost Grizzlies: A Search for Survivors in the Wilderness of Colorado.* **Boston: Houghton Mifflin, 1995.**
It is just possible that a very few grizzly bears, keeping rigorously to themselves, yet inhabit the San Juan Mountains in Colorado. This book describes attempts to find them. Along the way, Bass conveys a strong sense of the beauty and integrity of wilderness country, and of the interlinked fates of grizzlies and human beings.

————. *The New Wolves.* **New York: Lyons Press, 1998.**
An account of the beleaguered attempt in the 1990s to reintroduce Mexican wolves to the Blue Mountains of Arizona. Above all, threading through the

natural history information, political-corruption savvy, landscape description, and nervous, tenuous hope for the future in this interesting book, Bass prizes the mystery of wildness. From the magic of wild mountains, all health flows. "If the land is sick, nothing on top of it can be truly vital or healthy."

————. *The Ninemile Wolves.* Livingston, Mont.: Clark City Press, 1992; New York: Ballantine Books, 1993.
In the Ninemile Valley in Montana, northwest of Missoula, a litter of wolves was born in 1989, signaling that the immigrant pack had made a start on recovering some of their species' original territory. Bass traces the wolves' migrations, fortunes, and misfortunes, in the process writing the parallel story of our own species' behavior and outlook for the future.

Bates, Marston (1906–1974). *The Forest and the Sea: A Look at the Economy of Nature and the Ecology of Man.* New York: Random House, 1960.
An introductory (but challenging) course in the biosphere and the methods and theories of biology, conducted with wit and grace. The author recognized similarities between biological patterns in the tropical forest and the sea.

————. *A Jungle in the House: Essays in Natural and Unnatural History.* New York: Walker, 1970.
Two years' worth of Bates's columns from *Natural History* magazine, showing wonderfully broad scientific curiosity and the author's desire to communicate clearly and wittily. The "jungle" in the title is a conservatory and greenhouse he developed into a kind of outsized terrarium housing tropical plants and animals, including seven species of hummingbirds.

Bedichek, Roy (1878–1959). *Adventures with a Texas Naturalist.* Garden City, N.Y.: Doubleday, 1947; Austin: University of Texas Press, 1994.
J. Frank Dobie referred to Bedichek as "an earth man," his term of highest praise. This book regards simple items such as fences with an open, category-bridging attention; the "adventures" are thought-journeys into progressively deeper levels of relationship and complexity.

————. *Karankaway Country.* Garden City, N.Y.: Doubleday, 1950; Austin: University of Texas Press, 1974.
The Gulf Coast of Texas, and much, much else. Bedichek found that to intelligently discuss the decline in shellfish, he had to present facts on stream- and nutrient-flow; this opened up the subject of dams, and land use, and eventually humanity's role on earth. Everything is connected.

————. *The Sense of Smell.* Garden City, N.Y.: Doubleday, 1960.
The "most enduring of all the senses" is important to consciousness but lacks popular recognition of its importance and scientific standing. To correct this state of affairs, Bedichek presents a natural history of olfaction in immense detail from myriad sources, including remarkable accounts of "sensitives" like Helen Keller. His survey is not limited to humans. The concluding chapters examine some effects of industrialism and pollution.

Beebe, William (1877–1962). *Edge of the Jungle.* New York: Henry Holt, 1921; New York: Duell, Sloan and Pearce, 1950; Mattituck, N.Y.: Amereon, 1980.
A sequel to *Jungle Peace.* Beebe shares the "thrill of discovery and the artistic delight" of learning the labyrinthine diversity of Guiana. The area described here had been colonized and worked over at intervals, beginning around 1613, but the jungle was reestablishing itself as a wilderness, and the opportunities for study were endless. Beebe's attitude was, "Who can be bored for a moment . . . ?"

————. *High Jungle.* New York: Duell, Sloan and Pearce, 1949.
Beebe goes uphill here, to the Venezuelan cloud forest, and recounts interesting phenomena seen in three years of study during the 1940s. The account is evenly balanced between natural history and the sociology and humor of field-station naturalists' lives.

————. *Jungle Days.* New York: G. P. Putnam's Sons, 1925.
A "chain of jungle life" (predation, scavengers' consumption of carrion, and so on) takes on deeper implications when the author extends it to include his own comprehension and the making and reading of his book. The chapter on "Old-time People" is an interesting speculation on evolution and the earliest divergence of apes and hominids.

————. *Jungle Peace.* New York: Henry Holt, 1919.
The "great green wonderland" of the moist tropical forest in British Guiana, where Beebe established the Tropical Research Station of the New York Zoological Society. The peace of the jungle, which Beebe describes as "beyond all telling," contrasts greatly with popular images.

————. *The Log of the Sun: A Chronicle of Nature's Year.* Garden City, N.Y.: Garden City Publishing, 1927; Norwood, Pa.: Telegraph Books, 1982.
Short essays, most of them on the model of the ramble, appreciating on a fairly elementary level wildlife's adaptations to the seasons of the temperate zone.

Many of the pieces are about birds, and some adopt the bird's point of view, taking care to preserve logic and factuality.

————. *Unseen Life of New York As a Naturalist Sees It*. New York: Duell, Sloan and Pearce, 1953; Boston: Little, Brown, 1953.
Beebe examines the "creatures which pass in the night or swim in the depths, or which fly too high or too fast for our eyesight, or whose small size requires a microscope to become visible to us." In this unusual guide Beebe also covers prehistoric animals and more recently extirpated species such as the timber wolf and wood bison. This book helps to establish New York City as a bioregion.

Bent, Arthur Cleveland (1866–1954). *Life Histories of North American Birds*. 21 vols. Smithsonian Institution Bulletins. Washington, D.C.: U.S. Government Printing Office, 1919–68.
Immense compendiums of facts, travelers' and biologists' notes, aesthetic appreciations, curious incidents and anecdotes, and many passages of fine writing, passim. This is truly a life work. The volumes encompass so much and are referred to so often as a matter of course that they have attained among students of bird life the status of scripture. Although a few of the observers' reports need to be taken with a grain of salt, they are an indispensable resource for the study of American ecological history. The volumes are:

————. *Life Histories of North American Birds of Prey*. 2 vols. Smithsonian Institution Bulletins 167, 170. Washington, D.C., 1937–38; New York: Dover Publications, 1961.

————. *Life Histories of North American Blackbirds, Orioles, Tanagers, and Allies*. Smithsonian Institution Bulletin 211. Washington, D.C., 1958; New York: Dover Publications, 1965.

————. *Life Histories of North American Cardinals, Grosbeaks, Buntings, Towhees, Finches, Sparrows, and Allies*. Smithsonian Institution Bulletin 237. Washington, D.C., 1968; New York: Dover Publications, 1968.

————. *Life Histories of North American Cuckoos, Goatsuckers, Hummingbirds, and Their Allies*. Smithsonian Institution Bulletin 176. Washington, D.C., 1940; New York: Dover Publications, 1964.

————. *Life Histories of North American Diving Birds*. Smithsonian Institution Bulletin 107. Washington, D.C., 1919; New York: Dover Publications, 1963.

———. *Life Histories of North American Flycatchers, Larks, Swallows, and Their Allies*. Smithsonian Institution Bulletin 179. Washington, D.C., 1942; New York: Dover Publications, 1963.

———. *Life Histories of North American Gallinaceous Birds*. Smithsonian Institution Bulletin 162. Washington, D.C., 1932; New York: Dover Publications, 1963.

———. *Life Histories of North American Gulls and Terns*. Smithsonian Institution Bulletin 113. Washington, D.C., 1921; New York: Dover Publications, 1963.

———. *Life Histories of North American Jays, Crows, and Titmice*. Smithsonian Institution Bulletin 191. Washington, D.C., 1946; New York: Dover Publications, 1964.

———. *Life Histories of North American Marsh Birds*. Smithsonian Institution Bulletin 135. Washington, D.C., 1926; New York: Dover Publications, 1963.

———. *Life Histories of North American Nuthatches, Wrens, Thrashers, and Their Allies*. Smithsonian Institution Bulletin 195. Washington, D.C., 1948; New York: Dover Publications, 1964.

———. *Life Histories of North American Petrels and Pelicans and Their Allies*. Smithsonian Institution Bulletin 121. Washington, D.C., 1922; New York: Dover Publications, 1964.

———. *Life Histories of North American Shore Birds*. 2 vols. Smithsonian Institution Bulletins 142, 146. Washington, D.C., 1927, 1929; New York: Dover Publications, 1962.

———. *Life Histories of North American Thrushes, Kinglets, and Their Allies*. Smithsonian Institution Bulletin 196. Washington, D.C., 1949; New York: Dover Publications, 1964.

———. *Life Histories of North American Wagtails, Shrikes, Vireos, and Their Allies*. Smithsonian Institution Bulletin 197. Washington, D.C., 1950; New York: Dover Publications, 1965.

———. *Life Histories of North American Wildfowl*. 2 vols. Smithsonian Institution Bulletins 126, 130. Washington, D.C., 1923, 1925; New York: Dover Publications, 1962.

———. *Life Histories of North American Woodpeckers*. Smithsonian Institution Bulletin 174. Washington, D.C., 1939; New York: Dover Publications, 1964.

———. *Life Histories of North American Wood Warblers*. Smithsonian Institution Bulletin 203. Washington, D.C., 1953; New York: Dover Publications, 1963.

Berry, Wendell (1934–). *A Continuous Harmony: Essays Cultural and Agricultural.* New York: Harcourt Brace Jovanovich, 1972.

Berry affirms the possibility of moral and practical redemption and believes that this recovery, both personally and culturally, may begin in humble, working contact with nature. "What I have been preparing at such length to say is that there is only one value: the life and health of the world."

―――. *The Gift of Good Land: Further Essays Cultural and Agricultural.* Berkeley: North Point Press, 1981.

In this sequel to *The Unsettling of America,* the author goes traveling, to conferences where there isn't much of practical value being said, and to cared-for places where ecologically responsible farming has survived. In the title essay he proposes an interpretation of the Bible and Christianity in which land stewardship is central. This essay unifies all the travels and examples at a moral center. Berry asks, "Is there . . . any such thing as a Christian strip mine?"

―――. *The Long-Legged House.* New York: Harcourt, Brace and World, 1969; New York: Audubon Society, 1971; New York: Ballantine, 1971.

Berry had settled himself by 1969. This book shows both a related geographic and moral focus. From his position on the land, he rakes the false and destructive ways of placeless culture—"nature-consuming," the war in Vietnam, and the horror of strip mining. He also describes, positively, where he lives and what he lives for.

Beston, Henry (1888–1968). *Especially Maine: The Natural World of Henry Beston from Cape Cod to the Saint Lawrence.* Edited by Elizabeth Coatsworth. Brattleboro, Vt.: Stephen Greene, 1970.

An informative foreword and selections from many letters add biographical depth to this Beston reader. Coatsworth, the author's wife, offers useful insights. "He sometimes spent an entire morning on a single sentence, unable to go on until he was completely satisfied with both words and cadence, which he considered equally important."

―――. *Herbs and the Earth.* Garden City, N.Y.: Doubleday, Doran, 1935; Garden City, N.Y.: Doubleday, Dolphin Books, 1961, 1973; Boston: David R. Godine, 1990, 1996.

This is Beston at his most domestic, perhaps, tending and describing with delectation his herb garden and his twelve favorite herbs. But the fresh winds and the great swing of the seasons move through even this small, cultivated space. The outlook, that is the looking outward, is pure Beston, and his wife reported in *Especially Maine* that he "considered the last passages in this book the best he had ever written."

———. *Northern Farm: A Chronicle of Maine.* New York: Rinehart, 1948; New York: Henry Holt, 1995.
Rhythmically poetic prose, conveying the distinctive Beston sensitivity to weather and the seasons and the feel of the landscape. The author relishes what is earned and traditional, enjoys his neighbors, and anathematizes the machine era and its projected "chromium millennium"—"What a really appalling future!"

———. *The Outermost House: A Year of Life on the Great Beach of Cape Cod.* Garden City, N.Y.: Doubleday, 1928; New York: Rinehart, 1949, 1962; New York: Ballantine, 1971; New York: Henry Holt, 1995.
A year on the Great Beach of Cape Cod: one of our literature's classic evocations of just what a year might naturally mean.

———. *The St. Lawrence.* New York: Farrar and Rinehart, 1942.
The natural and human history of this great northern river, "flowing in vague and enormous motion to the east." This book also celebrates wildness: in some of the more remote stretches of the St. Lawrence, in 1942, "all sign and show of industrial perversion has melted from sight. It is the America of Audubon. . . ."

Bird, Isabella L. (1831–1904). *A Lady's Life in the Rocky Mountains.* New York: G. P. Putnam's Sons, 1879–80; Norman: University of Oklahoma Press, 1960, 1999.
A no-nonsense, non-Romantic account of the autumn and early winter of 1873, which Bird, an Englishwoman, spent in and around Estes Park, Colorado. She cowboyed some, and climbed Longs Peak, and appreciated the beauty of the mountains.

Bohn, David (1938–). *Rambles through an Alaskan Wild: Katmai and the Valley of the Smokes.* Santa Barbara: Capra Press, 1979.
Bohn, a photographer, records his strong feeling for wilderness and his desire that it be left alone. He is intensely conscious that even his photography and writing violate to some degree the leave-it-alone principle. The photographs reproduced here, though, will seem to most viewers acts of reverence.

Bolles, Frank (1856–1894). *From Blomidon to Smoky, and Other Papers.* Boston: Houghton Mifflin, 1894.
Tours in Nova Scotia and Cape Breton Island, prompting more reflection than the author's rambles in Massachusetts and New Hampshire. "The spell of the

wilderness grew stronger upon me, and when, suddenly, I thought how many wearied souls there were in great cities who would love to see this beautiful, hidden spot, something akin to shame for my own race came also into my mind. If man came here, would he not destroy?"

————. *Land of the Lingering Snow: Chronicles of a Stroller in New England from January to June.* Boston: Houghton Mifflin, 1901.
Brief essays in journal style, describing walks, carriage rides, and boating excursions, most of them in the vicinity of Boston. The author delights in atmospheric and psychological effects of seasonal changes and presents very fine evocations of birdsongs.

Bonta, Marcia (1940–). *Appalachian Autumn.* Pittsburgh: University of Pittsburgh Press, 1994.
An environmental diary, but more: a logger threatens to clear-cut neighboring land, eventually winning the right to do as he pleases with the Pennsylvania ridgetop he owns. Bonta is bittersweet in her observations, and the book goes deeper than you might expect.

————. *Appalachian Spring.* Pittsburgh: University of Pittsburgh Press, 1991.
The time of impetuous bursting forth, recorded on a Pennsylvania mountain top. If you were overcivilized, or maybe just sleepy, this book would be the cure.

————. *Appalachian Summer.* Pittsburgh: University of Pittsburgh Press, 1999.
Bonta has expanded her holdings to 648 acres, has become a grandmother, and though she feels "increasingly out of sync with the rest of humanity," writes feelingly of bears, deer, books, salamanders, and much else. A book that grows on you.

Borland, Hal (1900–1978). *Beyond Your Doorstep: A Handbook to the Country.* New York: Alfred A. Knopf, 1962.
A friendly guide to nature study, based on the Connecticut countryside near Borland's home and including interpretive commentary on land use. This is a primer on identification and on the observation of relationships.

————. *Countryman: A Summary of Belief.* Philadelphia: J. B. Lippincott, 1965.
A year's worth of observations and reflections, in which the author's land in Connecticut inspired him to consider human nature and our particular moment in time. This yearbook also sums up Borland's lifetime of philosophical affirmations.

—————. *The Enduring Pattern.* New York: Simon and Schuster, 1959.
Posing the questions, What is man? Where did he come from? What is his relationship to all the other forms of life around him? Borland sketches the earth's natural history and finds it a great, inclusive system, constantly developing. Many of the illustrations are drawn from the area surrounding the author's country home in Connecticut.

—————. *Hill Country Harvest.* Philadelphia: J. B. Lippincott, 1967.
Notes on natural history and country living in what the author describes as a "somewhat remote corner of New England." Borland writes that "most of man's troubles are man-made," and recommends a slower pace—walking or even sitting still.

—————. *Homeland: A Report from the Country.* Philadelphia: J. B. Lippincott, 1969.
These essays are columns from *The Progressive*, 1963–68, and may be seen as fever relief for the political mind. In these "dispatches," as Borland calls them, as if he were a kind of foreign correspondent, he affirms his belief that "the country—the uncultivated land and the remaining remnants of wilderness as well as the farmland—is essential to the whole nation's sense of proportion and its perspective."

—————. *Sundial of the Seasons: A Selection of Outdoor Editorials from the New York Times.* Philadelphia: J. B. Lippincott, 1964.
A year's worth of brief essays—most are just three paragraphs long—arranged in the traditional order, spring to spring.

Bowden, Charles (1945–). *Blue Desert.* Tucson: University of Arizona Press, 1986.
The dark side of Sun Belt hedonism. Violence and sleaze are held up against the ideal of desert clarity and sparseness. "Everything a desert tortoise is— calm, a homebody, long-lived, patient, quiet—the people of the Southwest are not."

—————. *Frog Mountain Blues.* Tucson: University of Arizona Press, 1987.
A spirited, frightening examination, on the evidence of Tucson and the mountain range just to the north, of what we have done to most of the American landscape, and why we have such difficulty changing our ways. The afterword, consisting mostly of the author's statement at a land-use hearing, is about as good as public speaking gets.

Bradbury, John (1768–1823). *Travels in the Interior of America in the Years 1809, 1810, and 1811.* London: Sherwood, Neely, and Jones, 1819; Lincoln: University of Nebraska Press, 1986.

Accompanying the Astorians partway, the English botanist Bradbury described some of the "wild productions of the Missouri Territory," such as grapes, persimmons, pawpaws, and strawberries, and recorded that a denizen of St. Louis could purchase a turkey or a quarter of venison for a quarter of a dollar. He was also one of the first to note that in the Midwest wolves were "already becoming scarce, and will soon disappear," and that "large tracts" of land were in the hands of speculators.

Brewer, William H. (1828–1910). *Up and Down California in 1860–1864: The Journal of William H. Brewer, Professor of Agriculture in the Sheffield Scientific School from 1864 to 1903.* Edited by Francis P. Farquhar. Berkeley: University of California Press, 1966.

Brewer, a member of the California Survey (whose charge was a complete geological accounting of the state's lands), was a graduate of the Sheffield Scientific School of Yale University. His descriptions of pristine, near-pristine, and already-besmirched California landscapes are always scientifically precise and often touched with enthusiasm.

Brewster, William (1851–1919). *Concord River: Selections from the Journals of William Brewster.* Edited by Smith O. Dexter. Cambridge: Harvard University Press, 1937.

Although he was a founder of the American Ornithologists' Union and served as president of the Massachusetts Audubon Society for several years, Brewster's prose suggests that these titles were of little importance to anyone whose goal was simply to watch a bird and see it truly. On his game-preserve farm, he saw and heard keenly. "Repeatedly of late I have heard a male Bluebird warbling to its mate in tones exquisitely soft and tender, and so low as to be audible only a few yards away."

———. *October Farm: From the Concord Journals and Diaries of William Brewster.* Cambridge: Harvard University Press, 1936.

Brewster owned about three hundred acres of varied, interesting land at Concord, Massachusetts, over which he walked with what must have been the greatest patience and watchfulness. His journal, which is the source of both *October Farm* and *Concord River,* has headings like "Sharp-shinned hawk catches a Robin" and "Remarkable Bird Concert." The episodes recorded are unadorned and unexpectedly moving.

Bromfield, Louis (1896–1956). *From My Experience: The Pleasures and Miseries of Life on a Farm.* New York: Harper and Brothers, 1955.

This is part 3 of the Malabar story (see *Malabar Farm,* below). A vision of a restored society, founded ultimately on humus- and mulch-enriched soil, is Bromfield's guiding thought, but he is no fanatic. He cautions against both chemicalism and organicism as religions. The final chapter, "The White Room," is a fine autobiographical essay in which the author looks beyond material success.

———. *Malabar Farm.* New York: Harper and Brothers, 1948; New York: Ballantine, 1970; Mattituck, N.Y.: Aeonian Press, 1978; Wooster, Ohio: Wooster Book Company, 1999.

This is part 2 of the Malabar story. The farm has grown to one thousand acres; the soil has been rejuvenated, largely by the "great healer," grass; and Bromfield has developed some ideas on how a family-sized farm might survive in the modern era. The keys, he predicts, will be planning and specialization. In the larger dimension, the author shows how the health of the land connects directly to world peace.

———. *Pleasant Valley.* New York: Harper and Brothers, 1945; Wooster, Ohio: Wooster Book Company, 1997.

A successful writer living in France in the late 1930s, Bromfield was looking for "real continuity, real love of one's country, real permanence." He returned to the Ohio countryside where he had grown up, bought three adjacent farms, set up a community modeled in part on the collective farm of Russia (but with himself, "as capitalist, . . . substituted for the state"), and began the agrarian ideal by restoring the soil's fertility.

Brooks, Paul (1909–1998). *Roadless Area.* New York: Alfred A. Knopf, 1964.

One of the early texts that contributed to the awakening to wilderness and environmental values in general in the 1960s. The framework here is narratives of trips into wilderness areas taken by the author and his wife. The gist of the book is a positive, ecological concept of wilderness, quietly radical.

Brown, Bruce (1950–). *Mountain in the Clouds: A Search for the Wild Salmon.* New York: Simon and Schuster, 1982.

The author walks and wades, mostly on the Olympic Peninsula, looking for wild salmon (as opposed to hatchery produced), and fills out his narratives with historical information. He brings our sorry history of mistreatment of the salmon and their habitat into immediate, unforgettable focus through strong images. Dams, logging, road building, nuclear power plants, and heavy commercial fishing have cut deeply into what was once a staggeringly beautiful abundance, but wherever conditions are at all favorable, the salmon still attempt to fulfill their ancient urges.

Brox, Jane (1956–). *Here and Nowhere Else: Late Seasons of a Farm and Its Family.* Boston: Beacon Press, 1995; Boston: G. K. Hall, 1999.
An immensely detailed sketch of present-day farm life in eastern Massachusetts. The author sees and hears well, from the parents' old-line farm wisdom to the yearly questions at the farmstand.

Bryson, Bill (1951–). *A Walk in the Woods: Rediscovering America on the Appalachian Trail.* New York: Broadway Books, 1998.
The author, a native of Iowa, had lived abroad for almost twenty years and, after moving to New Hampshire, thought to become "reacquainted with the scale and beauty of my native land" by hiking the entire Appalachian Trail. He persuaded a friend from Iowa to accompany him. Their adventures are told with great-spirited, often laugh-out-loud, humor, but in all the drollery Bryson doesn't neglect to pillory agency mismanagement and several culture-wide failings. A funny best-seller that is also a seriously good book.

Buchmann, Stephen L. (1952–), and Gary Paul Nabhan (1952–). *The Forgotten Pollinators.* Washington, D.C.: Island Press, 1996.
The "forgotten" in the title references our often-compartmentalized thinking, by which, for example, we might seek to preserve certain plants without recognizing the crucial role of pollinators in the plants' lives. Buchmann and Nabhan proceed by extensive, detailed case histories to show that the ecology of pollination is fundamental to nothing less than life on earth. They then describe manifold threats to pollinators, including rampant pesticide use.

Burdick, Arthur J. (1858–?). *The Mystic Mid-Region: The Deserts of the Southwest.* New York: G. P. Putnam's Sons, 1904.
The Mohave Desert and its peculiar, compelling attraction—beyond mineral riches, the author says—to the old-style prospectors.

Burroughs, John (1837–1921). *Locusts and Wild Honey.* Boston: Houghton, Osgood, 1879; reprinted in vol. 3 of *The Complete Writings of John Burroughs.* New York: Wm. H. Wise, 1924.
The focus on natural history is sharper and more particular than in *Wake-Robin*

or *Winter Sunshine* (see below). This collection includes a comparison of European and American birdsongs: ours are softer but wilder, according to the author. A week's camping in the Catskills had a bracing effect: "I was leg-weary and foot-sore, but a fresh, hardy feeling had taken possession of me that lasted for weeks."

————. *Signs and Seasons*. Boston: Houghton Mifflin, 1886; reprinted in vol. 8 of *The Complete Writings of John Burroughs*. New York: Wm. H. Wise, 1924. Sketches of how birds and other animals fare in a hard winter, of birds' nests and the dangers they are exposed to, and of camping in the Maine wilderness are notable here, but perhaps the most substantial chapter deals with the proper habits of observation.

————. *Time and Change*. Boston: Houghton Mifflin, 1912; reprinted in vol. 15 of *The Complete Writings of John Burroughs*. New York: Wm. H. Wise, 1924. Evolution is the theme. "I am sure I was an evolutionist in the abstract, or by the quality and complexion of my mind, before I read Darwin, but to become an evolutionist in the concrete, and accept the doctrine of the animal origin of man, has not for me been an easy matter." In a chapter on Yosemite, Burroughs stretches himself to take in the wild scene and writes a more excited prose than usual.

————. *Wake-Robin*. New York: Hurd and Houghton, 1871; reprinted in vol. 1 of *The Complete Writings of John Burroughs*. New York: Wm. H. Wise, 1924. Burroughs's first book of nature essays. *Wake-Robin* established him as the reader's congenial companion and observer of the near woods and fields. At this time, in 1871, he had not yet read Darwin, and his concept of nature lacked the acceptance of predation and death and the breadth and serenely comprehensive tone of his mature writings. Also at this time, he carried a gun and used it frequently.

————. *Ways of Nature*. Boston: Houghton Mifflin, 1905; reprinted in vol. 11 of *The Complete Writings of John Burroughs*. New York: Wm. H. Wise, 1924. Written soon after the "nature-faker" controversy, this volume sets forth Burroughs's thoughts on the instincts and probable consciousness of some of the other animals. His ideas represent an amalgam of native compassion and fellow-feeling, leanings toward a vitalist and transcendental view, and a recognition of the great powers of the scientific method and attitude.

————. *Winter Sunshine*. New York: Hurd and Houghton, 1875; reprinted in vol. 2 of *The Complete Writings of John Burroughs*. New York: Wm. H. Wise, 1924.
Early, charming sketches, including appreciations of the winter skies and atmosphere of Washington, D.C., and the activities of foxes and skunks. The last chapters are on England and Ireland, where Burroughs had gone on government business, and it is evident that the author much preferred his native land.

Cabeza de Vaca, Alvar Nuñez (1490–1558). *The Journey of Alvar Nuñez Cabeza de Vaca and His Companions from Florida to the Pacific, 1528–1536*. Edited by Ad. F. Bandelier. Translated by Fanny Bandelier. New York: A. S. Barnes, 1905; New York: AMS Press, 1922.
A brief, very brief, list of the birds and animals Cabeza de Vaca saw during his eight-year travail and the first report of bison to reach Europe. Cabeza de Vaca's account also gives evidence for a rather impressive population density of Indians, even in the dry Southwest.

Caras, Roger (1928–). *The Endless Migrations*. New York: E. P. Dutton, Truman Talley Books, 1985.
This book might profitably be read alongside Donald Griffin's *Bird Migration*. Caras's dramatic, narrative approach conveys the wonder and majesty of mass movements. Birds, butterflies, whales, turtles, eels, bats, salmon, and others are the actors. The book presents a strong image of the planet netted with complex routes, and living bodies and consciousnesses following them.

————. *The Forest*. New York: Holt, Rinehart and Winston, 1979.
Ecology lessons, given vividly through narratives centering on a two hundred-foot western hemlock and a golden eagle.

Carrighar, Sally (1898–1985). *Icebound Summer*. New York: Alfred A. Knopf, 1953; Lincoln: University of Nebraska Press, 1991; Lanham, Md.: Derrydale Press, 2000.
The blossoming of summer life in the Arctic as experienced by several birds and mammals. This book has a wider compass, both geographically and temporally, than *Beetle Rock* or *Teton Marsh* (see below), and thus suggests the earth's great patterns of wind and water more strongly. The human presence is also more evident. Carrighar took pains to make her writing ethologically and ecologically respectable; she also had a fine dramatic sense. The account here of the golden plover's migration is as compelling as many a novel.

————. *One Day at Teton Marsh.* New York: Alfred A. Knopf, 1947; Lincoln: University of Nebraska Press, 1969.
A September day's happenings at a beaver pond in Jackson Hole, Wyoming, given from various animals' points of view and recorded with a certain overall narrative push. Each actor's responses to the environment—the taste of a mayfly to a trout or of aspen bark to a beaver, or the feel of the water to an otter—seem realistically grounded in natural history facts, and in the aggregate give a remarkably vivid and complete picture of a biotic community.

————. *One Day on Beetle Rock.* New York: Alfred A. Knopf, 1944.
A June day on and around a two-acre outcrop of granite in the Sierra Nevada. The characters—Weasel, Coyote, Deer, Grouse, Lizard, and others—demonstrate the author's intense awareness of wild creatures and the way their lives impinge on one another's. The personalities described, and the inside views, appear as plausible extrapolations from observed behavior.

————. *The Twilight Seas.* New York: Weybright and Talley, 1975.
An inside narrative of a blue whale's life, told with imaginative feeling for the tactile delight of the ocean and with careful buttressing of scientific fact. "Whaleness was utter freedom, no gravity and no walls." A strong critique of whaling gives the book's title a disturbing dimension.

————. *Wild Heritage.* Boston: Houghton Mifflin, 1965.
An informed view of several aspects of animal behavior—courtship, aggression, play, dominance, and the effects of crowding, among other topics—that are both interesting in themselves and of possible application to the human circumstance.

————. *Wild Voice of the North.* Garden City, N.Y.: Doubleday, 1959.
Carrighar was engaged in a study of lemmings and was living in Nome, Alaska, when she acquired Bobo, a Siberian Husky. Over the years of their friendship she learned much from Bobo about animal behavior and the range of animal emotion and intelligence.

Carroll, David M. *Sleepwalker's Journal: A Wetlands Year.* Boston: Houghton Mifflin, 1999.
In the seven years it took to put this book together, Carroll spent a lot of time damp, studying salamanders, frogs, turtles, and much else. At one point, sitting still, he says he doesn't know how invisible he has become; a coyote, coming

within fifteen feet of Carroll, shows that when you become part of the surroundings, things happen.

Carson, Rachel (1907–1964). *The Edge of the Sea.* **Boston: Houghton Mifflin, 1955, 1998.**
The shoreline, one of the most interesting and productive ecotones on earth, is interpreted "in terms of that essential unity that binds life to the earth." Carson covers rock shores, sand beaches, and coral reefs, taking her examples from the Atlantic Coast of America. Her own response to beauty and her sense of the interconnecting patterns in nature are prominent here.

————. *Lost Woods: The Discovered Writing of Rachel Carson.* **Edited by Linda Lear. Boston: Beacon Press, 1998.**
Intelligently selected and well introduced, these writings, ranging from "My Favorite Recreation" for *St. Nicholas* magazine, to a speech to Kaiser-Permanente less than a year before her death, round out the picture we have of Carson. She was ahead of her time on many topics, and this book is of value for its portrait of courage.

————. *The Sea Around Us.* **New York: Oxford University Press, 1951; New York: Simon and Schuster, 1958; rev. ed., New York: Oxford University Press, 1961.**
A huge, encircling subject, given point and intelligibility by exposition of particulars and by carefully shaped and cadenced prose. There have been gains in knowledge since this book's most recent, revised edition, but there has been no clearer presentation of the big picture. The moral point of view is quiet but firm. Of oceanic islands like Laysan and Midway, where exotic and destructive species were casually introduced, Carson writes, "In a reasonable world men would have treated these islands as precious possessions, as natural museums filled with beautiful and curious works of creation, valuable beyond price because nowhere in the world are they duplicated."

————. *Under the Sea-Wind: A Naturalist's Picture of Ocean Life.* **New York: Oxford University Press, 1941; rev. ed., New York: Oxford University Press, 1952.**
Framed as a series of narratives and vignettes of shore and ocean life, this book dramatizes food chains and other ecological relationships. Focal animals—a pair of sanderlings, a young mackerel, and an eel—grant the coherence of a story line, but entirely without "nature faking." There is a moving account of purse seining at night, which might be read alongside Robinson Jeffers's great poem, "The Purse-Seine." The glossary consists of remarkably concise descriptions of

birds, fish, invertebrates, and geologic features—a kind of mini-encyclopedia of prominent elements in the littoral and pelagic realms.

Catesby, Mark (1682–1749). *Hortus Britanno-Americanus; or, A Curious Collection of Trees and Shrubs, the Produce of the British Colonies in North America; Adapted to the Soil and Climate of England.* London: W. Richardson and S. Clark, 1763.
A catalog of eighty-five American trees and shrubs, with instructions on transporting them to England for transplanting.

———. *The Natural History of Carolina, Florida and the Bahama Islands.* 2 vols. London: Printed at the expense of the author, 1731–43. Appendix published 1748.
One of the major primary texts of the presystematic era. Beautifully done plates and a text impressive for its thoroughness (given the state of science at the time) mark these volumes.

Catlin, George (1796–1872). *Letters and Notes on the Manners, Customs, and Conditions of the North American Indians, Written during Eight Years' Travel amongst the Wildest Tribes of Indians in North America.* New York: Wiley and Putnam, 1841; New York: Dover Publications, 1985.
Includes a prescient observation on the coming demise of the buffalo and a "splendid contemplation" of a *"nation's Park,"* in which Indians would be forever free to live as they had, "amid the fleeting herds of elks and buffaloes."

Chadwick, Douglas H. *A Beast the Color of Winter: The Mountain Goat Observed.* San Francisco: Sierra Club Books, 1983.
Oreamnos americanus and its perfect fit with the mountains it inhabits. The author's research in Montana began in 1971 and continued for seven years. The book gives a full natural history portrait of the mountain goat and makes a strong argument for wilderness in its presentation of the impacts of logging and road development.

Cohen, Michael P. (1944–). *A Garden of Bristlecones: Tales of Change in the Great Basin.* Reno: University of Nevada Press, 1998.
An unusual book, consisting of a history of the study of the bristlecone pine, several watercolors by the author's wife, Valerie, a proposal for two research natural areas, a meditative walk by the author, and much else. Cohen's ruminations on the various scientists' standpoints are unsparing and extensive, yet each man stands on his own feet. The passage on the cutting of the oldest tree is restraint at its best.

Cokinos, Christopher (1963–). *Hope Is the Thing with Feathers: A Personal Chronicle of Vanished Birds.* New York: Putnam, Jeremy P. Tarcher, 2000.
The Carolina parakeet, the ivory-billed woodpecker, the heath hen, the passenger pigeon, and the Labrador duck and the great auk: the stories are told with uncommon attention to every detail, and brought to date. The ivory-billed woodpecker's account leaves just enough room for hope.

Columbus, Christopher (1451–1506). *Journals and Other Documents on the Life and Voyages of Christopher Columbus.* Edited and translated by Samuel Eliot Morison. New York: Heritage Press, 1963.
The reactions of Columbus to his discovery of the New World: "Saturday, 13 October. This island is very big and very level; and the trees very green, and many bodies of water, and a very big lake in the middle, but no mountain, and the whole of it so green that it is a pleasure to gaze upon. . . ." Columbus was sorry, Morison tells us, that he didn't know the new plants and trees he was seeing, and wrote that this was "what [caused him] the greatest grief in the world. . . ."

Colvin, Verplanck (1847–1920). *Report on the Topographical Survey of the Adirondack Wilderness of New York, for the Year 1873.* Albany: Weed, Parsons, 1874.
Vicissitudes of survey work in a good cause (Colvin was a strong advocate of preservation for the Adirondacks), and in the midst of difficulties, appreciation for wilderness beauty. "The Adirondack wilderness may be considered the wonder and glory of New York. It is a vast *natural* park, one immense and silent forest, curiously and beautifully broken by the gleaming waters of a myriad of lakes, between which rugged mountain ranges rise as a sea of granite billows."

Comstock, Anna Botsford (1854–1930). *Handbook of Nature-Study.* Ithaca, N.Y.: Comstock Publishing, 1911; Ithaca: Cornell University Press, 1986.
A huge book (nine hundred-plus pages), dedicated to youth and clarity, and still in print. "Nature-study is science brought home. It is a knowledge of botany, zoology, and geology as illustrated in the dooryard, the cornfield or the woods back of the house." Lesson 135, "Outline for the Study of a Weed," begins, "1. Why do we call a plant a weed?"

Cooper, David J. (1952–). *Brooks Range Passage.* Seattle: Mountaineers Press, 1982.
A long solo adventure, including building and using a log raft. The author subsisted in part on roots and berries, and (after intentionally bringing only

minimal rain gear) came to terms with the Alaskan weather. The book has the flavor of solitude and wilderness, and little, if any, self-dramatization.

Cooper, Susan Fenimore (1813–1894). *Rural Hours.* New York: G. P. Putnam's Sons, 1850; rev. ed., Boston: Houghton Mifflin, 1887; Syracuse, N.Y.: Syracuse University Press, 1995; Athens: University of Georgia Press, 1998.
A distinct sense of place—the environs of Otsego Lake in New York—emerges from journal-like entries arranged on the classic seasonal basis. Miss Cooper walked a great deal and was not shy about taking moonlight rambles or venturing out in below-zero weather. She knew her birds, was acutely conscious of the feel of the day's atmosphere and light, and was a careful student of natural history. A memorable image is created when the author measures a large downed pine with her parasol. *Rural Hours* includes a detailed description of a New York farm household of the late 1840s and perceptive notes on local plant geography.

Craighead, Frank C., Jr. (1916–). *For Everything There Is a Season: The Sequence of Natural Events in the Grand Teton-Yellowstone Area.* Helena, Mont.: Falcon Press, 1994.
For all those who found the greatest pleasure of *A Field Guide to Rocky Mountain Wildflowers* in the matching of natural history events to the flowering of plants. This book does it for the entire year, and expands the species list, until you feel the light breeze ruffling the cottonwood leaves and see rufous hummingbirds arrive—that's when the scarlet gilia and Indian paintbrush bloom.

————. *Track of the Grizzly.* San Francisco: Sierra Club Books, 1979.
An immense amount of time in the field and carefully planned research procedures give this Yellowstone-based study its authority. It is also marked by broad knowledge of the ecosystem in general and its threatened integrity. "What is at stake is not just the grizzly, but the steady, often unnoticed attrition of the countless life forms, both plant and animal, that compose our complex biosphere and keep it functioning."

Crèvecoeur, Hector St. John de (1735–1813). *Letters from an American Farmer.* London: Thomas Davies, 1782; Philadelphia: Mathew Carey, 1793; New York: E. P. Dutton, 1912, 1951; New York: New American Library, 1963; New York: Oxford University Press, 1999.
The author's happy years (1769–1778) on his farm in Orange County, New York, set the dominant tone for these emotionally positive essays. There is both

evocative detail ("Often when I plough my low ground, I place my little boy on a chair which screws to the beam of the plough—its motion and that of the horses please him, he is perfectly happy and begins to chat") and broad generalization about farm life, the frontier, and America.

————. *Sketches of Eighteenth Century America*. **Edited by Henri L. Bourdin, Ralph H. Gabriel, and Stanley T. Williams. New Haven: Yale University Press, 1925.**
Here Crèvecoeur, the "emotional prototype" of the American, as D. H. Lawrence described him, puts the farm up against the reality of finance and graphically describes land abuse. He also notices the "most beautiful curves" made in the air by a bald eagle trying to escape a kingbird's attack, and sympathizes to a degree with blackbirds swarming onto the farmers' cornfields: "Are they not the children of the great Creator as well as we? They are entitled to live and get their food wherever they can get it."

Crisler, Lois (1896–1971). *Arctic Wild*. New York: Harper and Brothers, 1958; New York: Lyons Press, 1999.
The experiences of a husband and wife in the Brooks Range, as they gradually became more intimate with the wild and demanding place and with its wildlife, especially a group of wolves they came to know. A contribution to the debunking of the Little Red Riding Hood concept of wolves.

Darlington, William (1782–1863). *Memorials of John Bartram and Humphry Marshall*. Philadelphia: Lindsay and Blakiston, 1849.
Includes a history of American botany to the mid-nineteenth century, and a large, interesting selection of John Bartram's correspondence.

DeBlieu, Jan (1955–). *Wind: How the Flow of Air Has Shaped Life, Myth, and the Land*. Boston: Houghton Mifflin, 1998.
Centering on the Outer Banks of North Carolina, where she lives, and going forth to various places, the author has molded a portrait of what would seem impossible to portray. She writes well, and her prose is right on, whether depicting a light summer breeze or a tornado. The subject is far from completely known.

Dillard, Annie (1945–). *Pilgrim at Tinker Creek*. New York: Harper's Magazine Press, 1974; New York: McGraw-Hill, 2000.
Observation of nature here opens up profound questions about life and death, meaning, and identity. To the author, Tinker Creek in Virginia represents the

universe in all its spiritual complexity. A pilgrim watching for keys and signs, she examines very closely the experience of ostensibly small and ordinary things. One of the most influential of late twentieth-century books on natural history.

————. *Teaching a Stone to Talk: Expeditions and Encounters.* New York: Harper and Row, 1982.
Sensitive travel essays, carrying on many of the themes of *Pilgrim at Tinker Creek* in a wider geographic scope.

Dobie, J. Frank (1888–1964). *The Mustangs.* Boston: Little, Brown, 1952.
A paean to freedom above all, but also a work of historical and natural historical acumen and research. Should be read with Hope Ryden's *America's Last Wild Horses* as necessary background.

————. *Rattlesnakes.* Boston: Little, Brown, 1965; Austin: University of Texas Press, 1982.
As animals going about their business, rattlesnakes deserve the interested, evenhanded, folkloristically sophisticated treatment they get here. Of necessity, given the record of our relations with the rattlesnakes, this collection of experiences and tales offers almost as much material for an investigation of human nature as for a summary look at the pit vipers in genus *Crotalus.*

————. *The Voice of the Coyote.* Boston: Little, Brown, 1949; Lincoln: University of Nebraska Press, 1961.
A thoroughly maverick, thoroughly engaging work of scholarship and homage, in which Don Coyote is honored for being his clever, surviving self. Dobie blasts "jukebox culture" with glee and righteousness. The book is illustrated by Olaus Murie.

Douglas, Marjory Stoneman (1890–1998). *The Everglades: River of Grass.* New York: Rinehart, 1947; Englewood, Fla.: Pineapple, 1988, 1997.
A massive history of the glades, from the early Indians who lived with its slow, recycling, southward flow, to the latecomers who have slaughtered the plume bearers and set up enormous drainage projects. The latest edition includes "Forty More Years of Crisis" by Randy Lee Loftus, bringing us nearly up to date.

Douglas, William O. (1898–1980). *Farewell to Texas: A Vanishing Wilderness.* New York: McGraw-Hill, 1967.
A pained but still hopeful survey of the state, from the Big Thicket to the

western plains and mountains. As Douglas saw it, the frontier ethos was still firmly in the ascendant—in the saddle, so to speak: "Conservationists of Texas [are] a lonely lot." But there are *some,* and hope springs eternal.

———. *My Wilderness: East to Katahdin.* Garden City, N.Y.: Doubleday, 1961.
Rambles of a sensitive man in wild areas ranging from Utah to Maine, and plain talk about overgrazing, the political power of livestock interests, and governmental insufficiency and mistakes. Douglas believed in the restorative power of wilderness, individually and culturally. A forthright, simply written book, with sharp flashes of both poetic appreciation and rightful anger.

———. *My Wilderness: The Pacific West.* Garden City, N.Y.: Doubleday, 1960.
From the Brooks Range to Oregon's Wallowas, with stops in the Sierra Nevada, central Idaho, and lingering stays in the justice's home country of Washington state. As the author hikes and boats, he pays close attention to his surroundings and to threats against wilderness. Beautifully illustrated by Francis Lee Jaques.

Dubkin, Leonard (1904–). *Enchanted Streets: The Unlikely Adventures of an Urban Nature Lover.* Boston: Little, Brown, 1947.
Finding himself suddenly unemployed, the author returned to a youthful fascination, natural history. Even in Chicago, there was plenty to enchant him. Lying in the grass of a park, climbing a tree for a closer look at sparrows, then having a new job for four weeks and quitting it, Dubkin came to a certain perspective on himself as a potential interpreter of the importance of nature to the modern, working world.

———. *My Secret Places: One Man's Love Affair with Nature in the City.* New York: David McKay, 1972.
Reminiscences of Chicago when there were still "secret" (undeveloped) places. The book becomes the record of an awful decline, as the author attempts to revisit scenes of powerful experiences (the yard described so lovingly in *The Natural History of a Yard* is now a parking lot, for example). The result is a considerably darker book than *Enchanted Streets* or the *Yard* study (see below).

———. *The Natural History of a Yard.* Chicago: Henry Regnery, 1955.
The subject is the small grass plot of an apartment hotel on Chicago's north side, "surrounded by a [two-foot-high] privet hedge, with an elm tree in the back." Not a very promising subject, but Dubkin goes into it slowly and carefully over a three-year study, relying almost solely on his own observation, and

finds a surprising richness. This book is a testimony to the endurance of several species, our own included.

Dutton, Clarence E. (1841–1912). *Report on the Geology of the High Plateaus of Utah.* **Washington, D.C.: U.S. Government Printing Office, 1880.**
A government surveyor with a job to do, the author nonetheless responded deeply to the dramatic wilderness of southern Utah. He described the twelve thousand-foot Tushar range with both geological accuracy and poetic enthusiasm, as "a composite structure, its northern half being a wild bristling cordillera of grand dimensions and altitudes, crowned with snowy peaks, while the southern half is conspicuously tabular."

———. *Tertiary History of the Grand Cañon District.* **Washington, D.C.: U.S. Government Printing Office, 1882; Layton, Utah: Peregrine Smith, 1977.**
Geology and wilderness appreciation, along with an argument for a nontraditional mode of perception when viewing something as difficult to categorize as the Grand Canyon. "Forms so new to the culture of civilized races and so strongly contrasted with those which have been the ideals of thirty generations of white men cannot indeed be appreciated after the study of a single hour or day." Dutton recommended realism in description, over "fancy" or metaphor.

Dwight, Timothy (1752–1817). *Travels in New-England and New-York.* **New Haven, Conn.: Timothy Dwight, 1821–22; reprinted in 4 vols. Edited by Barbara Miller Solomon. Cambridge: Harvard University Press, 1969.**
Journals of a man with very wide interests and a keen eye. In his ecological history, *Changes in the Land,* William Cronon writes, "anyone interested in New England ecology could do no better than to read Dwight from cover to cover."

Eckert, Allan W. (1931–). *Wild Season.* **Boston: Little, Brown, 1967; Dayton, Ohio: Landfall Press, 1981.**
Astonishing activity in the month of May, unveiled at a modest, ordinary lake in the Midwest. Eckert describes growth, predation, human cruelty and pity, and the intricacy of ecological relationships with unsentimental objectivity.

Eckstein, Gustav (1890–1981). *Lives.* **New York: Harper, 1932.**
An unusual book, describing lives of laboratory rats, cockroaches, canaries, turtles, a green parrot, and a university groundskeeper with strong empathy and an uncompromising sense of democracy: these lives are just as vital and interesting and just as much to be respected as the observer's own. Eckstein writes

elliptically, which has the effect of removing the usual anthropomorphic and egoistic embroidery and putting the reader directly in touch with the subject at hand.

Ehrlich, Gretel (1946–). *The Solace of Open Spaces.* **New York: Viking Penguin, 1985.**
An appreciation of the vastness and rigor of Wyoming's High Plains country, and of the people whose lives have been shaped by its elemental forces.

————. *A Match to the Heart.* **New York: Pantheon Books, 1994.**
Struck by lightning in 1991, Ehrlich endures much, eventually flying from Wyoming to Santa Barbara and contacting a good cardiologist. She immerses herself in the world of the heart, in the end plunging into the Pacific—for the first time in thirty years—and glimpsing healing.

Eifert, Virginia (1911–1966). *Of Men and Rivers: Adventures and Discoveries Along American Waterways.* **New York: Dodd, Mead, 1966.**
A survey of major rivers and their travelers, with the final chapter offering a bit of hope through Lyndon Johnson's Wild and Scenic Rivers system.

Eiseley, Loren (1907–1977). *The Firmament of Time.* **New York: Atheneum, 1960; Lincoln: University of Nebraska Press, Bison Books, 1999.**
Six lectures on evolution, on man's perception of the process, and on mind and ideas, one of the most interesting of the last being the concept of "natural." Within these reflections, which are presented with Eiseley's great respect for the elusiveness of truth and his sense of the primacy of the inner life, there is a clear, biography-centered history of evolutionary interpretation over the past three centuries.

————. *The Immense Journey.* **New York: Vintage Books, 1957.**
A personal record of explorations into paleontological and anthropological time, back toward the *Urschleim* that was once thought to be a transitional form between nonliving and living matter. The investigations serve as map coordinates, so to speak, for placing man in the scheme of things. One of the author's central beliefs is that "the most enormous extension of vision of which life is capable" is "the projection of itself into other lives." This ability is necessary, Eiseley feels, for the imaginative and intellectual "immense journey" into evolutionary time.

————. *The Night Country.* **New York: Charles Scribner's Sons, 1971.**
There are dimensions to life, certain moments of unease in particular, that day-light thinking seemingly cannot encompass. This "night country," which the

author began entering at an early age, is perhaps the source of his slanted but thoroughly sane outlook.

―――. *The Star Thrower.* New York: Times Books, 1978; New York: Harcourt Brace Jovanovich, 1979.
An anthology of Eiseley's work, most of it chosen by Eiseley during the year before his death. The volume, edited by Kenneth Heuer, includes a fine appreciation by W. H. Auden, two interesting essays on Thoreau by Eiseley, and a selection of the author's early poems.

―――. *The Unexpected Universe.* New York: Harcourt, Brace and World, 1969.
The creativity of nature, its endless possibility and open-endedness, described with awe and with a poet's distrust of pat answers. "The world contains, for all its seeming regularity, a series of surprises resembling those that in childhood terrorized us by erupting on springs from closed boxes." These surprises may even be found in the study of the past; in one chapter Eiseley looks anew at Pleistocene and Permian glaciation, to find immense implications for human evolution.

Elder, John (1947–). *Reading the Mountains of Home.* Cambridge: Harvard University Press, 1998.
A bracing book, combining a reading of Frost's "Directive" with a bit of natural history, during the learning of which the writer becomes a Vermonter. The author lives slowly and thinks deeply. During the book, his father dies, he builds and tries out a canoe with a disaffected son, and he learns to think as cautiously as people contemplating an official third-growth wilderness must.

Emerson, Ralph Waldo (1803–1882). *Nature.* Boston: James Munroe, 1836; New York: Houghton Mifflin, 1902; Indianapolis: Bobbs-Merrill, 1948; Boston: Beacon Press, 1986 (facsimile reprint of 1836 edition).
One of the seminal texts in American nature writing and nature philosophy. Emerson argued persuasively that individual experience is universal in essence and that experience "in the woods" is full of potential for clarity and enlightenment. It was once fashionable to disdain Emerson for a certain alleged unreality, but the list of writers influenced by *Nature* would be very long indeed.

Errington, Paul L. (1902–1962). *Of Men and Marshes.* New York: Macmillan, 1957; Ames: Iowa State University Press, 1996.
An introduction to the study of wetlands, written with a strong sense of their beauty and importance. The text centers on the glaciated country of the

northcentral states and is founded on the idea that "greater familiarity with marshes on the part of more people could give man a truer and more wholesome view of himself in relation to Nature." Errington praises wildness and laments the fact that by 1957 more than three-fourths of the aboriginal wetlands of America had been damaged or drained.

———. *Of Predation and Life.* Ames: Iowa State University Press, 1967.
Many years of close observation, here focused chiefly on muskrats, mink, and bobwhite quail in northcentral locations, provided the author with remarkable opportunities for insight into the fluidity and complexity of predator-prey relationships. After what amounted to a lifetime in the field, all of his conclusions were tentative.

Evans, Howard Ensign (1919–). *Life on a Little-known Planet.* New York: E. P. Dutton, 1968; Chicago: University of Chicago Press, 1984.
We don't know much, and yet we presume so greatly. Evans, a museum curator and research entomologist, says, "Few groups are better suited to demonstrate how little we know about our planet than the insects—how little the experts know, and how very little of this knowledge has reached 'the man on the street.'" The author attempts to improve this by recounting in informal style some fascinating entomological items: flash patterns in male fireflies, mimicry in several species, the flight muscles of flies, the unusual mating habits of bedbugs, and much else, all written with clarity and wit. Evans concludes with a survey of pressing environmental matters, a plea for diversity, and a response to *Silent Spring* that seems oddly inadequate.

———. *Wasp Farm.* Garden City, N.Y.: Natural History Press, 1963; Garden City, N.Y.: Doubleday, 1973; Ithaca: Cornell University Press, 1985.
An engrossing natural history of wasps, based in part on the author's observations on an eight-acre farm in upstate New York. Evans says that "the twentieth century belongs to the laboratory scientists," but this course in wasp biology and evolution takes the reader into the field where the living wasps are.

Farb, Peter (1929–1980). *Living Earth.* New York: Harper and Brothers, 1959.
A lively introduction to the hidden world of soil, organized on the basis of forest, grassland, and desert, showing the complexity of "soil societies" and the importance of soil to manifold ecological relationships. "The soil is the seat of abundance on earth, a massive machinery for keeping the chemical stuff of the planet in constant circulation."

Finch, Robert (1943–). *Common Ground: A Naturalist's Cape Cod.* Boston: David R. Godine, 1981.

Every place, however extensively studied, is new to one who comes newly to it. Finch's impetus: "I felt that living with nature in the late twentieth century must mean more than turning down the thermostat and meeting state sanitary codes." So he explored Cape Cod at a walking pace, hearing the woodcock's spring vocalizations, trying to save an injured junco, and exploring the aftermath of the great winter storm of 1978, among other adventures in learning.

————. *Death of a Hornet and Other Cape Cod Essays.* Washington, D.C.: Counterpoint, 2000.

Brief essays, hitting one point, that somehow give the feeling of the cape. "On the Killing Fields" and "Brave New World" are memorable.

————. *Outlands: Journeys to the Outer Edges of Cape Cod.* Boston: David R. Godine, 1986.

These essays in personal experience are marked by a sharp, imagistic sense of place and a philosophically low-keyed, even antiportentous, tone. "North Beach Journal" is one of the finer contemporary essays on solitude.

————. *The Primal Place.* New York: W. W. Norton, 1983.

Concentrating upon the author's neighborhood, on Cape Cod but not especially near the ocean (the surf is rarely heard in this book—unusual for a Cape Cod natural history), these essays show a developing sense of home ground—a "primal place." From that center, one may venture outward with a certain authenticity and reference.

Flagg, Wilson (1805–1884). *Studies in the Field and Forest.* Boston: Little, Brown, 1857.

Rambles concentrating on the aesthetics of different scenes and landscapes. "What do we care for a scene, however beautiful, which is so tame as to afford no exercise for the imagination? Rocks, by increasing the inequalities of the surface, proportionally multiply the ideas and images which are associated with landscape."

————. *The Woods and By-Ways of New England.* Boston: James R. Osgood, 1872.

"It is delightful to enter by chance upon one of these old roads, when it will carry you half a day's journey on foot, without the intrusion upon your sight of a steam-factory or a railroad station." The book consists of short, three- to seven-page essays on such subjects as "Foliage" and "A Summer Night in the

Woods" and is marked by the author's fondness for the pastoral. But there is also some bite here, and a critical view of what was happening to the American landscape: "The preservation of the forests in a certain ratio over the whole territory ought to be the subject of immediate legislation in all the States."

Fletcher, Colin (1922–). *The Complete Walker: The Joys and Techniques of Hiking and Backpacking.* **New York: Alfred A. Knopf, 1968; rev. ed.,** *The New Complete Walker,* **1974; rev. ed.,** *The Complete Walker III,* **1984.**
This is a guide to equipment and techniques, but Fletcher makes it abundantly clear, through sharply drawn vignettes and extended philosophical commentary, that the real core of backpacking in the wilderness is not having tools or covering miles, but truly being there.

———. *The Man Who Walked Through Time.* **New York: Alfred A. Knopf, 1968; New York: Vintage Books, 1989.**
Walking the length of the Grand Canyon on a route at varying elevations from rim to river gave the author an ideal opportunity to ponder time and earth history, and his own place in and response to nature.

———. *River: One Man's Journey Down the Colorado, Source to Sea.* **New York: Alfred A. Knopf, 1997.**
If you have ever wondered what it's like—carrying a pack or solo rafting, day after day for better than six months—you will get no closer. Fletcher has a keen memory and an eye for detail, and he knows how to concentrate upon the things that will last. The three books, *The Thousand Mile Summer, The Man Who Walked Through Time,* and *The River,* make an outstanding contribution to our literature.

———. *The Thousand-Mile Summer: In Desert and High Sierra.* **Berkeley: Howell-North Books, 1964; New York: Vintage Books, 1987.**
Fletcher backpacked from the Mexican border to the California-Oregon line, traversing deserts and the length of the Sierra Nevada, relishing open country and open time, and especially enjoying evenings in camp after a long, capacity-stretching day.

Fosburgh, Hugh (1916–1976). *A Clearing in the Wilderness.* **Garden City, N.Y.: Doubleday, 1969.**
Baker's Clearing in the Adirondacks, created in 1854, is a seventy-acre opening. Living there gave the author opportunity to comment on the Adirondacks'

"incredible capacity to rejuvenate themselves." He argued that intelligent logging may make for a various and productive mix of environments.

Foster, David R. (1954–). *Thoreau's Country: Journey Through a Transformed Landscape*. Cambridge: Harvard University Press, 1999.
A generous selection from Thoreau's journals, arranged according to "The Cultural Landscapes of New England," "Firewood and Other Fuels," and "The Succession of Forest Trees," among other topics, and introduced to show how the reforestation of New England has proceeded. The author's perception of what has happened does credit to his reading of Thoreau. A fine bibliography.

Freneau, Philip (1752–1832). *The Prose of Philip Freneau*. Edited by Philip M. Marsh. New Brunswick, N.J.: Scarecrow Press, 1955.
A thoroughly political writer, and, in Marsh's words, a "thoroughgoing Rousseauistic romanticist," Freneau wrote a number of newspaper essays in the late-eighteenth and early-nineteenth centuries, criticizing civilization from the standpoint of the "Philosopher of the Forest" and that of "Tomo-Cheeki," a fictional Indian. Freneau's theme was that a simple life in the forest gave rise to democratic and tolerant feelings.

Fremont, John Charles (1813–1890). *Report on the Exploring Expedition to the Rocky Mountains in the Year 1842 and North California in the Years 1843–44*. Washington, D.C.: U.S. Senate, 1845.
Although Fremont was always going somewhere (in both a geographic and political sense), he did take the time to write some energetic descriptions of mountain scenery. The depictions of the Wind River Range of Wyoming are perhaps the high point, literarily, of this report.

Gilbert, Bil (1927–). *Our Nature*. Lincoln: University of Nebraska Press, 1986.
Written in a style that is both humorous and knowing when it deals with humanity and the self, and objective and respectful when nature is the subject, the magazine essays collected here are sophisticated but not slick. Gilbert takes pains to make personal contact with his subjects—retracing some of John Franklin's peregrinations in the Far North, for example—and he keeps our environmental moment firmly in the reader's mind.

———. *The Weasels: A Sensible Look at a Family of Predators*. New York: Pantheon Books, 1970.
The subtitle is accurate. With a comprehensive natural history of the weasel

family, Gilbert interweaves a logical, anti-anthropomorphic analysis of predation. He lays waste to several superstitions about the weasel family and holds up some human foibles to humorous witness.

Godman, John D. (1794–1830). *American Natural History.* 2 vols. Philadelphia: H. C. Carey and I. Lea, 1826; Philadelphia: Stoddert and Atherton, 1828–31; Philadelphia: R. W. Pomeroy, 1842; North Stratford, N.H.: Ayer Company, 1974.
Godman, a medical doctor, centered his descriptions of the quadrupeds of America on anatomy, building outward from the bodies of animals to their behavior and what would later be called their ecological niche. This careful and responsible work, which has been unfairly overlooked, also promotes the scientific approach—as opposed to folklore and prejudice—and displays an objective attitude toward predation. This enlightened view places Godman about a century ahead of his time.

———. *Rambles of a Naturalist.* Philadelphia: T. T. Ash, 1833; also in *American Natural History* 2 (1828–31) and *American Natural History* 2 (1842).
Careful instruction in the small and near-at-hand. This is one of the earliest examples of the ramble, a durable subgenre in American nature writing. As in later rambles, the lecture is based on paying close attention to common scenes that are usually passed over.

Gould, Stephen Jay (1941–). *Ever Since Darwin: Reflections in Natural History.* New York: W. W. Norton, 1977.
Pointing out that Darwinism is by no means fully accepted, or understood, the author examines what is so difficult about the theory. Darwin saw no purpose or direction to evolution; this helps make evolutionary theory an "antidote to our cosmic arrogance," as Gould says, and also helps make it a trying interpretation. The essays here (first published as columns in *Natural History* magazine) add up to a thorough treatment of evolution and its effects on human thought and self-concept.

———. *The Flamingo's Smile: Reflections in Natural History.* New York: W. W. Norton, 1985.
"Evolution is one of the half-dozen shattering ideas that science has developed to overturn past hopes and assumptions, and to enlighten our current thoughts." It is a more personal idea than quantum theory or relativity, Gould argues. In this collection of *Natural History* columns, a major theme is the possibility that a collision with an asteroid or a shower of comets brought about major changes

in earth's patterns of life. There follows an interesting discussion about "what it means to say that life is the product of a contingent past. . . ."

———. *The Panda's Thumb: More Reflections in Natural History.* New York: W. W. Norton, 1980.
Evolutionary theory, because it embodies the "duality in natural history—richness in particularities and potential union in underlying explanation," excites the author's mind profoundly. These essays, drawn from Gould's columns in *Natural History,* suggest natural history's rightful standing in intellectual life as a discipline demanding imagination and the highest powers of synthesis.

Graves, John (1920–). *From a Limestone Ledge: Some Essays and Other Ruminations about Country Life in Texas.* New York: Alfred A. Knopf, 1980; Dallas: Lone Star Books, 1984.
Essays originally published in *Texas Monthly,* describing life on a country place with a light, ironic touch.

———. *Goodbye to a River.* New York: Alfred A. Knopf, 1960; Dallas: Lone Star Books, 1984.
The author canoes down a stretch of the Brazos River in Texas, a section of the stream under sentence of dam construction, and reflects about time and loss and progress. He describes the rich and varied wildlife and calls up the lives of former inhabitants and settlers, weaving the elements of his story subtly, so that in the end the reader realizes that what is being lost is indeed nothing less than a world.

———. *Hard Scrabble: Observations on a Patch of Land.* New York: Alfred A. Knopf, 1974; Dallas: Lone Star Books, 1984.
Graves bought the first part of his country place in 1960 and over the years came to a sense of the requirements, and certainly the pleasures and pains, of living beyond the easy-service zone. He writes of his acquisition of knowledge entirely without self-praise.

Grayson, David [Ray Stannard Baker] (1870–1946). *The Countryman's Year.* Garden City, N.Y.: Doubleday, Doran, 1936.
Journal entries and quietly offered aphorisms, based on life in rural Massachusetts. This may be one of the most modest of the books on country life; the author keeps his eye on small matters and common things, and the cumulative effect is of a profound, alert calmness.

Greene, Harry W. (1945–). *Snakes: The Evolution of Mystery in Nature*. Berkeley: University of California Press, 1997.
A comprehensive natural history, covering locomotion, feeding habits, defense strategies, reproduction, and much else, followed by a review-survey of snake species of the world. A large number of high-quality photographs by Michael and Patricia Fogden, and excursions into narrative natural history by the author, enliven an already lively text. The writer, a teacher and field biologist of much experience, says humbly, "Writing this book taught me a lot." The reader is likely to enjoy a parallel experience.

Griffin, Donald R. (1915–). *Bird Migration*. Garden City, N.Y.: Doubleday, 1964; New York: Dover Publications, 1974.
The facts on velocity, range, altitude, timing, navigation, and the theories on why and how birds migrate are set forth patiently and thoroughly. But the author is also aware of the deeper dimensions of life's fit with the earth and its seasons. One of the book's most stirring passages describes Griffin's flight in a light plane alongside some migrants, trying to learn, trying to sense their world.

———. *Animal Thinking*. Cambridge: Harvard University Press, 1984.
"The aim of this book," Griffin explains, "is to rekindle scientific interest in the conscious mental experiences of animals." To do this, Griffin must subvert the reigning behaviorist-mechanist theories by presenting voluminous data showing that the thoughts and feelings of other species are real, verifiable items. There are, of course, some profound philosophical questions inherent in this investigation. A remarkably provocative study.

Gruchow, Paul (1947–). *Boundary Waters: The Grace of the Wild*. Minneapolis: Milkweed Editions, 1997.
Modestly written narratives of canoeing, skiing, and camping in northern Minnesota grow subtly into reflections on wildness, mystery, spiritual aliveness, dreaming and coming awake, and other profound subjects. This book is a sleeper.

———. *Grass Roots: The Universe of Home*. Minneapolis: Milkweed Editions, 1995.
By going back and examining his farm boyhood, not all that long ago, Gruchow is able to criticize agribusiness in this eloquent testimony. He offers a twelve-point program for revitalizing small towns that is very interesting.

————. *The Necessity of Empty Places.* New York: St. Martin's, 1989; Minneapolis: Milkweed Editions, 1999.
The author motors west from Minnesota, looking for emptiness. What he finds is conducive to his heart, and right at the border of language.

Haines, John (1924–). *Living Off the Country: Essays on Poetry and Place.* Ann Arbor: University of Michigan Press, 1981.
Twenty years on a homestead in Alaska gave Haines a standpoint. He came into his own as a poet there ("there" means Alaska, and also what he describes as "the hard irreducible world of natural things—of rock and water, fire and wood, flesh and blood") and from that place and state of mind come his estimates of what is not centered or tied to any sense of place, in particular modern culture and a good deal of modern poetry. The essays here seem to be without illusion about both wilderness and civilization. They also vivify the "old ways" of mankind in sudden, poetic images.

————. *Other Days: Selections from a Work in Progress.* Port Townsend, Wash.: Graywolf Press, 1982.
Succinct, lyrical vignettes and reflections drawn from the author's life in Alaska. He describes the coming of spring, the singing of wolves, and the suddenness with which getting lost can occur. The images carry a weight of thought and a certain dreamlike quality, as if what is perceptible to the eye or ear stopped just short of explaining itself and yet unmistakably indicated meaning, leading the mind on.

Hakluyt, Richard (1552–1616). *The Principal Navigations, Voyages, Traffiques, and Discoveries of the English Nation Made by Sea or Overland to the Remote and Farthest Distant Quarters of the Earth at Any Time within the Compass of These 1600 Years.* New York: E. P. Dutton, 1927.
Volume 6 includes Thomas Heriot's "A briefe and true report of the new found land of Virginia," a sixteenth-century man of science's attempt to describe paradise soberly. "Walnut trees, as I have said before very many, some have bene seene excellent faire timber of foure and five fadome [fathoms], and above fourescore foote streight without bough."

Hall, Donald (1928–). *String Too Short to Be Saved.* New York: Viking Press, 1961; Boston: David R. Godine, 1992.
The old ways and character of small-farm America. The author spent his

childhood summers on his grandparents' farm in New Hampshire, watching and listening. In maturity, he returned and found that it all still rang true.

Halle, Louis J., Jr. (1910–1998). *Birds Against Men.* **New York: Viking Press, 1938.**
Halle is sensitive to the impact of modern man on the natural world, and entirely sympathetic to his bird subjects here, whose natural innocence and simple following of the dictates of their natures he finds instructive. As for man, Halle observes, "By his own militant energy, by the sweat of his brow and the labor of his hands, he has found riches. But he has not found peace." In these essays there is a strong feeling for the individual selves of the birds described.

————. *Spring in Washington.* **New York: William Sloane Associates, 1947; New York: Harper and Brothers, 1957; Baltimore: Johns Hopkins University Press, 1988.**
"To snatch the passing moment and examine it for signs of eternity is the noblest of occupations. It is Olympian. Therefore I undertook to be monitor of the Washington seasons, when the government was not looking." This beautiful book is a tribute to the nature threading through even the most chest-thumpingly monumental of cities. "The discovery of spring each year, after the winter's hibernation, is like a rediscovery of the universe."

Hamilton, Gail [Mary Abigail Dodge] (1833–1896). *Country Living and Country Thinking.* **Boston: Ticknor and Fields, 1862.**
Confiding, spirited essays, more or less well connected to country life. The author's proclivities were for philosophy and social comment rather than nature study. The essay on "Men and Women," whose connection to country living is not evident, is a strong assertion of the author's feminist point of view.

Hasselstrom, Linda (1943–). *Feels Like Far: A Rancher's Life on the Great Plains.* **New York: Lyons Press, 1999.**
Autobiography, but with such a strong sense of place that one can see and hear the nighthawks. This is her best book yet.

————. *Land Circle: Writings Collected from the Land.* **Golden, Colo.: Fulcrum Publishing, 1991.**
Working a small, at times one-woman, ranch in South Dakota, Hasselstrom somehow found time to write these original, iconoclastic essays, and the heartfelt poems placed between chapters. The root of the book is her independent, feisty allegiance to her home place and her life on it. The manifestations of this theme are various—from "Confessions of a Born-Again Pagan" to "Why One

Peaceful Woman Carries a Pistol"—but always solidly within the nervy consciousness of a woman standing on her own two feet, on the land.

Hay, John (1915–). *The Bird of Light*. New York: W. W. Norton, 1991.
If there is such a thing as an epic poem of nature writing, this is it: a natural history of terns, a plea for ecological responsibility, a passionate thanksgiving to the earth and wildness.

————. *The Great Beach*. Garden City, N.Y.: Doubleday, 1963.
The Outer Beach of Cape Cod, where light and space and the sounds of the surf and the birds conspire to awaken an elemental consciousness. In one memorable chapter, the author takes a three-day walk down the beach, between the dunes and the sea, responding to the wild and evocative scene.

————. *The Immortal Wilderness*. New York: W. W. Norton, 1987.
The myriad signals and adjustments of species and habitats, complexly and perfectly tuned to each other; the inspiring odysseys of alewives, terns, and monarch butterflies; the fit and health of the whole, and the dismaying estrangement from this of the modern human way. Hay affirms, "We do not own intelligence; it is an attribute of the planet, together with all of the fine degrees of perception and awareness in living things. . . ."

————. *In Defense of Nature*. Boston: Little, Brown, 1969.
The author, recognizing certain symptoms in himself, makes a critique of progress-engrossed, uprooted, "free agent" modern humanity and affirms what could be a saving allegiance to nature and wildness. "As we diminish our environment, both physically and in terms of our attitude toward it, so we diminish our range of attention. Half the beauties of the world are no longer seen." Hay wonders, "What will we be when left to nothing but our own devices!"

————. *In the Company of Light*. Boston: Beacon Press, 1998.
The author lets us into his consciousness—sometimes beautifully lyric, singing the weather, the light, the winging birds, and other times dark, noting the destruction of an oceanic fishery or the overdevelopment of a shoreline—in such a forthright, companionable way that we do not stop at Hay's self, but rather enter a kind of common sensibility. An enlarging book.

————. *Nature's Year*. Garden City, N.Y.: Doubleday, 1961.
"I drove to Cape Cod with travelers from everywhere" is this book's first sentence. What follows is a record of learning a place and coming to be at home

there. One of the early texts, possibly, in the modern literature of bioregionalism and reinhabitation.

————. *The Run.* New York: W. W. Norton, 1979; Boston: Beacon Press, 1999.
Hay describes the alewives' great journeys, emblematic of nature's long cycles and patterns, abundance, and survival despite remorseless attrition. As he looks down into a New England brook in springtime, he stands in awe of what might be learned from these patterns.

————. *Spirit of Survival: A Natural and Personal History of Terns.* New York: E. P. Dutton, 1974.
A gathering of information on migration, courtship, nesting, communication, care and feeding of young, and other matters, illuminated by a profound personal response to this attractive family of birds. "I kept moving toward them, listening to them, not as if they were entirely alien factors, but as if we had a collateral relationship whose depths were beyond conscious knowledge."

————. *The Undiscovered Country.* New York: W. W. Norton, 1981.
This is a book about learning "the proprieties of the earth," the living system of connections of each to all. Hay describes his own movement toward recognition of these proprieties. "How wild and wonderful it is," he exclaims, "to be out in open territory with everything to learn!" This, precisely, is the undiscovered country.

Heinrich, Bernd (1940–). *Mind of the Raven: Investigations and Adventures with Wolf-Birds.* New York: Cliff Street Books, 1999.
Everything about the raven. "Partnership and Social Webs," "Hunting and Foraging," "Adoption," "Communication," "Fears," and "Play" are a few of the chapters. This book is given depth and interest by the author's personal contact with the birds.

————. *The Trees in My Forest.* New York: Cliff Street Books, 1997.
A love song to a natural neighborhood (three hundred acres in Maine, purchased by the author in 1977), and along with the lyric, a smoothly delivered compendium of facts on forest ecology. The area was logged before the author bought it, and he is now managing its regrowth according to ecological principles.

Higginson, Thomas Wentworth (1823–1911). *Outdoor Studies: Poems.* Vol. 6 of *The Writings of Thomas Wentworth Higginson.* Cambridge, Mass.: Riverside Press, 1900.
Six essays are added here to a reprinting of *The Procession of the Flowers.* In

"Saints and Their Bodies," the author praises physical fitness and activity and accuses Americans of becoming a soft, indoor breed. The essay was originally published in 1858. "Footpaths," another notable essay, is built on the idea that "civilization is tiresome and enfeebling, unless we occasionally give it the relish of a little outlawry, and approach, in imagination at least, the zest of a gypsy life."

─────. *The Procession of the Flowers, and Kindred Papers.* New York: Longmans, Green, 1897.

Higginson is wary of affectation and sentimentality, and holds that "Nature is not didactic, but simply healthy." The author's impressionistic style seems appropriate to his refusal to pin nature down too tightly. "My Out-Door Study" touches on some of the same ground, genteelly, as Thoreau covered in "Walking."

Hinchman, Hannah. *A Trail Through Leaves: The Journal As a Path to Place.* New York: W. W. Norton, 1997, 1999.

Hinchman is not a writer but an artist, though you see the basic things confirmed. "The detachment required for meditation worthy of its name, and for journal entries that are fearless and lucid, creates a healthy uncertainty about the self." Autobiographically, she traces her own trail to where she is, enriching the account by thousands of drawings from her journal. A full book.

Hoagland, Edward (1932–). *The Courage of Turtles.* New York: Random House, 1970; San Francisco: North Point Press, 1985; New York: Lyons Press, 1993.

The author is energized by his two-part existence, one in New York City and the other in Vermont, and derives sophisticated insights from playing the parts off one another. Four of the essays here touch on this gray-green dialectic. Attracted to country characters and old-time ways, the author nevertheless has no sentimental desire to turn the clock back.

─────. *Notes from the Century Before: A Journal of British Columbia.* New York: Random House, 1969; San Francisco: North Point Press, 1982; San Francisco: Sierra Club Books, 1995.

The author spent a glorious season—the summer of 1966—in backcountry British Columbia, interviewing old-timers. Surrounded by lush greenness and seemingly limitless wilderness, their lives had been slow paced and self-sufficient and in some ways rangier than they might have been "outside." Hoagland realizes such richness is being cut back swiftly, and hurries to get the record down. The situation has obvious tragic dimensions, but in the face of our dark progress the account glows with affirmation.

————. *Red Wolves and Black Bears.* New York: Random House, 1976; New York: Lyons Press, 1995.

Hoagland gives a sharp sense of where we are, in our rush into what certainly looks to be a tamer future. In Hoagland's hands, a subject like the difference between field study and "black box" biology blossoms into a subtly done commentary on our entire relationship with nature. The author's subjects here could be temptations to preach, but he resists.

————. *Tigers and Ice: Reflections on Nature and Life.* New York: Lyons Press, 1999.

Hoagland in his sixties. His naturally upbeat manner increased by a fifteen thousand dollar eye operation (he had been legally blind for two years), the author is hard to keep down. "I Have Seen the Elephant," a fifty-page essay celebrating Antarctica, and "Wild Things," even longer, about India, are both superb. But, "frogs are disappearing worldwide in a drastic fashion, perhaps because of ultraviolet rays or acid rain; and I may finally cease to believe that heaven is on earth, if they do."

————. *Walking the Dead Diamond River.* New York: Random House, 1973; San Francisco: North Point Press, 1985.

Five essays in this collection, including the outstanding "Hailing the Elusory Mountain Lion," convey the keen, pleasurable sense of a long hike in good country. Hoagland straightforwardly warns, "All factions have reason to worry if the broad majority of citizens lose that mysterious sense of felicity and exuberance they once had in the presence of natural grandeur—the feeling of having known it before, of being linked to it via thousands of centuries before they were born—and simply stop caring."

Hogan, Linda (1947–). *Dwellings: A Spiritual History of the Living World.* New York, W. W. Norton, 1995.

A Chickasaw Indian woman, Hogan revives here the ancient meaning and moral depth in storytelling. The essays are about bats, corn, eagles, wolves, and water, among other natural subjects, and the core concern is for our spiritual connection and contract with the world. Hogan writes in a disarming style in which profound insights sneak up quietly.

Hoover, Helen (1910–1984). *The Gift of the Deer.* New York: Alfred A. Knopf, 1966; Minneapolis: University of Minnesota Press, 1998.

The author describes herself as an alien in the Minnesota forest, separated from it by many generations of civilized humanity, but her knowledgeable sympathy for wild creatures does not speak of alienation. This is an account of the relationship Hoover and her husband Ade (who illustrated the book) developed with a family of white-tailed deer. Though attached to the deer, the author understands and values the role of the predators in the area, especially, and crucially, the wolves.

————. *A Place in the Woods.* New York: Alfred A. Knopf, 1969; Minneapolis: University of Minnesota Press, 1999.
The day-to-day changes involved in moving from Chicago to a cabin in the North Woods are not small things, but they did not prevent the Hoovers from coming to an appreciative relationship with the wilderness around them.

————. *The Years of the Forest.* New York: Alfred A. Knopf, 1973; Minneapolis: University of Minnesota Press, 1999.
A chronicle of the Hoovers as they find and improve their place in the north woods of Minnesota. There are life-enhancing adventures with wild animals, very considerable practicalities to master, and a reorientation toward work and money. This book contains, in between the lines, an interesting essay on freedom.

Hubbell, Sue (1935–). *A Book of Bees . . . and How to Keep Them.* New York: Random House, 1988; Boston: Houghton Mifflin, 1998.
"I have had bees now for fifteen years, and my life is the better for it." *A Book of Bees,* framed on the seasons and what each demands of bees and beekeepers, expands on the relish for natural history, for open-air work, and for a loved home place, all of which, centered on the bees, did apparently make Hubbell's life better. The practical details of how to keep bees, given in the author's low-key prose, become poetic in the best pastoral tradition.

————. *A Country Year: Living the Questions.* New York: Random House, 1986; New York: Harper and Row, 1987; Boston: Mariner Books, 1999.
A record of living in the Ozarks, tending some three hundred hives of bees, and looking well at the natural world. At fifty, the author was divorced and set about "building a new kind of order . . . *at peace* with herself and the world around her." She does her own truck maintenance, knows how to use a come-along, and writes in a plain, untranscendental style. There is good natural history information here on bats, bees, copperheads, brown recluse spiders, and much else; autobiographical revelations come slowly, in patches, as the account develops.

———. *Waiting for Aphrodite: Journeys Into the Time Before Bones*. Boston: Houghton Mifflin, 1999.

Each chapter is built on finding and learning more about an example of invertebrate life: sponges and sea urchins, pill bugs and fireflies, and finally the sea mouse, whose picture graces this book's title page. The accounts are given in a conversational voice, mixed in with a record of moving from Missouri to Washington to Maine, so the story is seamless. The chapter on the sea urchin deals with their mysterious rise and fall, recently, and draws a conservation ethic out of this precarious existence.

Huntington, Cynthia (1951–). *The Salt House: A Summer on the Dunes of Cape Cod.* Hanover, N.H.: University Press of New England, 1999.

The author, a poet, moved to the small shack on the far end of Cape Cod, and began living. "Only gradually was I able to take it into myself and let it remake me." A record of the inner, secret life that is satisfying in its honest record.

Jackson, Wes (1936–). *Becoming Native to This Place.* Lexington: University Press of Kentucky, 1994; Washington, D.C.: Counterpoint Press, 1996.

At work in Matfield Green, Kansas, Jackson develops a sense of community—which means, in the end, an ecological worldview.

James, George Wharton (1858–1923). *California: Romantic and Beautiful.* Boston: Page, 1914.

James was perhaps more of a booster than a serious or reflective writer, but he did respond to wilderness. The theme of what might be called renewal of the self through scenery is prominent in his work, and has autobiographical roots.

———. *Utah: The Land of Blossoming Valleys.* Boston: Page, 1922.

In this book, something like an extended travel brochure, James praises the "good work" of irrigation.

———. *The Wonders of the Colorado Desert.* Boston: Little, Brown, 1906.

In the desert, James had found recovery and health after a personal crisis. He recommended the desert for its absolute honesty. "There is no knowing of self in the whirl of the cities." This is his most substantial book.

Janovy, John, Jr. (1937–). *Back in Keith County.* New York: St. Martin's Press, 1981; Lincoln: University of Nebraska Press, 1981.

Occasional glimpses of the Nebraska sandhills and their natural history, but the concentration here is on the author and his friends and students, on their way to or from the field.

———. *Keith County Journal.* New York: St. Martin's Press, 1980.
Nuggets of Nebraska prairieland natural history set within, and partially integrated with, personal notes and stories.

Jefferson, Thomas (1743–1826). *Notes on the State of Virginia.* London: J. Stockdale, 1787; Philadelphia: Prichard and Hall, 1788; Chapel Hill: University of North Carolina Press, 1955; New York: Penguin, 1981, 1998.
A careful, diplomatic demolition of the Comte de Buffon's suppositions on the degeneracy of American life-forms, a compilation of natural history facts from the author's own study and reading, and a bit of personal narrative relating an experience at the Virginia Natural Bridge probably qualify parts of this wide-ranging book as early natural history essays.

Johnson, Josephine W. (1910–1990). *The Inland Island.* New York: Simon and Schuster, 1969.
The journal of a year on an old Ohio farm, in which the beauty and encouragement and essential sanity of nature are somewhat darkened by the author's sense of human and national decline. She states, "We are dying of preconceptions, outworn rules, decaying flags, venomous religions, and sentimentalities. We need a new world." The Vietnam War casts a shadow over this account, but on December 31, the last entry reads, "It went down to zero in the night. And the new year began with awesome clarity."

Jones, Charles (1932–). *The Gifting Birds: Toward an Art of Having Place and Being Animal.* Salt Lake City: Dream Garden, 1985.
Notes on various places, including southern Arizona ("finest solitude I had ever known"), San Gregorio Beach in California, the Arctic coast near Point Barrow, and Hawaii. The theme is the impact that place has on consciousness and the mind.

Josselyn, John (?–1675). *An Account of Two Voyages to New-England.* London: Giles Widdows, 1674; Boston: William Veazie, 1865.
A haphazard diary of odd little occurrences and adventures, mixed in with natural history notes. An example of the author's curious approach: "I never heard of any mischief that snakes did [Josselyn differentiates "snakes" from "Rattlesnakes"], they kill them sometimes for their skins and bones to make hatbands

of, their skins likewise worn as a Garter is an excellent remedie against the cramp." But there are also passages of what should probably be called ecological insight.

————. *New-England's Rarities Discovered.* London: G. Widdows, 1672; reprinted in vol. 4 of *Transactions and Collections of the American Antiquarian Society.* Edited by Edward Tuckerman. Boston: John Wilson and Son, 1860; Boston: Massachusetts Historical Society, 1972 (facsimile reprint of 1672 edition); Bedford, Mass.: Applewood Books, 1986.
In this book, his first, Josselyn presents rather brief lists of birds and animals, and quaint ideas ("The skin of a gripe [bald eagle], drest with the doun on, is good to wear upon the stomach, for the pain and coldness of it"), and also good detail on plants and their virtues, and a useful account of changes in the land already under way.

Kalm, Peter (1716–1779). *Peter Kalm's Travels in North America.* 2 vols. Edited by Adolph B. Benson. New York: Wilson-Erickson, 1937; New York: Dover Publications, 1966.
A most useful historical reference. The Delaware River was still of drinking-water quality in 1748, but the forests of New Jersey were being hard hit to supply the market for "black walnut and oak planks for ships." The countryside around Philadelphia, as seen by Kalm, confirms the most positive agrarian traditions, but already there were losses in wildlife, perceptible to old-timers whom he met and interviewed. Kalm was a traveler with a utilitarian eye (looking out for plants that could be transported to Sweden), and his account has a sober, factual solidity.

Kappel-Smith, Diana (1951–). *Desert Time: A Journey through the American Southwest.* Boston: Little, Brown, 1992; Tucson: University of Arizona Press, 1994.
A year and a half, and twenty-five thousand miles by car, form the bare bones of this tour. The sketches are surprisingly beautiful, as are the occasional moments of insight.

————. *Night Life: Nature from Dusk to Dawn.* Boston: Little, Brown, 1990; Tucson: University of Arizona Press, 1996.
Beginning her studies of nightlife in Arizona, she recognizes and partially overcomes her fears. North Dakota and Hawaii are further stops. By the time her journeys reach Connecticut, in her mother's backyard, she is fully of the night, able to hear the trilling of toads and the belling of peepers.

————. *Wintering.* Boston: Little, Brown, 1984; New York: McGraw-Hill, 1986.
From a farm in northern Vermont, emotionally forthright reflections on the experience of the seasons. Moments of contact with the earth provide sustenance through the winter. After an earthquake, and after drilling for a water well and finding limestone 120 feet down, "Suddenly everything that I am exploring—live, surface, things—seems fragmentary, insecurely perched, hardly worth the ticket. I am seated on miles of living rock."

Kaufman, Kenn (1956–). *Kingbird Highway: The Story of a Natural Obsession That Got a Little Out of Hand.* **Boston: Houghton Mifflin, 1997.**
In the early 1970s, when birdwatching was becoming *birding,* the author, having recently dropped out of high school, followed his bliss over a good deal of North America, living frugally, hitchhiking everywhere, and searching for birds new to his list of species. He earned seasoned naturalists' respect for his knowledge and, with this account, impresses the reader with both the purity of his passion and the subtlety of the retrospective portrayal of his younger self.

Kaza, Stephanie (1947–). *The Attentive Heart: Conversations with Trees.* **New York: Fawcett Columbine, 1993; Boston: Shambhala, 1996.**
The author goes to individual trees, spends quiet time with them, researches their individual history and that of their species, and then goes back to the trees themselves, paying them the gift of complete attention. She listens well, describing the specific trees beautifully, and then expands the field of concern to suggest a world where trees and persons have equal stake and equal standing.

Kent, Rockwell (1882–1971). *N by E.* **New York: Random House, 1930; New York: Harcourt Brace, 1930; Middletown, Conn.: Wesleyan University Press, 1996.**
A stormy and difficult passage by sail to Greenland, climaxing in shipwreck on a rocky shore. The denouement, however, is Kent's post-disaster awakening to the beauty of the wild, spare surroundings. Camping out on the tundra, walking in occasionally to a tiny settlement, the author found perception renewed. "How rich in everything was Greenland! ... [T]hen human kind seemed what it ought to be."

————. *Wilderness: A Journal of Quiet Adventure in Alaska.* **New York: G. P. Putnam's Sons, 1920; Middletown, Conn.: Wesleyan University Press, 1996.**
The artist and his son, Rockwell III (nine years old at the time), spent six months on Fox Island, just off the Kenai Peninsula, in the winter of 1918–1919. Kent's informal, forthright style conveys the sense of place and weather with

clarity, and characterizes the relationship between father and son simply and profoundly. "The still, deep cup of the wilderness is potent with wisdom. Only to have tasted it is to have moved a lifetime forward to a finer youth." A beautiful book.

Kieran, John (1892–1981). *Footnotes on Nature.* Garden City, N.Y.: Doubleday, 1947.
Rambles with a strolling group of friends, mostly in the vicinity of New York City, suggesting the delight in nature and the flavor of camaraderie of Izaak Walton's *The Compleat Angler.* The quarry here is usually birds. Written with charmingly self-effacing wit.

————. *A Natural History of New York City: A Personal Report after Fifty Years of Study and Enjoyment of Wildlife within the Boundaries of Greater New York.* Boston: Houghton Mifflin, 1959; New York: Fordham University Press, 1982.
Modestly, the author writes that he has "touched on some of the easily observed divisions of plant and animal life that occur within the city limits." One might wonder how a place with twenty-five thousand people per square mile, notoriously overtopped with asphalt and concrete, could be of much natural history interest. This book shows how it could, in detail.

King, Clarence (1842–1901). *Mountaineering in the Sierra Nevada.* Boston: James R. Osgood, 1871; New York: Charles Scribner's Sons, 1902; New York: W. W. Norton, 1935; Philadelphia: J. B. Lippincott, 1963; Lincoln: University of Nebraska Press, 1997.
Entertaining adventures in the Sierra, clear lectures on geology, and perceptive and humorous accounts of mountain characters. The most consciously literary production of the California Survey team.

————. *Systematic Geology.* Washington, D.C.: U.S. Government Printing Office, 1878.
A remarkably lucid overview of the landscape between Cheyenne, Wyoming, and Carson City, Nevada, covering a one hundred-mile swath of country as representative. King's vigorous prose conveys the drama of geologic history as revealed by present landforms.

King, Thomas Starr (1824–1864). *The White Hills: Their Legends, Landscape, and Poetry.* Boston: Crosby, Nichols, 1859.
Concentrating upon views and viewpoints, this book guides the traveler toward New Hampshire's White Mountains from every point of the compass. The emphasis is entirely visual. "One can hardly conceive what heightened charm a very little cultivation on the sides of a mountain will add to the landscape."

Kingsolver, Barbara (1955–). *High Tide in Tucson: Essays from Now or Never.* New York: HarperPerennial, 1995.
Twenty-five essays on subjects ranging from the museum of atom bomb relics to a battle of wills with a two-year-old. The Arizona novelist shows her talent in nature writing.

Kinkead, Eugene (1906–). *A Concrete Look at Nature: Central Park (and Other) Glimpses.* New York: Quadrangle, New York Times Books, 1974.
Most of the pieces here describe rambles in New York City, including bird walks and tree walks that may surprise the reader with the richness of things to see.

Knowler, Donald (1946–). *The Falconer of Central Park.* New York: Karz-Cohl, 1984.
A British birder comes to New York City and is mugged early on, but continues birding in Central Park, making sharp observations on the human scene and entering in this journal-like account lyrical descriptions of birds, weather, and the seasons.

Krutch, Joseph Wood (1893–1970). *The Best Nature Writing of Joseph Wood Krutch.* New York: William Morrow, 1970; New York: Pocket Books, 1971; Salt Lake City: University of Utah Press, 1995.
A good selection, made by the author and introduced by an essay that describes nature writing as science with a human, caring face and that also recounts Krutch's own beginnings in the genre.

———. *The Desert Year.* New York: William Sloane Associates, 1952; New York: Viking Press, 1963.
Essays in desert natural history, derived from the author's life-changing sabbatical year in Arizona. A major pleasure here is Krutch's growing sense of wonder and delight, and his depth of response to other creatures' consciousness and emotions. The chapter "A Bird in the Bush," in which Krutch writes, "A bird in the bush is worth two in the hand," is a penetrating examination of the unfeeling kind of biological science.

———. *The Forgotten Peninsula: A Naturalist in Baja California.* New York: William Sloane Associates, 1961; Tucson: University of Arizona Press, 1986.
Baja California, when it *was* forgotten. Krutch described himself as a traveler "so struck by its wildness and its beauty that he returned again and again." This travel book contains astute observations on progress, inspired by Krutch's glimpses into a slower, materially poorer, yet richer world.

————. *The Grand Canyon: Today and All Its Yesterdays.* New York: William Sloane Associates, 1958.

Instruction in ecology—for example, the differentiation between squirrels that live on the north and south rims of the canyon—and the canyon's clear demonstration of Merriam's "life-zone" theory. Krutch declares himself among those "who find themselves seeing it more vividly when nature is not merely a spectacle but a phenomenon interpretable in terms of the infinitely complex and subtle processes of which the spectacle is an outward and visible sign. And I have never found either the beauty or the wonder diminished."

————. *The Great Chain of Life.* Boston: Houghton Mifflin, 1956, 1978.

The author's immense command of historical and literary reference is brought to bear on some of the most instructive aspects of the biosphere. Working from an evolutionary standpoint, Krutch attempts to place consciousness and feeling within the overall biological context. His reflections on happiness and joy are provocative.

————. *The Voice of the Desert: A Naturalist's Interpretation.* New York: William Sloane Associates, 1955.

The adaptations of desert wildlife to heat and aridity lead the author to considerations on humanity's place, and to a critique of mechanical behaviorism as a theory of nature. The book also includes a plea for an attitude more profound than mere conservation. Krutch argues, "The wisest, the most enlightened, the most remotely long-seeing exploitation of resources is not enough, for the simple reason that the whole concept of exploitation is so false and so limited that in the end it will defeat itself and the earth will have been plundered no matter how scientifically and farseeingly the plundering has been done."

LaBastille, Anne (1938–). *Beyond Black Bear Lake.* New York: W. W. Norton, 1987, 2000.

In this sequel to *Woodswoman,* a stronger environmental concern is evident. Much had happened in ten years, but the central themes remain in place. The author built a second cabin for $130.75 and called it "Thoreau II."

————. *Woodswoman.* New York: E. P. Dutton, 1976, 1991.

Getting to know the Adirondacks close-up, in all seasons, learning how to live alone, and learning how to live in "an ecologically sound manner" in the wilderness. The author honestly relates her fears and occasional loneliness, and her impatience for spring.

Lambourne, Alfred (1850–1926). *Our Inland Sea: The Story of a Homestead.* Salt Lake City: Deseret News, 1909.
Lambourne, a poet of some power and a landscape artist in the tradition of Albert Bierstadt, lived alone for fourteen months on Gunnison Island in the Great Salt Lake. "I shall see the great phenomena of nature," he wrote early in his stay, and though he did spend some time looking at the mainland through his telescope, he also responded to the spareness of the island and to the dramatic movement of storms across the lake.

Lanner, Ronald (1930–). *Made for Each Other: A Symbiosis of Birds and Pines.* New York: Oxford University Press, 1996.
A study of the coevolution of nut pines—bristlecone pines, limber pines, whitebark pines, Jeffrey pines, Korean stone pines, and others—and the group of birds known as nutcrackers. Lanner marvels at the knit of interbeing demonstrated here, but also recognizes that it isn't impregnable. Loss of a keystone mutualist such as whitebark pine (threatened presently by several inadvertent effects of human action) could bring about major changes, well beyond those affecting the codependent bird species.

————. *The Piñon Pine: A Natural and Cultural History.* Reno: University of Nevada Press, 1981.
A good example of how to write popular natural history without writing down. This forestry professor's account of a most interesting tree examines its ecological settings and describes its uses and its beauty and appeal. The book includes pine-nut recipes supplied by the author's wife, Harriette.

————. *Trees of the Great Basin: A Natural History.* Reno: University of Nevada Press, 1983.
A thorough survey, illustrated with drawings by Christine Rasmuss as well as several fine photographs, and studded with little-known facts revealing the ecological complexity of an area often regarded as a wasteland or military testing ground. This is a basic reference text and, for its clarity and depth of appreciation for its subject, a pleasure to read.

Lawson, John (1674–1711). *A New Voyage to Carolina.* London: n.p., 1709; edited by Hugh T. Lefler. Chapel Hill: University of North Carolina Press, 1967, 1994.
In the first decade of the eighteenth century, Lawson went inland into Carolina on a journey of over five hundred miles, going from one Indian tribe to the next. His journal gives plentiful information on animals' lives (though he did not

look as closely as Catesby would, later, at the hog-nosed snake, and though he believed female opossums bore their young at the nipples). He studied Indians minutely, describing their physiques and their ways of life in vivid detail.

LeConte, Joseph (1823–1901). *A Journal of Ramblings Through the High Sierras of California.* San Francisco: Francis and Valentine, 1875; San Francisco: Sierra Club Books, 1930, 1960.
A summer pack trip in the year 1870, with a geology professor from the University of California. The author describes the lay of the land and its likely geological history, and pays an early tribute to the charisma and intelligence of John Muir, whom LeConte met in Yosemite Valley.

Lehmberg, Paul (1946–). *In the Strong Woods: A Season Alone in the North Country.* New York: St. Martin's Press, 1980.
From the kitchen table of a cabin at Nym Lake in Minnesota, the author reflects on solitude, work and its relation to contemplation, and his own life, and finds himself able to come to a major decision.

Leopold, Aldo (1887–1948). *Round River: From the Journals of Aldo Leopold.* Edited by Luna Leopold. New York: Oxford University Press, 1953, 1972.
Early journals, with many of the entries about hunting. This would be a good text for the argument that a hunter's awareness is related to ecological consciousness.

————. *A Sand County Almanac.* New York: Oxford University Press, 1949, 1993.
One of the modern classics, setting forth in elegantly economical prose the author's own journey toward ecological understanding, the necessity of wilderness to civilization, and (perhaps most revolutionary of his ideas) the need for a "land ethic."

Leydet, Francois (1927–). *The Coyote: Defiant Songdog of the West.* Norman: University of Oklahoma Press, 1977, 1988.
Focusing on the relationship between coyote and man, and more pointedly on "predator control," Leydet describes the wonderful adaptability of the coyote. On the human side are those who respect and appreciate the animal, and also those who dedicate much of their lives and a good deal of the public's money to a campaign of eradication. The extent of the war on coyotes, and the perverse energy with which it is prosecuted, may surprise some readers.

Linnea, Ann (1949–). *Deep Water Passage: A Spiritual Journey at Midlife*. Boston: Little, Brown, 1995.

In the summer of 1992, the author paddled her kayak some eighteen hundred miles, around almost the entire shoreline of Lake Superior. In the course of many days on the cold and often stormy water, and a like number of nights camped on mostly wild shores, she experienced a full gamut of states—exaltation, loneliness, hypothermia, exhaustion, and a strong sense of her own power among them. Great issues in her life became clearer.

Longgood, William (1917–). *The Queen Must Die: And Other Affairs of Bees and Men*. New York: W. W. Norton, 1985.

A beekeeper's thoughts on the life of the hive, with interesting, nonclichéd comparisons and contrasts to human life. The descriptions of bee physiology and behavior are splendidly clear, yet suggest the mystery and poetry, which the author believes are at the heart of the subject.

Lopez, Barry (1945–) *About This Life: Journeys on the Threshold of Memory*. New York: Alfred A. Knopf, 1998.

There isn't a classic nature essay in here—in fact, there isn't much about nature—but there is a rapt sense of the surroundings, of the light and the air, that most nature writers would die for. The essays are so beautifully written, so calm and so measured, and fit together so well, that we await the author's autobiography impatiently. "Searching for Depth in Bonaire," "In a Country of Light, Among Animals," and "The American Geographies," if I had to pick three, are superb. But "Speed" and "Theft" make a great way to end this book: the author isn't so different from us after all.

———. *Arctic Dreams: Imagination and Desire in a Northern Landscape*. New York: Charles Scribner's Sons, 1986; New York: Bantam Books, 1996.

This is a book with much to say about perception. Perception, Lopez explains, may be shaped and limited by preconceptions, psychic needs, and material wants—these are some of our dreams. It may also, on occasion, and revealing an admirable human potential, simply be clear. The author travels over great stretches of the Arctic, meditating upon the great choice that is behind our eyes.

———. *Crossing Open Ground*. New York: Charles Scribner's Sons, 1988.

A collection of essays unified by Lopez's stance of passionate respect for the natural world and by the exquisite attention he pays to things like the sound of music in the Grand Canyon, a wolverine story in Alaska, and an actual wolverine entering his camp. "Bob and I stood up, as though someone important had walked in. . . ." Similes seem to leap up before his wide-awake perception. The spectacle of nature does not appear here so much as a resource for writing, but as intense moral instruction. "The Passing Wisdom of Birds" has the weight of a major essay in the quest for an ecologically responsible human position.

————. *Of Wolves and Men.* New York: Charles Scribner's Sons, 1978.
A wide-ranging book that brings in biology, ethology, mythology, folklore, and history. The author's insights into the relationship between wolves and men from each angle of vision are penetrating. A strong indictment of human shortsightedness and fear emerges, but the fellow-feeling that permeates the book offers evidence of a different, better attitude. The section on American antiwolf hysteria, both individual and government sponsored, makes its point by understatement.

Lueders, Edward (1923–). *The Clam Lake Papers: A Winter in the North Woods.* New York: Harper and Row, 1977; Ellison Bay, Wis.: William Caxton, 1996.
In a small cabin near Clam Lake in Wisconsin, the author becomes intensely self- and word-conscious as winter deepens. "I am less and less stimulated by the observation of my surroundings, and I find myself turning my observations more and more inward." A major quest here is for an understanding of metaphor and the basic processes of consciousness.

Madson, John (1923–). *Up on the River.* New York: Schocken Books, 1985.
Madson describes the Mississippi between St. Louis and St. Paul as the heart of the country, the home of wildlife, and an abundance of human characters.

————. *Where the Sky Began: Land of the Tallgrass Prairie.* Boston: Houghton Mifflin, 1982; San Francisco: Sierra Club, 1985; Ames: Iowa State University Press, 1996.
A natural and recent human history of the easternmost grasslands of North America, covering soils, weather, ecological complexity, and the impact of settlement and conversion. A most useful appendix lists natural and restored tallgrass reserves in twelve states.

Marshall, Ian (1954–). *Story Line: Exploring the Literature of the Appalachian Trail.* Charlottesville: University Press of Virginia, 1998.
Narrative criticism, mixing extended quotations from such writers as William

Bartram, Henry David Thoreau, Horace Kephart, and Annie Dillard with Marshall's reponses to their writing and to the Appalachian Trail itself. The result is an example of ecocriticism at a high level. Among other fresh insights, Marshall lays to rest the hoary interpretation that Thoreau was "scared spirit-less" on top of Mt. Katahdin in 1846.

Marshall, Robert (1901–1939). *Arctic Wilderness.* Edited by George Marshall. Berkeley: University of California Press, 1956; reprinted as *Alaska Wilderness.* Berkeley: University of California Press, 1970
In his youth, Marshall lamented being born too late for Lewis-and-Clark-style adventure and exploration. But four expeditions to the Brooks Range gave him plenty of opportunity to ford rivers, hike enormous distances, be tested by weather, and climb nameless mountains to gaze off over thousands of square miles of wilderness. This is a fast-moving, exhilarating account.

Maslow, Jonathan Evan (1948–). *Bird of Life, Bird of Death: A Naturalist's Journey Through a Land of Political Turmoil.* New York: Simon and Schuster, 1986.
A search for the resplendent quetzal, ancient symbol of freedom and the na-tional symbol of Guatemala, a country where vultures now prosper famously. The author reports that the highland cloud-forest habitat of the quetzal has shrunk to some twenty-five hundred square kilometers.

Matthiessen, Peter (1927–). *Sand Rivers.* New York: Viking Press, 1981.
An expedition in 1979 into the Selous Game Reserve in Tanzania, the largest wildlife reservation in Africa and a wilderness of almost primeval intactness.

————. *The Snow Leopard.* New York: Viking Press, 1978; New York: Penguin USA, 1996.
The story of a long, physically and spiritually demanding trek in a remote sec-tion of Nepal, undertaken not long after the death of the author's wife. The narrative is bell-clear and strongly evocative of a world of bright mountain light, snow, and rock.

————. *The Shorebirds of North America.* Edited by Gardner D. Stout. New York: Viking Press, 1967; reprinted in part as *The Wind Birds.* New York: Viking Press, 1973; Shelburne, Vt.: Chapters Publishing, 1994.
A most interesting group of birds, given thorough and appreciative treatment. Matthiessen's eleven chapters covering the history, physiology, and habits of the "wind birds" are written in a prose as elegant and precise as a flight of phalaropes. Robert Clem's paintings and Ralph S. Palmer's "Species Accounts,"

found in the 1967 edition, are also scientifically trustworthy and touched with the poetry that shorebirds seem to inspire. A beautiful book in all respects. The revised edition, *The Wind Birds,* is illustrated by Robert Gillmor.

————. *Tigers in the Snow.* New York: North Point Press, 2000.
To far eastern Russia, the Sikhote-Alin region, land of Dersu the hunter and home of the last few tigers in the snow. The political changes in Russia have opened the door to the poaching of tigers (with a street value of $25,000).

Matthiessen, Peter, and Eliot Porter. *The Tree Where Man Was Born: The African Experience.* New York: E. P. Dutton, 1972.
In preserved portions of East Africa we can still see a "glimpse of the earth's morning." The author conveys this auroral freshness not only in descriptions of wildlife but also in portraits of humans. A book revealing high awareness of both the moment and the ancient, interlocked story of Africa and humans. Eliot Porter's photographs are also superb.

Maximilian, Alexander Philip (1782–1867). *Travels in the Interior of North America, 1832–1834.* Vols. 22, 23, 24 of *Early Western Travels.* Edited by Reuben Gold Thwaites. Cleveland: Arthur H. Clark, 1906.
The Prince of Wied-Neuwied on the Rhine, Maximilian had the means and the leisure to take a slow journey up the Missouri and to winter over at the Mandan villages on his way home. He studied the abundant wildlife and the Indians with deep interest, and recorded one of the most compelling accounts of early travel in the West. His descriptions of cranes, buffalo, and wolves are memorable, in part because his writing speaks to the ear as well as the eye.

McMullen, James P. (1943–). *Cry of the Panther: Quest of a Species.* Englewood, Fla.: Pineapple Press, 1984; New York: McGraw-Hill, 1985.
A Vietnam veteran throws his guns into a river, then spends years searching for the Florida cougar, hoping to see and know the health that a living big cat in a living ecosystem would epitomize.

McNamee, Thomas (1947–). *The Grizzly Bear.* New York: Alfred A. Knopf, 1984; New York: McGraw-Hill, 1986; New York: Lyons Press, 1997.
The author's style is nearly conversational, and the organization somewhat episodic, but this book offers a solid natural history of grizzlies and a stimulating interpretation of bear-man interaction. The book focuses on the greater Yellowstone ecosystem and includes criticism of the Park Service and of lax local prosecution of poachers.

————. *The Return of the Wolf to Yellowstone.* New York: Henry Holt, 1997.
"The fact of the matter is that a lot of conservation is at heart sentimental," says the author forthrightly. He brings the story up to February 1998, when a U.S. District Judge said all of the wolves—a hundred in Yellowstone, and eighty in Idaho—had to go back. A patent absurdity.

McNulty, Faith (1918–). *The Wildlife Stories of Faith McNulty.* Garden City, N.Y.: Doubleday, 1980.
Close-up accounts of animals the author has encountered, studied, and in some cases lived with, written in high consciousness of the great, endangering power of the modern human way of life. This is an informative and reflective book of essays, in which "The Whooping Crane," a gem of concerned reportage, is perhaps the centerpiece. The book ought to have a more accurately descriptive title.

McPhee, John (1931–). *Assembling California.* New York: Farrar, Straus and Giroux, 1993; New York: Noonday Press, 1994.
The author accompanies the plate tectonics specialist Eldridge Moores around California, taking what amounts to a graduate course in geology, and then assembles his notes into a sparkling, seeable narrative of the deep-down history of the state. Six main pieces of plate, some of them uneasily joined, make up what a road map shows as one state. The information, for McPhee, is not academic: "Great earthquakes are all over the geology. A big one will always be in the offing."

————. *Basin and Range.* New York: Farrar, Straus and Giroux, 1981; New York: Noonday Press, 1990.
A wide-ranging introductory course in earth history, strung along Interstate 80 in part and using its roadcuts to make lecture points. The focus is on Nevada and the Great Basin, where the parallel, north-south mountain ranges appear to McPhee like stretch marks on the earth's crust. Highly informative prose, with sentences taking unforeseen but eminently logical turns.

————. *Coming into the Country.* New York: Farrar, Straus and Giroux, 1977; New York: Bantam, 1979; New York: Noonday Press, 1991.
A portrait of Alaska, including a wilderness idyll (a float trip on the Salmon River), telling snapshots of movers and shakers, and more extended accounts of backcountry settlers—many of whom appear to desire both wilderness and a fossil-fuel powered lifestyle.

―――. *The Control of Nature.* New York: Farrar Straus Giroux, 1989; New York: Noonday Press, 1990.

The Mississippi River, McPhee points out, has in its delta wanderings created the state of Louisiana. But now we want the river to stay put. Similarly, Iceland and Hawaii were created by volcanoes, and now it is necessary to manage that power, keep it within bounds. Many people want to live at the edge of the Los Angeles Basin, where flows of mud and rock, under the right conditions, have for millenia roared out of the canyons of the San Gabriel Mountains. McPhee surveys these conflicts with wit and a strong sense of the ironies in human behavior.

―――. *The Pine Barrens.* New York: Farrar, Straus and Giroux, 1968, 1981 (special edition with photographs by Bill Curtsinger).

A surprisingly intact quasi wilderness in the center of the northeast industrial corridor, with a cast of interesting characters. The focus here, and typically so for McPhee, is sociological and personal, but there is also information on such matters as berries, the giant aquifer underneath the Barrens, fire and its effects upon forest succession, and the birds of the area.

―――. *Rising from the Plains.* New York: Farrar Straus Giroux, 1986; New York: Noonday Press, 1991.

A fascinating geological tour of Wyoming, with biographies of David Love (the "Grand Old Man of Rocky Mountain Geology") and his mother, a Wellesley graduate turned rancher.

Mech, L. David (1937–). *Wolves of the High Arctic.* Stillwater, Minn.: Voyageur Press, 1992.

Magnificent photographs, spanning five years. The captions are so information filled, they amount to nature writing.

Meloy, Ellen (1946–). *The Last Cheater's Waltz: Beauty and Violence in the Desert Southwest.* New York: Henry Holt, 1999.

What binds a person to place? is a tough question. Meloy took a tour around her western place and found herself concentrating on the nuclear industry at Los Alamos. Her humor quieted down; her seriousness grew. Finally, despite a well having been dug and eight acres surrounding it bought, she finds no easy answers. Trinity will do that to you.

―――. *Raven's Exile: A Season on the Green River.* New York: Henry Holt, 1994.

Much of the way here, the author is right where she wants to be, floating with her river-ranger husband as he oversees the recreational boater high time on the Green River in Utah. She has great love for place, biting satiric wit, upwelling good humor and acceptance, and a fund of historical and natural history knowledge. This book is rich in information and also has the feel of water, sandstone grit, and strong sun.

Merriam, Florence A. (1863–1948). *A-Birding on a Bronco*. Boston: Houghton, Mifflin, 1896.
Two springtimes in southern California just north of San Diego were the source of these pleasant, well-written birdwatching narratives. Merriam, the author of authoritative bird guides and later the winner of a major scientific prize in ornithology, knew her birds. Her writing expresses strong fellow-feeling as well.

Michaux, F. André (1770–1855), and Thomas Nuttall (1786–1859). *The North American Sylva, or, A Description of the Forest Trees of the United States, Canada, and Nova Scotia.* 5 vols. Philadelphia: D. Rice and A. N. Hart, 1867. (Vols. 1–3 by Michaux, 4, 5 by Nuttall.)
Two great field men survey the trees of North America with scientific thoroughness and with delight. Nuttall's preface expresses his love for the wild, American places he had known, as do his narratives of events during his botanical explorations in the West.

Mills, Enos A. (1870–1922). *The Spell of the Rockies*. Boston: Houghton Mifflin, 1911.
High adventures in the mountains, including a race with an avalanche that may test readers' credulity, mingled with excellent descriptions of wildlife and logical arguments for forest preservation. Mills was self-educated, an amateur in the high sense, and endlessly curious. "To spend a day in the rain at the source of a stream was an experience I had long desired, for the behavior of the waters in collecting and hurrying down slopes would doubtless show some of Nature's interesting ways."

———. *Wild Animal Homesteads*. Garden City, N.Y.: Doubleday, Page, 1923.
Narratives of animal interaction by a most patient and understanding observer. Mills emphasizes the importance of territory and familiarity with a home range in the lives of his subjects. Two of the essays here demonstrate a talent for satire, when the author compares animal and human ways.

———. *Wild Life on the Rockies*. Boston: Houghton Mifflin, 1909.
This energetic book of observations and adventures was dedicated to John

Muir, and contains many expressions that hark back to Muir, such as, "I lived intensely through ten strong days and nights, and gave to my life new and rare experiences." There are also detailed accounts of the distribution and ecology of various tree species.

————. *Your National Parks*. Boston: Houghton Mifflin, 1917.
A rather general travel guide, supplemented by occasional quotations from John Muir or John Charles Van Dyke. Mills's stand is clear: "Without parks and outdoor life all that is best in civilization will be smothered."

Milne, Lorus J. (1910–), and Margery J. Milne (1914–). *The Balance of Nature*. New York: Alfred A. Knopf, 1960.
Modern ecological studies, several of which are reported in detail here, provide concepts, and standards for environmental health, that might help humans adjust our numbers and activities to the earth. A valuable handbook, illustrated by Olaus Murie.

————. *A Multitude of Living Things*. New York: Dodd, Mead, 1947.
Clear explications of small, usually unnoticed phenomena: the work of burying (carrion) beetles, the importance of water film (surface tension) on small bodies of water, the lives of animals who spend the daytime under rocks, and more. The opening chapter, not surprisingly, is a guide to slowed-down, patient observation.

————. *The Valley: Meadow, Grove, and Stream*. New York: Harper and Row, 1963.
The commonplaces of one's local surroundings—in this case a river valley in New England—reinforce the web of all life. The subtitle is from Wordsworth's "Ode on Intimations of Immortality," and this book provides a scientific gloss on that poem's theme. The immortality is the ecological wholeness in which every mollusk, bird, fish, or human observer participates.

————. *The World of Night*. New York: Harper and Brothers, 1956.
What happens at night on the desert, in the ocean, in polar regions, in the forest, on the beach, in the jungle, and elsewhere, described in expository prose that is a model of clarity. The often-neglected half of natural history.

Milton, John P. (1938–). *Nameless Valleys, Shining Mountains: The Record of an Expedition into the Vanishing Wilderness of Alaska's Brooks Range*. New York: Walker, 1970.
A three hundred-mile, thirty-eight day trek in 1967, across the mountains and

down the North Slope to the Arctic Ocean, with the awareness that the oil companies were close behind.

Mitchell, Donald Grant (1822–1908). *My Farm of Edgewood: A Country Book.* **New York: Charles Scribner, 1863.**
Careful planning (including the matter of just how far from a city a farm ought to be) enabled the author to make Edgewood, his farm near New Haven, Connecticut, something of a model. This is mainly a how-to book, but Mitchell's many references to literature and philosophy help put the matter of going back to the country into a larger perspective.

———. *Wet Days at Edgewood: With Old Farmers, Old Gardeners, and Old Pastorals.* **New York: Charles Scribner, 1865.**
Rain and snow keep the author indoors here, and he takes the opportunity to renew his acquaintance with Virgil and other writers of the classical era, medieval and Renaissance authors, and near contemporaries—writers who all dealt with agricultural and pastoral matters in one way or another.

Mitchell, John Hanson (1940–). *Ceremonial Time: Fifteen Thousand Years on One Square Mile.* **Garden City, N.Y.: Doubleday, Anchor Press, 1984.**
The story of Scratch Flat, an area near Boston, from the era of the last glaciation. Mitchell covers the known historical events, and renders the area's ecological history clearly, but what interests him most is "that undiscovered country of the nearby, the secret world that lurks beyond the night windows and at the fringes of cultivated backyards."

———. *Trespassing: An Inquiry into the Private Ownership of Land.* **Reading, Mass.: Addison-Wesley, 1998.**
A meditation on one of the pillars of our land-sense (or beams in our eye, if you will). Mitchell traces the history of Nashoba, a piece of land about thirty-five miles west of Boston, as it moves from common land among the Pawtucket Indians to private holding, and in our time back toward something like commonality. This is a relaxed, leisurely book, dramatizing the pace of a cross-lots walker with time to think.

———. *Walking Towards Walden: A Pilgrimage in Search of Place.* **Reading, Mass.: Addison-Wesley, 1995; Reading, Mass.: Perseus Press, 1997.**
With two companions, Mitchell sets out to walk fifteen miles through eastern Massachusetts on the way to Walden. In the course of the journey, they reflect

on the idea of pilgrimage, and many other things. They saunter and trespass freely, but contemplate with care.

Montgomery, Sy (1958–). *Journey of the Pink Dolphins: An Amazon Quest.* New York: Simon and Schuster, 2000.
The author travels to Amazonia to see the amazing freshwater dolphins. She overcomes the environment and gets quite close to the strange, compelling, pink cetaceans, still marveling at their mystery. Much folklore, much straight science, and much wonder.

————. *Seasons of the Wild: A Year of Nature's Magic and Mysteries.* Shelburne, Vt.: Chapters Publishing, 1995.
A collection of short essays from the *Boston Globe,* which prove that nature is endlessly interesting. The fact-per-inch rate is high here, especially in the chapters on lichens, robins, and blackflies, but the writing is good all the way.

Moore, Kathleen Dean (1947–). *Riverwalking: Reflections on Moving Water.* New York: Lyons and Burford, 1995.
Essays with strong autobiographical content, framed on trips to rivers the author and her family have walked along and in or floated on. Feeling for family catalyzes reflection and insight in these essays.

Morton, Thomas (1575–1646). *New English Canaan.* London: Charles Green, 1632; reprinted in *Tracts and Other Papers, Relating Principally to the Origin, Settlement, and Progress of the Colonies in North America, from the Discovery of the Country to the Year 1776.* Washington: Peter Force, 1838; North Scituate, Mass.: Digital Scanning, 2000.
Morton says he arrived in the month of June 1622, with thirty servants "and provision of all sorts fit for a plantation. . . ." While the houses were being built, he "did endeavour to take a survey of the Country: The more I looked, the more I liked it." His book lists prominent wildlife species and makes observations on forest cover, which are useful to later ecological historians.

Muir, John (1838–1914). *John Muir: To Yosemite and Beyond.* Edited by Robert Engberg and Donald Wesling. Madison: University of Wisconsin Press, 1980; Salt Lake City: University of Utah Press, 1999.
A valuable collation of letters, journal entries, and lesser-known writings, extending Muir's own *Story of My Boyhood and Youth* through 1875. The editors' framing of the selections and their interpretations of Muir's thought are informative.

————. *John of the Mountains: The Unpublished Journals of John Muir.* Edited by Linnie Marsh Wolfe. Boston: Houghton Mifflin, 1938; Madison: University of Wisconsin Press, 1979.

Muir's shortest entries here (probably reflecting the level of his interest) describe dinner parties and meetings with well-known people, which come late in the journal. The record of the earlier years, particularly the early 1870s, is steadily focused on the wilderness, as fruitfully as in any American book.

————. *Letters to a Friend.* Boston: Houghton Mifflin, 1915; Dunwoody, Ga.: Norman S. Berg, 1973.

Jeanne Carr, the wife of Muir's science professor at the University of Wisconsin and something very like a mentor herself to the young Muir, encouraged him to write, both to her and more generally for publication. These letters stand with the early journal as primary sources on Muir's inner life and developing knowledge of wilderness.

————. *The Mountains of California.* New York: Century, 1894; Garden City, N.Y.: Doubleday, 1961; New York: Penguin USA, 1997.

Muir's first book, well controlled and put together. It moves from the overview to the particulars with logic, and yet remains mysteriously radiant and ebullient—wild. "A Near View of the High Sierra," "A Wind-Storm in the Forests," and "The Water-Ouzel" are classic essays, epitomizing Muir's highly individual, yet transparent, wilderness-engrossed outlook.

————. *My First Summer in the Sierra.* Boston: Houghton Mifflin, 1911, 1979, 1998.

The journal of the baptismal summer of 1869, edited by a Muir who is older but very much alive. In these months he saw his first water ouzels and glacial erratics, crossed the Sierra Nevada for the first time, stared with awe at summer thunderheads, crept to the edge of Yosemite Falls, and stood face to face with a bear. Muir directed his ecstasy into his notebook, there being no one else to discuss it with: "June 13. Another glorious Sierra day in which one seems to be dissolved and absorbed and sent pulsing onward we know not where. Life seems neither long nor short, and we take no more heed to save time or make haste than do the trees and stars. This is true freedom, a good practical sort of immortality."

————. *Steep Trails.* Edited by William Frederic Badè. Boston: Houghton Mifflin, 1918; San Francisco: Sierra Club Books, 1994.

A posthumous collection of essays that includes the important piece "Wild

Wool," an early effort to describe wilderness not as chaotic or in need of human correction but as reflecting the pure order of the universe. Muir roams to Nevada and Utah, among other places.

————. *The Story of My Boyhood and Youth.* Boston: Houghton Mifflin, 1913, 1938; Madison: University of Wisconsin Press, 1965.
Muir's early years, as seen from the vantage point of a seventy-year-old, appear as a drama of emergence. His innate love of wild things and wild places, with freedom of spirit, survive punishingly narrow circumstances.

————. *John Muir's Studies in the Sierra.* Edited by William E. Colby. San Francisco: Sierra Club, 1960.
These are Muir's glacier articles, originally published in the 1870s in the *Overland Monthly.* Even at his most scientific, working out the proofs for Sierran glaciation, Muir managed to convey the wild, thrilling beauty of ice-sculptured mountains.

————. *A Thousand-Mile Walk to the Gulf.* Edited by William Frederic Badè. Boston: Houghton Mifflin, 1916, 1981; San Francisco: Sierra Club Books, 1992.
This is a journal record of Muir's first great solo adventure, a hike from southern Indiana to the Gulf Coast of Florida in the fall of 1867. Less polished literarily than Muir's other works, it records his delight in new botanical scenes and, most interestingly, his growing philosophical independence.

————. *Travels in Alaska.* Boston: Houghton Mifflin, 1915, 1979; San Francisco: Sierra Club Books, 1988.
The wild southeastern coast of Alaska, with its gigantic fjords and ice rivers, provided scope for Muir's expansive love of wildness and up-to-date texts for his understanding of glaciation and his sense of the ongoing creation of the world. He reveled in the great land, canoeing eight hundred miles in one trip, climbing mountains, and taking a theretofore greater interest in native peoples.

————. *The Yosemite.* New York: Century, 1912; Garden City, N.Y.: Doubleday, 1962.
A guidebook that names the most spectacular features and directs interested walkers to them, but also urges readers to realize the spiritual dimensions of a sacred place. The book concludes with a passionate, biblically thundering defense of Hetch Hetchy as wilderness that ought to be left alone and undammed.

Murie, Adolph (1899–1973). *Ecology of the Coyote in the Yellowstone.* U.S. National Park Service, Fauna Series, no. 4. Washington, D.C.: U.S. Government Printing Office, 1940.
An important contribution to the adoption of a more ecological point of view

in the National Park Service's attitude toward predation. The author walked the backcountry, observing the behavior of coyotes and documenting their diet by examining several hundred scats. A baseline type of study that should be read in conjunction with Dobie's *The Voice of the Coyote* and Leydet's *The Coyote, Defiant Songdog of the West.*

————. *The Grizzlies of Mount McKinley.* Scientific Monograph Series, no. 14. Washington, D.C.: U.S. Government Printing Office, 1981; Seattle: University of Washington Press, 1981, 1996.
A natural history and historical treatment based upon many seasons in Denali, and written with a depth of feeling and understanding not always seen in professional reports: "On our initial day in the field in McKinley National Park in 1922, my brother and I were crossing from Jenny Creek over a rise to Savage River on our way to the head of the river. In those days there was no road, the park was all a blessed wilderness, and I have often thought since what a wonderful people we would have been if we had wanted to keep it that way."

————. *A Naturalist in Alaska.* New York: Devin-Adair, 1961; Tucson: University of Arizona Press, 1990.
Encounters with wildlife, showing what kind of adventures a person might have, and what sense of nature and wilderness he or she might develop, if willing to spend a lifetime in the field.

————. *The Wolves of Mount McKinley.* U.S. National Park Service, Fauna Series, no. 5. Washington, D.C.: U.S. Government Printing Office, 1944; Seattle: University of Washington Press, 1985.
The first extended scientific study of wolves in the wild, conducted (in the days before radio collars and aerial tracking) by going out and watching and listening.

Murie, Margaret E. (1902–). *Two in the Far North.* New York: Alfred A. Knopf, 1962; Portland, Oreg.: Graphic Arts Center Publishing, 1997.
The author gives a vivid reminiscence of her early life in Alaska, her marriage to Olaus Murie, and several of their wilderness trips together, including one to the Sheenjek River in 1956. The feel of untrammeled country and of caring, uncrowded human relationships is strong in these pages.

Murie, Margaret E., and Olaus J. Murie. *Wapiti Wilderness.* New York: Alfred A. Knopf, 1967; Boulder: University of Colorado Press, 1986.
A sequel to *Two in the Far North,* covering the authors' life together in Jackson

Hole, Wyoming, with a strong sense of place. This book contains some of Olaus Murie's best plain-style writing, and conveys throughout the Muries' deep response to wild country.

Murie, Olaus J. (1889–1963). *The Elk of North America.* Harrisburg, Pa.: Stackpole, 1951, 1957; Jackson, Wyo.: Teton Bookshop, 1979.
An authoritative natural history, with a clear presentation of the historical-political record and a consideration of the impacts of modern settlement upon a formerly wide-ranging species. The author's sense of what might constitute intelligent management of a wilderness animal in a nonwilderness world is the result of long pondering of a difficult, many-sided subject.

————. *Journeys to the Far North.* Palo Alto: Wilderness Society and American West Publishing, 1973.
Over a span of forty-seven years of field work, the author made trips to Labrador, the Hudson Bay country, and several parts of Alaska studying wild-life where it lived and experiencing the challenges of the old-time naturalist's way of life. The essays and journal entries here record explicitly what many of Murie's technical and professional papers could not dwell upon, his powerful feelings for wilderness and his artistic response to line, color, and sound.

Murphy, Alexandra (1963–). *Graced by Pines: The Ponderosa Pine in the American West.* Missoula, Mont.: Mountain Press Publishing, 1994.
Murphy believes in the reverence-creating power of story and here enacts that belief. This compact but great-hearted book gives the ponderosa's natural history and ecological relationships and covers the checkered time the species has endured at the hands of modern culture.

Murphy, Robert Cushman (1887–1973). *Fish-Shape Paumanok.* Philadelphia: American Philosophical Society, 1964.
A brilliantly ordered lecture on some of the major factors that shaped the natural history of Long Island, from glaciation to the 1960s, with particular stress on the effects of Euro-American settlement and population growth over the past three centuries.

Murphy, Robert (1902–1971). *The Peregrine Falcon.* Boston: Houghton Mifflin, 1963.
The first year in the life of a female peregrine, hatched on the Barren Grounds of Canada. After the arctic summer she flies southward into a strange, dangerous world crowded with humans. The story is told credibly from the falcon's point of view.

Nabhan, Gary Paul (1952–). *Cultures of Habitat: On Nature, Culture, and Story.*
Washington, D.C.: Counterpoint, 1997.
A collection of twenty-six essays from various periodicals, this book makes
valuable connections between plants and their pollinators, and communities
and their biodiverse surroundings.

―――. *The Desert Smells Like Rain: A Naturalist in Papago Indian Country.* San
Francisco: North Point Press, 1982, 1987.
A description of the old ways of the Papago Indians, stressing their adaptations
to seasonal abundance and scarcity and their knowledge of the desert's fine
points. The Papagos live in "raw intimacy" with the dry land, and take nothing
for granted.

―――. *Enduring Seeds: Native American Agriculture and Wild Plant Conservation.*
San Francisco: North Point Press, 1989.
Industrial agriculture's bent is to maximize profit by concentrating on highly
productive varieties. Nature's way is toward long-term health through diversity.
In twelve essays, Nabhan argues that a sophisticated injection of the vigor of
wildness into our food production (first requiring that we respect the wild and
the native people who have kept it alive in their fields) would be a prudent
course. This is a text in ecological responsibility.

―――. *Gathering the Desert.* Tucson: University of Arizona Press, 1985.
Although the author describes edible plants of the Sonoran Desert, his focus
expands from natural history to a general consideration of the ways we get our
food and what this tells of our whole inhabitation of the earth. "Gathering"
here means taking in, trying to understand, and being ready in the mind.

Nathan, Leonard (1924–). *Diary of a Left-Handed Birdwatcher.* St. Paul, Minn.:
Graywolf Press, 1996.
The author, a poet, is hoping to see one of the most poetic of birds, the snow
bunting. While on the quest, he carries on a running, funny dialogue with a
rational-skeptical ornithologist friend, on the subjects of epiphany, the shock
of recognition, truth, quantity versus quality, and perception. This book brings
us close to the mysterious attractiveness of birds, and some people's compelling need to see and hear them.

Nelson, Richard K. (1941–). *Make Prayers to the Raven: A Koyukon View of the
Northern Forest.* Chicago: University of Chicago Press, 1983, 1986.
An account of research in Alaska in the 1970s, expressed in terms of what might

be called deep anthropology: "Through the Koyukon, I became aware of a rich and eloquent natural history that extends into realms unknown or ignored in my own culture." Subsistence and the natural history knowledge it depends upon are seen here as a fundamentally spiritual way of life.

————. *The Island Within*. San Francisco: North Point Press, 1989; New York: Vintage Books, 1991.
Dense with almost palpable natural history detail, this book tells of an island in Southeast Alaska, the author's abiding attraction to it, and his ecological state of consciousness when wandering along the island's shores or penetrating its forests.

————. *Heart and Blood: Living with Deer in America*. New York: Alfred A. Knopf, 1997.
Narrative natural history, recording the interactions of deer and humans ("two quick-minded creatures") in North America, and bringing into play the author's Native American-influenced sensitivity. A Koyukon man once told him, "Every animal knows way more than you do," and Nelson took that sentence to heart. This book conveys an immense amount of information, but something else as well—a humble readiness to learn more, to step beyond data.

Nollman, Jim (1947–). *The Charged Border: Where Whales and Humans Meet*. New York: Henry Holt, 1999.
Consisting of pieces from various periodicals and books, and slow to develop, this book nevertheless provides insights, and may support the conclusion: "Few dispute the fact that the cetaceans have coalesced a new environmental consciousness."

————. *Why We Garden: Cultivating a Sense of Place*. New York: Henry Holt, 1994.
We garden because doing so grounds us. Gardeners aren't as likely to fly from earth, spiritually, or be unrealistic politically. His garden (in Friday Harbor, Washington) is where Nollman, as he says, meets nature halfway, seeing himself as part of a natural neighborhood. Out of this sense of place he offers garden-related ruminations on such matters as wilderness, European gardening traditions, anthropocentrism, and organic agriculture.

Nuttall, Thomas (1786–1859). *A Journal of Travels into the Arkansa Territory, During the Year 1819*. Philadelphia: Thos. H. Palmer, 1821; reprinted in vol. 13 of *Early Western Travels, 1748–1846*. Edited by Reuben Gold Thwaites. Cleveland: Arthur H. Clark, 1905; Fayetteville: University of Arkansas Press, 1999.

Extensive notes on frontier settlements, Indians, and the flora of both riverine forest and prairie. Nuttall forgot his gun at least once, and was known to use the barrel as a digging stick. Parts of this journal have a Garden of Eden flavor.

————. *A Manual of the Ornithology of the United States and of Canada.* Cambridge, Mass.: Hilliard and Brown, 1832; Boston: Hilliard, Gray, 1840; North Stratford, N.H.: Ayer Company Publishers, 1974.
The standard bird book for most of the nineteenth century. The introduction is an important ecological essay, and several of the descriptions are enlivened by Nuttall's extensive field experience and his good ear for songs and calls.

————. *Nuttall's Travels into the Old Northwest: An Unpublished 1810 Diary.* Edited by Jeannette E. Graustein. Vol. 14 of *Chronica Botanica.* Waltham, Mass.: Chronica Botanica Company, 1950-51.
The record of a long, difficult, and lonely journey, from Philadelphia to Detroit, to the Mandan villages, and downstream to St. Louis and New Orleans. It is the travel diary of a young man, as yet rather inexperienced in the American fauna and flora, and its natural history consists mainly of lists. But the author's dedication and bravery shine through. Suffering from ague (malaria), he tried bleeding, cathartics, and emetics, somehow managing to keep traveling and continue learning.

O'Brien, Dan (1947–). *Equinox: Life, Love, and Birds of Prey.* New York: Lyons and Burford, 1997.
A lover of falcons and of the Great Plains, and of a woman who has gone to New Hampshire for a year, describes in a candid manner just how he attempts, at the turn toward the autumn of his life, to make a coherent whole of his passions. There is beautiful writing here about grass and healthy land, food, and above all the powerful stoops of peregrines.

————. *The Rites of Autumn: A Falconer's Journey Across the American West.* New York: Atlantic Monthly Press, 1988; New York: Lyons Press, 1997.
In the 1970s, the author participated in the re-establishment of peregrine falcons after their near extirpation. In this strongly felt account he tells of trying to return a young falcon to the wild by taking it southward down the western edge of the Great Plains, imprinting the bird with what would be its natural autumnal migration route.

Ogburn, Charlton (1911–1998). *The Adventure of Birds.* New York: William Morrow, 1975.
What is it about birds, Ogburn asks, that "gave them meaning to man, in the

needs of his soul?" Ogburn attempts no abstract formulation, but answers the question from the inside by revealing his own grand passion, a life passion, for birds. This feeling makes the chapters on avian physiology and behavior come alive. Here, and in a most fascinating essay on birdsong, Ogburn enlarges and poeticizes these subjects with a sense of earth and woods and weather. Much of the book derives from the author's own experience, a good deal of that in the vicinity of Washington, D.C.

————. *The Winter Beach.* New York: William Morrow, 1966; New York: Simon and Schuster, 1971; New York: William Morrow, 1979.
Winter tours of Mt. Desert Island, Cape Ann, Cape Cod, Long Island, Assateague, and the Outer Banks with informed commentary on the areas' geological history and present ecological condition. The quiet (all of these East Coast areas are crowded in summer), the sense of impending storm, and the hardiness of wintering birds are prominent themes, as is the meretriciousness of development. The author also speculates on the ultimate philosophical origins of the calamitous changes he recounts.

Olson, Sigurd F. (1899–1982). *Listening Point.* New York: Alfred A. Knopf, 1958; Minneapolis: University of Minnesota Press, 1997.
Home in the North Woods, on a point of shelving granite at the edge of a lake bordered by pines and birches. The sounds come clearly—far-off rapids in the quiet of the night, the call of a loon, and the distance-sweetened hooting of a steam locomotive. The peacefulness of wild country is conveyed well by Olson's unadorned sentences.

————. *Runes of the North.* New York: Alfred A. Knopf, 1963; Minneapolis: University of Minnesota Press, 1997.
Runes, to Olson, are narratives with the touch of the wilderness, awakening the inner world, the "earth wisdom which since the beginning of man's rise from the primitive has nourished his visions and dreams." The personal accounts here come from northern lands—northern waters, more precisely—from Minnesota to Alaska, and speak of the elemental attractiveness of clean lakeside rock, clear water, wind in the pines, and the voice of the loon.

————. *The Singing Wilderness.* New York: Alfred A. Knopf, 1956; Minneapolis: University of Minnesota Press, 1997.
The Quetico-Superior country of northern Minnesota and Ontario, still a wilderness, sings to the spirit: ". . . the music can even be heard in the soft

guttering of an open fire or in the beat of rain on a tent, and sometimes not until long afterward when, like an echo out of the past, you know it was there in some quiet place or when you were doing some simple thing in the out-of-doors." Here Olson records moments like that in his notably straightforward prose, arranging them on the calendar of the northern seasons.

Packard, Winthrop (1862–1943). *Wild Pastures.* Boston: Small, Maynard, 1909.
The soul of gentility. "The most beautiful place which can be found on earth of a June morning is a New England pasture. . . ." The author noted, however, that the "trolley tripper" had come to even the most secluded ponds near the hallowed pastures, and now "builds his bungalows on its shore, sinks his tin cans in its waters, and scares the bullfrogs with his phonograph."

———. *Wildwood Ways.* Boston: Small, Maynard, 1909.
Pleasant rambles with a *Boston Transcript* columnist, out into the winter countryside. Packard made forthright, copious use of the pathetic fallacy and looked always for what could quicken the sense of magic, what he called "fairyland." But he also paid close attention to the building of a hornets' nest, and protested against the pollution of streams.

———. *Wood Wanderings.* Boston: Small, Maynard, 1910.
Relaxed, agreeable, genteel essays, mostly about rural and semirural parts of eastern Massachusetts. "Among Autumn Leaves" has some fine descriptions of trees and colors.

Page, Jake (1936–). *Pastorale: A Natural History of Sorts.* New York: W. W. Norton, 1985.
Observations on keeping pets, gardening, and modern technology, and on various curiosities of nature and hairsplitting predilections of human nature, such as the American Ornithologists' Union's imperial renaming of several bird species. Much of the commentary is written with wry wit, and most of it is drawn from the author's country life on an acre in Virginia.

Peacock, Doug (1942–). *Grizzly Years: In Search of the American Wilderness.* New York: Henry Holt, 1990, 1996.
As a medic in Vietnam, Peacock carried with him a well-worn map of Wyoming and Montana. When he returned to the U.S., traumatized and with "no talent for reentering society," he headed for the wilderness. Gradually, on the ground, he began to study the icon of wildness, the grizzly bear, and over years of

resolutely independent work, found an organizing point for his life. This book, written in truth-telling, bell-clear prose, radiates a passionate concern for the wild earth as a whole.

Peattie, Donald Culross (1898–1964). *An Almanac for Moderns*. New York: G. P. Putnam's Sons, 1935; Boston: David R. Godine, 1980.
In 1950, Joseph Wood Krutch thought that Peattie was "perhaps the most widely read of all contemporary American nature writers." The *Almanac* consists of 365 one-page essays, most suggested by the date or season. Many reveal the author's concern with evolution and other theories of life's origin and development. He interweaves thoughts on philosophical matters with descriptions of birdsong and the progression of the seasons, and with excellent thumbnail sketches of figures like Linnaeus, Thoreau, and Muir, occasioned by their birthdays. The book is for moderns by virtue of its up-to-date understanding of the natural universe and its realization that science has changed the very ground of thought.

————. *A Book of Hours*. New York: G. P. Putnam's Sons, 1937.
One contemplative spring day: the special, natural quality of each of the hours, as marked by the activity of birds and animals and recorded in the mythic, anciently derived thoughts of men. At each hour something is noted that might, to a receptive mind, reveal the meaningfulness abiding in the world.

————. *Flowering Earth*. New York: G. P. Putnam's Sons, 1939; Bloomington: University of Indiana Press, 1991.
A vision of earth as knit together by the green society of plants that makes animal life possible. In this essay on ecology, a strongly participative point of view (which makes this book something different from mere autobiography) enlivens the text. Peattie makes topics such as photosynthesis indubitably real, and also miraculous.

————. *A Natural History of Trees of Eastern and Central North America*. Boston: Houghton Mifflin, 1950; Boston: Houghton Mifflin, 1991.
An immensely detailed handbook, giving clear descriptions (including a key to genera and species) and full historical information. For certain species of large utilitarian importance, such as white pine and sugar maple, the descriptions amount to essays on human ecology.

————. *A Natural History of Western Trees*. Boston: Houghton Mifflin, 1953, 1991.
The first words of this 750-page manual are "The sylva of western North America is the most impressive and humanly significant in the world." The

text, both poetically evocative and deep with scholarly information, lives up to the charge implicit in those words.

———. *The Road of a Naturalist.* Boston: Houghton Mifflin, 1941; New York: G. K. Hall, 1986.
The road here is the author's life, described in terms of formative moments, and concurrently an account of a trip by car through several western habitat types. "Since Walden," the penultimate chapter, offers reflections on nature writing in which Peattie defends science and realism. In the shadow of impending war (World War II), science and realism seemed to the author the most substantial grounds for hope.

Perrin, Noel (1927–) *First Person Rural: Essays of a Sometime Farmer.* Boston: David R. Godine, 1978; New York: Penguin, 1980.
Emphasis on practical matters, described with a droll, self-deprecating attitude, as Perrin learns how to choose a pickup truck, sell firewood in New York City (a funny tale), and buy a chainsaw.

———. *Second Person Rural: More Essays of a Sometime Farmer.* Boston: David R. Godine, 1980; New York: Penguin, 1981.
There is relaxed wit here, much of it playing off the contrast between native New Englander and recent arrival, and an occasional sharp comment serving to keep the back-to-the-country scene firmly real.

———. *Third Person Rural: Further Essays of a Sometime Farmer.* Boston: David R. Godine, 1983.
Regional mystique is very evident in these pieces, but not slavishly revered. "Country Calendar" is a record of the New England seasons, as the author has known them, acutely and practically. The subsequent essays, gathered from various journals, continue Perrin's humorous, astute autobiography and his examination of farm and country mores.

Petersen, David (1946–). *Elkheart.* Denver: Johnson Books, 1998.
The author is Elkheart, and the book is his tribute to wapiti. The picture of young Petersen, growing up in Oklahoma and being driven by his father to a hunting and camping ground, is affecting.

———. *Ghost Grizzlies.* New York: Henry Holt, 1995; rev. ed., Denver: Johnson Books, 1998.
The Round River San Juan Grizzly Project has faith, and so does Petersen, that

a few bears have managed to hang on, sequestered in the Colorado wilderness. This book surveys the scene. A memorable essay by Doug Peacock is included, and Petersen is to be credited with a bulldog's search for truth. In the updated edition, a reliable observer is pinned down, in July 1995, and swears it was a grizzly.

————. *Heartsblood: Hunting, Spirituality, and Wildness in America.* Washington, D. C.: Island Press, 2000.
This is a book that will shake up those already convinced against hunting. "The hunt is, or should be, a quiet, deeply personal rite, an active sacrament that re-connects us to our human/humane roots and realigns us with wild (being the only true) nature, our one and only home: past, present, forever."

————. *The Nearby Faraway.* Boulder, Colo.: Johnson Books, 1997.
This collection of essays begins with a loving tribute to a home ground—a piece of mountain land near Durango, Colorado—and moves outward to in-clude adventures in Arizona, Utah, Wyoming, and Washington, among other places. What unifies the collection is the writer's sensibility, an instance of love bringing all places near. Petersen's critique of our time, in which "the spiritual quality of our lives atrophies while our material 'standard of living' continues to bloat," is sharp but not despairing. He still hopes to see a grizzly in Colorado.

————. *Racks: The Natural History of Antlers and the Animals That Wear Them.* Santa Barbara: Capra Press, 1991.
Petersen hopes that *Racks* is ". . . the first and sole effort to present in a detailed, technically accurate yet easily digestible and perhaps even modestly entertain-ing manner," the high points of research. In an afterthought, he presents an argument that the silent majority of hunters "are at least serious and con-scionable if not downright reverential about their hunting."

Peterson, Brenda (1950–). *Living by Water.* Seattle: Alaska Northwest Books, 1990; New York: Fawcett, 1994.
Living by Puget Sound, Peterson tries hard to live by water in other senses. On a trip to swim with dolphins, she dives and delves and comes pretty close. But the closest she comes is in describing her writing study, and you can feel, right there, the closeness of the water.

Peterson, Roger Tory (1908–1996). *Birds Over America.* New York: Dodd, Mead, 1948.
Birding rambles from many parts of the country, showing that the sense of dis-covery inherent in birding is there even for an authority. Peterson observes, "The

appeal of birds seems to be greater the more life is restrained." Illustrated with over a hundred photos by the author.

Platt, Rutherford (1894–1975). *The Great American Forest.* **Englewood Cliffs, N.J.: Prentice-Hall, 1965.**
Annie Dillard has called this "one of the most interesting books ever written." Done in an energetic, informal style, it covers forest ecology, the mechanics of water and trace-element transport, photosynthesis, and the importance of soil and humus. Interspersed with this information are several dramatic renderings of historical incidents (such as Alexander Mackenzie's great overland trip to the Pacific in 1793) that took place in forested country. The final chapter, "Our Vanishing Wilderness," is a passionate cry for preservation.

———. *This Green World.* **New York: Dodd, Mead, 1942.**
A course in botany, taught with enthusiasm. Platt creates a large, ecological understanding of what a plant is and does. A simple and useful key to tree identification is included.

Pollan, Michael. *Second Nature: A Gardener's Education.* **New York: Atlantic Monthly Press, 1991; New York: Dell Books, 1995.**
Via tales of his own gardening and landscaping adventures in the suburbs, and general commentary on gardening as a kind of philosophical middle way, the author undercuts the dualism of wilderness purists. This book fits well with Cronon's attack on what he sees as wildernessism in *Uncommon Ground* (1996).

Powell, John Wesley (1834–1902). *Exploration of the Colorado River of the West and its Tributaries.* **Washington, D.C.: U.S. Government Printing Office, 1875; Chicago: University of Chicago Press, 1957; New York: Dover Publications, 1961; New York: Penguin USA, 1997.**
A present-tense account of the great downriver adventure of Powell and his men in 1869, full of drama and suspense. Powell appreciated the splendor and sublimity of the great canyons he drifted through.

Proenneke, Richard. *One Man's Wilderness.* **Edited by Sam Keith. Anchorage: Alaska Northwest Publishing, 1973, 1999.**
Proenneke did what many have dreamed of. He built a cabin by himself in the wilderness of the Alaska Peninsula and lived sensibly and well for many years, abiding by the constraints of the land and weather. His journal reflects calmness and practicality and a deep, compassionate interest in wildlife.

Pruitt, William O., Jr. (1922–). *Animals of the North*. New York: Harper and Row, 1967.
Pruitt shows the rugged North in its true fragility, via narratives describing what a sharply seasonal life is like for voles, hares, wolves, caribou, and others. The Moose People of former times are contrasted pointedly with modern-day invaders having little or no knowledge of taiga and tundra ecology.

Pyle, Robert Michael (1947–). *Chasing Monarchs: Migrating with the Butterflies of Passage*. Boston: Houghton Mifflin, 1999.
Pyle, who has been chasing butterflies for almost forty years, follows his favorite here, the monarch, accompanied by his trusty net and his old Honda. (Only the monarch regularly shifts north in the spring and south in the fall.) A loose, anecdotal style enables him to gain "a clearer sense of how these creatures actually live their remarkable lives. . . ."

———. *Wintergreen: Listening to the Land's Heart*. New York: Charles Scribner's Sons, 1986; Boston: Houghton Mifflin, 1988.
The author lives among the Willapa Hills, a small, cutover range near the mouth of the Columbia River, a place not much studied by naturalists nor hiked in by recreationists. In the tradition of Gilbert White of Selborne, Pyle finds much to study and enjoy on his chosen home ground. He also finds much to lament, in particular the brutal destructiveness of clearcut logging carried on by corporate giants. Though the area has been ravaged, and its human culture, now that the logging boom is over, appears senescent, its grass does revive in beautiful greenness each winter, a metaphor for hope.

Quammen, David (1948–). *Natural Acts: A Sidelong View of Science Nature*. New York: Nick Lyons Books, 1985.
Most of the pieces here are from the author's columns in *Outside*. Quammen has an eye for odd facts, and delights in revealing how even the oddest may become instructive of nature's ways. The essays are written in an informal, sidelong manner; Quammen, whose main vocation is writing novels, states that he is a follower of science rather than a scientist.

———. *The Song of the Dodo: Island Biogeography in an Age of Extinctions*. New York: Scribner, 1996.
"Islands give clarity to evolution," Quammen writes. As he points out in this remarkably clear, ominously factual book, islands also give a frightening clarity to extinction. Species inhabiting islands are extremely vulnerable. Exactly why this is so, and what are the implications for our fragmented world—in which

mainland natural areas have in fact become islands—makes a story to awaken the most complacent.

———. *Wild Thoughts from Wild Places.* New York: Scribner, 1998.
Sincere and informed essays, originally published in various sources over the years, now as a whole making clear the author's care for the earth and earnest desire for learning. Includes an appreciation of Gilbert White and a fine tribute to Edward Abbey.

Rawlins, C. L. (1949–). *Broken Country: Mountains and Memory.* New York: Henry Holt, 1996.
A summer in the unfamous but beautiful and mostly wild Salt River Range of Wyoming, working as a sheepherder, became a watershed season for the author, imprinting on him mountains and wilderness and confirming his core values. The retrospect here (looking back almost twenty-five years), and the vision of what backcountry means in a life, are realistic and without sentiment.

———. *Sky's Witness: A Year in the Wind River Mountains.* New York: Henry Holt, 1993.
Looking for evidence of acid rain, the author (a paid inspector of snowstorms) made long treks to collect snow samples and water from alpine lakes, in the process engaging about every kind of mountain weather, learning a good deal about geology and hydrology, and reflecting on wildness and tameness.

Ray, Janisse (1962–). *Ecology of a Cracker Childhood.* Minneapolis: Milkweed Editions, 1999.
A compelling memoir about growing up in Georgia at the edge of a junkyard, becoming interested in the longleaf pine woods, and coming to recognize destruction of that forest as the concomitant of a disappearing culture.

Ribaut, Jean (c. 1520–1565). *The Whole and True Discouerye of Terra Florida.* Deland, Fla.: The Florida State Historical Society, 1927 (facsimile reprint of 1563 London edition).
Cruising northward along the Florida coast in May 1562, Ribaut (in good European explorer fashion) named the rivers he came upon: the "Seine," the "Somme," the "Loire," etc. But at another level he responded deeply to the teeming wildlife of "this incomperable lande," and to its utter, as he saw it, "God endued" wildness.

Rich, Louise Dickinson (1903–1991). *The Natural World of Louise Dickinson Rich*. New York: Dodd, Mead, 1962.

Essays covering the author's life in three environments: southeastern Massachusetts; northwestern Maine, where she spent fifteen years in wild country; and the coast of Maine, where she moved after her husband's death. Rich displays humor and a slightly ironic view of herself as a countrywoman, and quietly reflects on our place in the natural scheme of things: "Perhaps all [of man's] other achievements are less than this, that he watches, and makes the record, and tries to find the meaning."

————. *We Took to the Woods*. Philadelphia: J. B. Lippincott, 1942; Cutchogue, N.Y.: Buccaneer Books, 1992.

A full life, lived with relish, in northwestern Maine: pines, water, storms, and the delicious quiet after a forty-inch snowfall; hot summer days, "characters," and making-do.

Richardson, Wyman (1896–1953). *The House on Nauset Marsh*. New York: W. W. Norton, 1955; Woodstock, Vt.: Countryman Press, 1997.

Brief essays on life at a vacation place in Cape Cod, by a Boston physician and Harvard Medical School professor. Encounters with birds, including several with the rare gyrfalcon, tally the seasons.

Roberts, David (1943–). *Moments of Doubt, and Other Mountaineering Writings*. Seattle: Mountaineers Press, 1986.

A collection of twenty essays spanning the author's career as a climber and stressing motivations and feelings—the human element. The title essay recounts, soberly, the climbing accidents that Roberts has witnessed or been a part of.

————. *The Mountain of My Fear*. New York: Vanguard Press, 1968; Seattle: Mountaineers Press, 1991.

An ascent of Mt. Huntington in the Alaska Range, rendered in intense prose. The author describes "an unwitnessable challenge in an inhuman place," where a snow cave illuminated by candles "seemed the only island of safety in a limitless sea of night."

Robinson, Rowland Evans (1833–1900). *In New England Fields and Woods*. Boston: Houghton Mifflin, 1896; Rutland, Vt.: Charles E. Tuttle, 1937.

Sinclair Lewis, in a foreword to the 1937 edition, praised Robinson's work for keeping alive the "simplicities of the old democratic life" found in the country in Vermont. The sketches here cover the seasonal changes and some of the familiar birds and animals of Vermont and describe an excursion to view once again the vivid and whole woods of youth, only to find them logged off.

Ronald, Ann (1939–) and Stephen Trimble (1950–). *Earthtones: A Nevada Album.* **Reno: University of Nevada Press, 1995.**
This is a surprising book, like its subject: you get close to Nevada, and find there is much you have missed. Ronald's hiking diary, including being surprised by Nevada's episodes of wintry weather in summer, gets you on the ground. Trimble's photographs show you how much beauty there is without the color green.

Roosevelt, Theodore (1858–1919). *Hunting Trips of a Ranchman: Hunting Trips on the Prairie and in the Mountains.* **New York: Review of Reviews Company, 1904 (Statesman Edition); New York: Modern Library, 1998; originally published New York: Cooperative Publication Society, 1882; New York: G. P. Putnam's Sons, 1885.**
There are hints of the condition of the northern plains in the 1880s—bison and wolves almost gone, coyotes rare, elk diminishing rapidly—and some natural history information, such as the habits of sharp-tailed grouse. But the weight of detail here is on the techniques of the hunt.

———. *The Wilderness Hunter: An Account of the Big Game of the United States and Its Chase with Horse, Hound, and Rifle.* **New York: G. P. Putnam's Sons, 1893.**
Although Roosevelt boasts that "it has been [his] good-luck to kill every kind of game properly belonging to the United States," he tempers his enthusiasm with a certain amount of restraint: "It is always lawful to kill dangerous or noxious animals, like the bear, cougar, and wolf; but other game should only be shot when there is need of the meat, or for the sake of an unusually fine trophy."

Roueché, Berton (1911–1994). *The River World and Other Explorations.* **New York: Harper and Row, 1978.**
Essays that first appeared in the *New Yorker,* including interesting accounts of the fossil beds in Florissant, Colorado, bananas, apples, and an exciting ocean voyage with a group of Eskimos.

———. *What's Left: Reports on a Diminishing America.* **Boston: Little, Brown, 1968.**
These essays, which originally appeared in the *New Yorker,* have a point: some beautiful places (such as the C. & O. towpath along the Potomac River, the Islandia Keys in Florida, and the Current River in the Ozarks) are indeed left, but urgently in need of protection.

Rowell, Galen A. (1940–), ed. *The Vertical World of Yosemite: A Collection of Photographs and Writings on Rock Climbing in Yosemite.* Berkeley: Wilderness Press, 1974.
An anthology of writing about climbing that offers more than vertigo and derring-do.

Rudloe, Jack (1943–). *The Living Dock at Panacea.* New York: Alfred A. Knopf, 1977.
Engaging narratives based on Rudloe's marine-specimen business in the fishing village of Panacea, Florida. Adventures featuring sharks and heavy weather, coping with bureaucracy and barnacles, and other elements in the working day of the author provide natural history information and show the writer's sense of wonder at the Gulf's abundant life. Upon inspection, the company dock itself is revealed as an interesting ecosystem.

———. *Time of the Turtle.* New York: Alfred A. Knopf, 1979.
Personal encounters with sea turtles are the framework here for the author's presentation of the natural history of these animals, their powerful presence in folklore, and their too-often shabby treatment at the hands of *Homo sapiens.* A brief but telling description of Haiti, where Rudloe had gone to look for the beautiful hawksbill turtle, presages a world overcrowded with desperately needy humans.

Ruess, Everett (1914–1934). *Everett Ruess: Vagabond for Beauty.* Edited by W. L. Rusho. Layton, Utah: Gibbs M. Smith, 1983.
The solitary wanderings of Everett Ruess in the desert remain emblematic of the quest for wilderness and the ultimate. In this "life and letters," Ruess's artistic talent and moral sincerity come through as clearly as the country he walked and rode through.

Russell, Franklin (1922–). *The Hunting Animal.* New York: Harper and Row, 1983.
Narratives on hunting, stalking, predation, and aloneness. Gradually the picture widens to suggest the deep importance of predation in maintaining healthy ecosystems, and beyond that to speculate on the kinds of bonds that may exist between hunted and hunter.

———. *Searchers at the Gulf.* New York: W. W. Norton, 1970.
Fictionalized and poeticized natural history of the Gulf of St. Lawrence, built on the central metaphor of the Gulf itself as a superorganism. Russell brings out the time-tested synchronicity of all aspects of the ecosystem. "Interdependence was the touchstone. . . ."

————. *Watchers at the Pond*. New York: Alfred A. Knopf, 1961; Boston: David R. Godine, 1981.

Alternately sliding into the viewpoints of red-tailed hawk, snowshoe hare, muskrat, or raven, then giving information in straight, expository style, the author makes the complex life of the pond intensely interesting. This novelistic treatment has been criticized on certain factual points.

Russell, Franklin, and Thase Daniel. *Wings on the Southwind: Birds and Creatures of the Southern Wetlands*. Birmingham, Ala.: Oxmoor House, 1984.

A celebration of the teeming marshes, bayous, bays, lagoons, swamps, and lakes of the South, particularly the Gulf Coast—"places where the lushness of American nature is still on display." Photographs by Thase Daniel.

Russell, Osborne (1814–1892). *Journal of a Trapper, or Nine Years in the Rocky Mountains*. Glendale, Calif.: Arthur H. Clark, 1921; New York: Fine Communication, 1997.

There are some poetic appreciations of wilderness here, apparently written in the field (that is, the Rocky Mountain wilderness, 1834–1843). The appendix consists of quaint thumbnail sketches of various animals this trapper encountered. A sensitive journal, evidence that at least one mountain man was not hampered in his responses by the necessities of a dangerous way of life.

Ryden, Hope. *America's Last Wild Horses*. New York: E. P. Dutton, 1970; rev. ed., New York: E. P. Dutton, 1978; New York: Lyons Press, 1999.

A history of the wild horse in America and a survey of the modern controversy, written with enthusiasm and forthrightly stated personal involvement: "When I first saw wild horses sweeping across a mountain slope, tails and manes streaming, screaming with an exuberance never heard in any pasture, my whole view of modern America brightened."

————. *God's Dog: A Celebration of the North American Coyote*. New York: Lyons and Burford, 1979; New York: Lyons Press, 1997.

A highly sympathetic natural history and tribute, much of it based on old-fashioned field observation.

————. *Lily Pond: Four Years with a Family of Beavers*. New York: William Morrow, 1989.

Hope Ryden practices a meditative kind of natural history: she goes quietly to the subject animal's habitat, sits down, and watches. Over the course of her study at a pond in Rockland County, New York, she gained insights about the personalities of individual beavers, a fund of detailed knowledge about beaver behavior (including their remarkable problem-solving abilities), and a thorough sense of the animal in its habitat. She herself was at home there.

Sanders, Scott Russell (1945–). *The Country of Language.* **Minneapolis: Milkweed Editions, 1999.**
Part of the *Credo* series (a succession of books explaining how and why writers write about the natural world), this book argues for "at-homeness" with the natural world as a necessary starting point for addressing life's larger questions and for living well and fully amid the griefs of human experience.

———. *Staying Put: Making a Home in a Restless World.* **Boston: Beacon Press, 1993.**
"I am all the more committed to know and care for the place I have come to as an adult because I have lost irretrievably the childhood landscapes that gave shape to my love of the earth." Thus Sanders describes Bloomington, the adult home, and Wayland, the Ohio origin land. But Wayland arouses some pretty strong memories, the reader is likely to think. The writing about it is as strong, in its way, as the more philosophical pieces dealing with Indiana.

Schaller, George B. (1933–). *Stones of Silence: Journeys in the Himalaya.* **New York: Viking Press, 1980.**
High adventures (1969–1975) described in a sober, modest, intense style. The author's quest to observe a snow leopard is a quest to know the complete wilderness. After a fruitless night camped near the object of his search, he writes, "I had learned nothing new that night, but the hours of silence, the celestial beauty of the mountains in the moonlight, and, above all, the knowledge of having been a part of the snow leopard's world filled me with quiet ecstasy."

———. *The Year of the Gorilla.* **Chicago: University of Chicago Press, 1964; New York: Ballantine Books, 1965, 1971.**
The result of a pioneering investigation, this book is a demonstration of what may be accomplished in a humane, nonintrusive way in the study of animals, and is a testimony to scientific openness on the part of the author. It stands with Adolph Murie's *The Wolves of Mount McKinley* as revisionist natural history. Schaller's own response to the gorillas and their wilderness home is integral to the account.

Scherman, Katharine (1915–). *Spring on an Arctic Island.* **Boston: Little, Brown, 1956.**
Scherman and her husband, with half a dozen other birders and scientists, spent six eventful weeks on Bylot Island, north of Baffin, watching and listening to the

incredible burgeoning of life that marks the Arctic spring. Although the tundra looked "depressingly barren" at first sight, she later wrote, "I can feel it under my feet, bouncy and full of life."

Schorger, A. W. (1884–1972). *The Passenger Pigeon: Its Natural History and Extinction.* **Madison: University of Wisconsin Press, 1955; Norman: University of Oklahoma Press, 1973.**
A necessary text, and necessarily a sad one: "Viewed from all angles, the passenger pigeon was the most impressive species of bird that man has known. Elegant in form and color, graceful and swift of flight, it moved about and nested in such enormous numbers as to confound the senses. Equally dramatic was its disappearance from the earth due to the thoughtlessness and insatiable greed of man."

Servid, Carolyn (1953–). *Of Landscape and Longing: Finding a Home at the Water's Edge.* **Minneapolis: Milkweed Editions, 2000.**
This is a rich book, full of trees and water. Servid marks off her prime places and things, until finally you are looking down through trees at a red dory. The dory is a well-built little craft, essential to her life in Sitka, Alaska. An imaginative, surprising book.

Seton, Ernest Thompson (1860–1946). *The Arctic Prairies: A Canoe-Journey of 2,000 Miles in Search of the Caribou; Being the Account of a Voyage to the Region North of Aylmer Lake.* **New York: Charles Scribner's Sons, 1911.**
A strongly flavored account of travel and adventure in the vast, wild neighborhood of Great Slave Lake. The subtitle grants Seton plenty of opportunity to demonstrate his sincere love of beauty and wildness, especially in beautiful portraits of his favorite rivers, the Nyarling and the Little Buffalo. He also displays sarcastic wit (usually at the Indians' expense), rails at mosquitoes, and usually shows himself in good light.

————. *Lives of Game Animals: An Account of Those Land Animals in America, North of the Mexican Border, Which Are Considered "Game," Either Because They Have Held the Attention of Sportsmen, or Received the Protection of Law.* **4 vols. Garden City, N.Y.: Doubleday, Doran, 1925.**
A complete natural history, constructed of data on size, habits, distribution, "Record Heads" (of hoofed animals), food, enemies, diseases, and more, with illustrative narratives of the author's own experiences, these last given with his customary verve.

Sharp, Dallas Lore (1870–1929). *The Face of the Fields.* Boston: Houghton Mifflin, 1911. This is perhaps Sharp's most substantial and penetrating book, containing essays on death and fear, on his own growth in self-knowledge when forced to deal with skunks' depredations upon his chickens, on literary nature writing, on John Burroughs (whom he compares more than favorably with Thoreau), and on what has later come to be known as the "tragedy of the commons."

————. *The Lay of the Land.* Boston: Houghton Mifflin, 1908. Rambles on the author's fourteen-acre Massachusetts farm, and thoughts on the joy and simplicity of country living: "A farm, of all human habitations, is most of all a home. . . ." Sharp takes particular delight in coziness, as exemplified in animals' preparations for winter and his own provisions for the season as a farmer.

————. *A Watcher in the Woods.* New York: Century, 1901. Sharp appreciated the near and accessible scenes that included orchards and woods roads. Thirty-six species of birds nested within a quarter-mile of his New England home, and he thought a similar density and variety could not be achieved in the wilderness. Thus, he felt, there was hope for a harmonious fitting-in of man.

————. *The Whole Year Round.* Boston: Houghton Mifflin, 1915. A gathering of essays arranged by the seasons and directed at younger readers, advising them of special delights to watch for.

Sheldon, Charles (1867–1928). *The Wilderness of Denali: Explorations of a Hunter-Naturalist in Northern Alaska.* New York: Charles Scribner's Sons, 1930; Lanham, Md.: Derrydale Press, 2000. Although Sheldon killed an appalling number of animals, he was the earliest promoter of national park status for the Mt. McKinley (Denali) area. He also had a strong yen for the sublime: "Alone in an unknown wilderness hundreds of miles from civilization and high on one of the world's most imposing mountains, I was deeply moved by the stupendous mass of the great upheaval, the vast extent of the wild areas below, the chaos of the unfinished surfaces still in process of moulding, and by the crash and roar of the mighty avalanches."

————. *The Wilderness of the North Pacific Coast Islands: A Hunter's Experiences While Searching for Wapiti, Bears, and Caribou on the Larger Coast Islands of British Columbia and Alaska.* New York: Charles Scribner's Sons, 1912.

Independently wealthy, the author was able to devote several months of each year to hunting. In this book, he describes quests for wapiti, grizzly bears, and caribou. Although he shot a number of grizzlies, he thought that if the bears were exterminated, it would be a deep loss to the wilderness, "perhaps the loss of its very essence."

————. *The Wilderness of the Upper Yukon: A Hunter's Explorations for Wild Sheep in Sub-Arctic Mountains*. New York: Charles Scribner's Sons, 1919.
Self-consciously aware of contradiction in his values, Sheldon declared his love for the animals he killed. A frighteningly assiduous trophy hunter and museum collector, he could foresee a time when lovers of the wilderness would go there strictly for contemplation. This book records his response to the untracked mountains of the Yukon, where he hunted in 1904.

Skutch, Alexander F. (1904–). *A Bird Watcher's Adventures in Tropical America*. Austin: University of Texas Press, 1977.
Travels in the neotropics, before the advent of good roads and field guides. Skutch did not use a gun, nor was he out to make a big list; he moved at a leisurely, studying pace and came into close acquaintance with the lush habitats described here.

————. *The Imperative Call: A Naturalist's Quest in Temperate and Tropical America*. Gainesville: University Presses of Florida, 1979.
Travels and studies in an autobiographical framework. Skutch describes his good fortune in being able to respond to the call of nature study and to know tropical environments before their modern decimation. "A Wanderer's Harvest" describes his nonintrusive methods of field study—tedious, but fulfilling.

————. *Life of the Woodpecker*. Santa Monica: Ibis Publishing, 1985; Ithaca: Cornell University Press, 1988.
A natural history of one of the most interesting and attractive of bird families, delineating habits, habitats, and ecological information on several prominent species.

————. *Nature Through Tropical Windows*. Berkeley: University of California Press, 1983.
The windows of the author's home at Los Cusingos in Costa Rica are screenless and glassless, enabling unobstructed views of the forest outside and the birds who nest close by. Close observation, and consideration of such matters as the

ecology of size, the "gentler side of nature," and altruism distinguish this interesting book. "Windows of the Mind," the concluding chapter, is a meditation on isolation and its possible cures.

Slocum, Joshua (1844–1909). *Sailing Alone Around the World*. New York: Century, 1900; New York: Dover Publications, 1956; Boston: Shambhala Publications, 1999.
The critic Van Wyck Brooks called this book a "nautical equivalent" to *Walden*, and Slocum asserted after his epic circumnavigation of 1895 to 1898 that he had been "in touch with nature as few have ever been," though the great bulk of his writing is wrapped up in practical details of seamanship—getting from one place to another. He does describe how whales catch small fish, and records that the farther he went, the less able he was to kill, even for the table. Slocum wrote with understated wit. For many readers, *Sailing Alone* is a compelling statement of self-reliance.

Smith, John (1580–1631). *The Generall Historie of Virginia, New England and the Summer Isles, Together with the True Travels, Adventures and Observations, and a Sea Grammar*. 2 vols. London: Michael Sparkes, 1624; New York: Macmillan, 1907.
In major part a promotional tract, this narrative nevertheless presents information rarely encountered elsewhere, such as the size of the Indians' cultivated fields: "some 20 acres, some 40. some 100. some 200." Also: "Neare their habitations is little small wood or old trees on the ground by reason of their burning of them for fire. So that a man may gallop a horse amongst these woods any way, but where the creekes or Rivers shall hinder."

Snyder, Gary (1930–). *Earth House Hold: Technical Notes and Queries to Fellow Dharma Revolutionaries*. New York: New Directions, 1969.
Early journals from a fire lookout, along with several penetrating essays, including "Poetry and the Primitive" and the influential "Buddhism and the Coming Revolution," place this book within the philosophically radical wing of American nature writing. An important, influential text.

———. *A Place in Space: Ethics, Aesthetics, and Watersheds*. Washington, D.C.: Counterpoint, 1995.
A collection of essays, reminiscences, and talks drawn from forty years of free-minded thinking, and constituting (despite later publication date) a kind of prequel to *The Practice of the Wild*.

———. *The Practice of the Wild*. New York: North Point Press, 1990.
"Wildness is not just the 'preservation of the world,' it *is* the world." Thus the

author brings his synthesis of Buddhism and ecology to bear on American nature thought and its Thoreau-reference, suggesting a further level of insight. The essays in this collection, especially "The Etiquette of Freedom" and "Good, Wild, Sacred," seem inarguably solid and sensible, and at the same time point toward a philosophical and psychological territory still ahead of us. One of the important books of the decade.

————. *Turtle Island*. New York: New Directions, 1974.
A book of poetry in the main, this volume also contains "Four Changes" and "The Wilderness," two significant essays on mind, nature, and human ecology.

Stadtfeld, Curtis K. (1935–). *From the Land and Back*. New York: Charles Scribner's Sons, 1972.
A heartfelt remembrance of the ways and values of the family farm: "We remember forever that we were once a part of something whole. . . ."

Stansbury, Howard (1806–1863). *Exploration and Survey of the Valley of the Great Salt Lake of Utah, Including a Reconnoissance of a New Route through the Rocky Mountains*. Philadelphia: Lippincott, Grambo, 1852.
A difficult survey, during which, at times, the author had to dole out water to the party's mules by the cupful. In spite of heat, cold, wind, and thirst, Stansbury appreciated the severe beauty of the Great Basin desert.

Stanwell-Fletcher, Theodora Cope (1906–). *Driftwood Valley*. Boston: Little, Brown, 1946; New York: Viking, 1989; Corvallis: Oregon State University Press, 1999.
Accompanying her husband to some of the wildest land in British Columbia, the author dispensed with the civilized self. The best thing is that she can write: "We spent three days wandering over open peaks that rose some two thousand feet above camp. Miles and miles of steep grassy uplands stretched to high rocky peaks and, in every direction, falling and rising in blue sheets so vast the eye could scarcely compass them, were views undescribable of great new ranges, wooded valleys, countless lakes. Never a trace of man, or of anything made by man."

Stegner, Wallace (1909–1993). *The Sound of Mountain Water*. Garden City, N.Y.: Doubleday, 1969; Lincoln: University of Nebraska Press, 1985.
A collection of searching, humanistic essays on the broad theme of man and nature, including the quiet and unforgettable "Glen Canyon Submersus." A statement about the permanent flooding of Utah's Glen Canyon (behind Glen

Canyon Dam) and the creation of Lake Powell, this essay might make even the most wilderness-indifferent pause.

Steinbeck, John (1902–1968). *The Log from the Sea of Cortez.* New York: Viking Press, 1951, 1962, 1995.
Originally published in 1941 as part of *Sea of Cortez.* A biological expedition to the Gulf of California, on which the author and his mentor Edward Ricketts discussed ecology, evolution, teleology, and much else. Of particular interest are the Darwinian, nonteleological conclusions the men reach.

Steinhart, Peter (1943–). *The Company of Wolves.* New York: Alfred A. Knopf, 1995.
A very high order of natural history journalism, surveying in detail the history of human-wolf interaction, conveying along the way a great deal of biological and ethological information, withal rising to a philosophically subtle suggestion of the many-sided closeness of wolves and humans. Even when depicting the hysterical anger that many people direct against wolves, Steinhart sticks with his understated, factual style. He knows what he's up against: "We seem to have freighted the wolf with too much meaning for mere discussion to encompass." A powerful accounting.

Swain, Roger B. (1949–). *Earthly Pleasures: Tales from a Biologist's Garden.* New York: Charles Scribner's Sons, 1981; New York: Penguin, 1985; New York: Lyons Press, 1994.
In these essays from *Horticulture,* the author begins with his small farm and garden in southern New Hampshire and weaves interconnections with all manner of topics, including dung beetles, lightning, road salting, and energy use.

Tall, Deborah (1951–). *From Where We Stand: Recovering a Sense of Place.* New York: Alfred A. Knopf, 1993.
"Looking for the play between land and people," the author settles in Penn Yan, New York, and eventually moves to Ithaca. She has two daughters and studies gardening and recounts story after story, accumulating a pretty good history of the Seneca Lake region.

Tallmadge, John. *Meeting the Tree of Life: A Teacher's Path.* Salt Lake City: University of Utah Press, 1997.
A candid spiritual-natural autobiography, in which wild places like Minnesota's Boundary Waters, the Deep Creek Mountains of Utah, and the Wind River Range of Wyoming give context and deeper dimension to the author's learning about self and society. Both exaltation and despair are known and incorporated, finally, within the reference of specific, wild places. An interesting,

sometimes surprising, forthright example of what might be termed the natural history of experience.

Teal, John (1929–), and Mildred Teal (1928–). *Life and Death of the Salt Marsh.*
Boston: Little, Brown, 1969; New York: Ballantine, 1969, 1991.
A complex and thorough book, paying the tribute of close attention to the "green ribbon" of salt marshes along the East Coast of America. These marshes, "some of the most productive natural areas known," have been underappreciated and often abused. This book's discussions on filling, pollution, and insect control are amazingly temperate, under the circumstances, but nonetheless alarming.

Teale, Edwin Way (1899–1980). *Autumn Across America.* **New York: Dodd, Mead, 1956.**
A Tealean journey—that is, relaxed, digressive, and eminently informative—from Cape Cod to the California Coast, mostly in the northern tier of states. Thomas Nuttall's impressive contributions, the butterfly concentration at Point Pelee on Lake Erie, Kirtland's warbler in Michigan, and the life history of the pika are some of the many topics held up for the pleasure of leisurely inspection. A strong environmental consciousness surfaces in the author's remarks on the once-proposed Echo Park Dam in Utah.

————. *Journey Into Summer.* **New York: Dodd, Mead, 1960.**
From New England to the Colorado Rockies, via the Great Lakes, showing the immense variety of summers in America. Teale shows us the best way to travel by car: prepare well, with maps and extensive notes; go easy, looping around; and learn new things each day.

————. *The Lost Woods: Adventures of a Naturalist.* **New York: Dodd, Mead, 1945.**
Teale notes, "It is curious how some moments have abnormal vitality, how they live on in memory long after later events have faded from the mind." For Teale, the touchstone experience came on a winter day at his grandfather's farm in Indiana, when he and the old man went to the woods by sleigh to gather firewood. Years later, the author was unable to find the exact place—thus the title of this book—but his career, in effect, continually sought to re-create it. (During the journey recorded in *Autumn Across America,* Teale finally learned that the woods had been cut down in 1911).

————. *North with the Spring.* **New York: Dodd, Mead, 1951.**
Spring advances gloriously about fifteen miles per day northward through eastern America. Teale and his wife, Nellie, kept pace, covering some seventeen

thousand miles and twenty-three states. The narrative is laced with a vast number of natural history facts and historical notes, recording well the drama of what, for most observers, is the most exciting season.

————. *A Walk Through the Year.* New York: Dodd, Mead, 1978.
Home base was the author's pleasant Connecticut house, and the acres of woods, meadows, brooks, and ponds where he and his wife, Nellie, walked every day when not on farther travels. The diary-like entries are framed on natural history observations made by an excellent observer. The sheer room in the author's life, the leisurely, engaged quality of his consciousness, and the unspoiledness of his neighborhood give this book a Shangri-la-like feel. On the final page, Teale wrote, "I sit here wondering if the time will ever come when such a book as this will seem like a letter from another world."

————. *Wandering Through Winter.* New York: Dodd, Mead, 1965.
The last in the American Seasons series, and the most given to reflection. The natural history information is just as rich as in the previous books—how sand dunes move, how shrikes and sparrow hawks (kestrels) space themselves out on their winter territories, how sleet is formed, and a great deal more—but there is a heightened sense of the historical moment, and more comment on humanity and nature. Teale warns, "Those who become aroused only when *man* is endangered become aroused too late."

Terres, John K. (1905–), ed. *Discovery: Great Moments in the Lives of Outstanding Naturalists.* Philadelphia: J. B. Lippincott, 1961.
"I believe that all naturalists at some time in their lives have had one great adventure, and that the shock, ecstasy, beauty, wonder, tragedy, or intellectual illumination of that moment, hour, or day, they carry with them the rest of their lives." Operating on that premise, Terres persuaded thirty-six naturalists to describe their own outstanding experiences. The sense of discovery is strong here; these adult experiences might be studied alongside those discussed in Edith Cobb's *The Ecology of Imagination in Childhood* (1977).

————. *From Laurel Hill to Siler's Bog: The Walking Adventures of a Naturalist.* New York: Alfred A. Knopf, 1969; Chapel Hill: University of North Carolina Press, 1993.
An eight hundred-acre nature preserve in North Carolina, taken in at a walking pace or better still from within a blind, becomes a wilderness of large proportions. Terres argues, and demonstrates here, that it is the receptive mind that

makes the last frontier. Informative natural history essays on foxes, flying squirrels, the golden mouse, turkeys, and others.

Thaxter, Celia (1835–1894). *An Island Garden.* Boston: Houghton Mifflin, 1894.
On Appledore, an island off Portsmouth, New Hampshire, Thaxter found her work and her place. The garden itself was only fifteen feet by fifty feet, but it had an "altar" and a "shrine," and paths to the sea. The daily round of work became a source of true understanding.

Thomas, Lewis (1913–1993). *The Lives of a Cell: Notes of a Biology Watcher.* New York: Viking Press, 1974; New York: Bantam Books, 1975; New York: Penguin USA, 1995.
A justly famed book of essays. Thomas begins by noting that man's effort to imagine himself "above the rest of life" has been "his most consistent intellectual exertion down the millennia," and proceeds to describe hundreds of connections that demolish the fantasy of separateness while suggesting a beautiful vision of possibility in expanding consciousness.

———. *The Medusa and the Snail: More Notes of a Biology Watcher.* New York: Viking Press, 1979; New York: Penguin USA, 1995.
Brief but penetrating reflections, most of them originally published in the *New England Journal of Medicine,* showing how the study of nature can raise disturbing and humbling questions. The author is keenly aware of the limits of human consciousness and the mutability of nature, and suggests by this awareness a properly humble position toward the world. Thomas states: "The only solid piece of scientific truth about which I feel totally confident is that we are profoundly ignorant about nature. Indeed, I regard this as the major discovery of the past hundred years of biology."

Thomson, Betty Flanders (1913–). *The Changing Face of New England.* New York: Macmillan, 1958; Boston: Houghton Mifflin, 1977.
An ecological history of a familiar, yet still appealing, landscape. Thomson suggests something of the broad subject of the agency of humans on earth in her description of tree succession on abandoned fields. She also responds personally to her subject, creating the "home" feeling of place. "Other plants turn red, but none quite equals the inner light of a sugar maple in full gold and scarlet glory." An absorbing and valuable study.

Thoreau, Henry David (1817–1862). *Cape Cod.* Boston: Ticknor and Fields, 1865; New York: Crowell, 1966.
Three long walks on Cape Cod, in 1849, 1850, and 1855, described with zest,

humor, and sociable fellow-feeling for old-timers. Thoreau's images, as in the opening scenes describing the remains of a shipwreck, are sharp with the sense of discovery. On the Great Beach, "ever and anon a higher wave caused us hastily to deviate from our path, and we looked back on our tracks filled with water and foam. The breakers looked like droves of a thousand wild horses of Neptune, rushing to the shore, with their white manes streaming far behind; and when at length the sun shone for a moment, their manes were rainbow-tinted."

————. *Faith in a Seed: The Dispersion of Seeds and Other Late Natural History Writings.* Edited by Bradley P. Dean. Washington, D.C.: Island Press, Shearwater Books, 1993.
A recovery project in which Bradley Dean painstakingly assembled vast and disorderly manuscript sources, putting together something probably much like the book Thoreau would have, had he lived longer; the underlying fieldwork, the ecologically sophisticated theories, and the writing itself, scattered though its parts were, belong to Thoreau. This book is testimony to the commitment Thoreau made to natural history, especially evident in the last twelve years of his life. It shows (contrary to the speculations of some critics, over the years) that far from being a mechanical recorder of facts in those latter years, Thoreau was engaged in a passion.

————. *Journals.* Vols. 7–20 of *The Writings of Henry David Thoreau.* Boston: Houghton Mifflin, 1906; new ed., Princeton: Princeton University Press, 1981–.
The examined life, in the form of a kind of continuing letter to the higher self, and a continuing and intensifying study of nature. The entries of the later years have been criticized as too scientific or as reflecting a drying up of transcendental motivation, but William Howarth's *The Book of Concord: Thoreau's Life as a Writer* (1982) and Robert Richardson's *Henry Thoreau: A Life of the Mind* (1986), and more recently the edited books, *Faith in a Seed* (1993) and *Wild Fruits* (2000) show that Thoreau was engaged in a high, sincere attempt to know himself and his place, a life project which simply needed science to be complete.

————. *The Maine Woods.* Boston: Ticknor and Fields, 1864; New York: Crowell, 1961, 1966; Princeton: Princeton University Press, 1972.
A record of three trips, in 1846, 1853, and 1857, on foot and in a "birch" into the wildest portion of New England. Thoreau was sharply conscious of the contrast between the shaggy wilderness of Maine and the smoothed landscapes

back home in Concord. He watched his Indian guides closely, and noted trees, flowers, moose, birds, and the techniques of route finding. "You carried so much topography in your mind always. . . ."

—————. *Walden.* Boston: Ticknor and Fields, 1854; edited by Walter Harding (Variorum Edition). New York: Twayne, 1962; Princeton: Princeton University Press, 1971. A world-famous text on simple living as the means and the expression of enlightenment, and one of the purest appreciations of place and the natural that we have. This is a carefully developed, clarified book, which the author put through several drafts, but which retained through the course of refinement its original inspiration and force.

—————. *Wild Fruits.* Edited by Bradley P. Dean. New York: W. W. Norton, 2000. This is Thoreau's last manuscript, gathered and succinctly introduced. It is accompanied by Abigail Rorer's beautiful drawings, and by the editor's careful explanations of how Thoreau managed. By itself *Wild Fruits* strengthens the idea that Thoreau's last decade was busy, and more than that, dedicated, and that his knowledge was great. The passages on wildness are worth reading over.

Thwaites, Reuben Gold (1853–1913), ed. *Original Journals of the Lewis and Clark Expedition, 1804–1806.* New York: Dodd, Mead, 1904–1905; New York: Antiquarian Press, 1959. A document rich in itself, and potent in its ability to suggest the measure of what has happened since. Meriwether Lewis's entries are often reflective and aesthetically sensitive, shaped in a way that approaches at times the intentional quality of more formal essays.

Torrey, Bradford (1843–1912). *Birds in the Bush.* Boston: Houghton Mifflin, 1885. Pleasant bird rambles, mostly in the Boston area. The author had an excellent ear for birdcalls and songs, and in a fine essay describes the opening of his eyes and ears by birds.

—————. *The Foot-Path Way.* Boston: Houghton Mifflin, 1892. Genial, chatty essays for the most part, commenting on rural scenes the author walks through. But there is acid too, in Torrey's outrage at hunting, particularly the shooting of shorebirds. "But a man of twenty, a man of seventy, shooting sanderlings, ring plovers, golden plovers, and whatever else comes in his way, not for money, nor primarily for food, but because he enjoys the work! 'A little lower than the angels'!"

Townsend, John Kirk (1809–1851). *Narrative of a Journey Across the Rocky Mountains, to the Columbia River, and a Visit to the Sandwich Islands, Chili, &c.* Philadelphia: Henry Perkins, 1839; also in vol. 21 of *Early Western Travels*. Edited by Reuben Gold Thwaites. Cleveland: Arthur H. Clark, 1905; Lincoln: University of Nebraska Press, 1978. The author made the western crossing in the company of Thomas Nuttall in 1834. His account is smooth and urbane, and is focused on pictorial scenes, amounting to something like a tourist's view of the West during the mountain man era.

Traver, Robert [John Voelker] (1903–1991). *Anatomy of a Fisherman.* New York: McGraw-Hill, 1964; Santa Barbara: Peregrine Smith, 1978. "I fish because I love to; because I love the environs where trout are found, which are invariably beautiful, and hate the environs where crowds of people are found, which are invariably ugly. . . ."

Trefil, James (1938–). *Meditations at 10,000 Feet: A Scientist in the Mountains.* New York: Charles Scribner's Sons, 1986. Interesting lessons in geohistory, loosely based, in part, on walks in the Beartooth Mountains of Montana.

———. *A Scientist at the Seashore.* New York: Charles Scribner's Sons, 1984. The edge of the sea as seen by a physicist pursuing law, or the physical principles behind phenomena. "Something as ephemeral and inconsequential as a bubble in the foam leads us to consider the forces that hold the nucleus of the atom together."

Trimble, Stephen (1950–). *Longs Peak: A Rocky Mountain Chronicle.* Estes Park, Colo.: Rocky Mountain Nature Association, 1984. Among local natural histories and nature guides, books most often sold in visitor centers and nearby bookstores, one may encounter not only useful facts and good photographs, but sometimes a deeper sense of the history and meanings of a place, and even a poetic apprehension of its sacredness. *Longs Peak* tells the ecological story of the famous mountain, and the human history (with particular detail on climbing), and goes on to suggest the significance of the peak as a numinous presence in our civilized, flatland lives.

———. *The Sagebrush Ocean: A Natural History of the Great Basin.* Reno: University of Nevada Press, 1989, 1999. The whole thing: sweep of country, aspen-tree graffiti by Basque sheepherders, and the feel of lonely distance. Trimble provides the text and photographs.

Turner, Jack (1942–). *The Abstract Wild*. Tucson: University of Arizona Press, 1996.
A forthright argument—better said, a manifesto—against our attempts at management of the wild, and the blithe arrogance behind such efforts. The title
piece, which Turner refers to as a rant, and another chapter, "Economic
Nature," have the feel of landmark essays, carving out a radical position that
other, more moderate, or perhaps less passionate, essayists will be obliged to
respond to.

————. *Teewinot: A Year in the Teton Range*. New York: St. Martin's, 2000.
A carefully written, specific, detailed look at the author's life in place. Well
aware of his own limits, Turner paces himself on climbs and knows how to
enjoy what is before him. The writing is splendid throughout, but chapter 13,
"Early Winters," in which a cougar trails the author, is especially good.

Tweit, Susan J. (1956–). *Barren Wild and Worthless: Living in the Chihuahuan Desert*.
Albuquerque: University of New Mexico Press, 1995.
"It [the desert near her Las Cruces, New Mexico, home] looks shabby." But the
author, having recently arrived in the area, looks closer and finds much of interest, including spadefoot toads, weeds (this chapter includes an interesting
meditation on human migration), and the local history of extirpations.

————. *Seasons on the Pacific Coast: A Naturalist's Notebook*. San Francisco:
Chronicle Books, 1999.
Intimate, personal portraits of thirty-nine creatures, ranging from eelgrass to
grey whales, with good bibliographic help. Informative and ranging far beyond
its short table of contents.

Underhill, Linda. *The Unequal Hours: Moments of Being in the Natural World*.
Athens: University of Georgia Press, 1999.
Slowed-down, apperceptive, deceptively simple writing. The subjects are the
common miracles to be experienced at and near the author's home in rural,
upstate New York: water, fire, trees, seasons. The essence of what is communi-
cated is attention itself.

Van Dyke, John Charles (1856–1932). *The Desert: Further Studies in Natural
Appearances*. New York: Charles Scribner's Sons, 1901; Tucson: Arizona Historical
Society, 1976; Layton, Utah: Peregrine Smith, 1980.
This is a primary text in the aesthetic and spiritual appreciation of wilder-
ness, written out of solitude, illness, hardship, and exaltation: "What is it that
draws us to the boundless and the fathomless? Why should the lovely things of

earth—the grasses, the trees, the lakes, the little hills—appear trivial and insignificant when we come face to face with the sea or the desert or the vastness of the midnight sky?"

————. *The Grand Canyon of the Colorado: Recurrent Studies in Impressions and Appearances.* New York: Charles Scribner's Sons, 1920; Salt Lake City: University of Utah Press, 1992.
The author is modest about how closely words or art may approach this particular subject, and his reticence creates an artistic distance from the subject that draws our attention. One of the more successful treatments of a canyon whose scale and wildness make it the archetype of the sublime.

————. *The Mountain: Renewed Studies in Impressions and Appearances.* New York: Charles Scribner's Sons, 1916; Salt Lake City: University of Utah Press, 1992.
"The great spaces of the wilderness have a quality of beauty about them that no panorama of civilized lands can equal or even suggest." One of the high points of this book is Van Dyke's impressionistic account of a long horseback journey across the plains of Montana toward the Rockies. The text also includes a good deal of the natural history of mountains: mountain-building forces, glaciers, avalanches, and the flora and fauna of high places.

————. *Nature For Its Own Sake.* New York: Charles Scribner's Sons, 1898.
Polished lectures on the aesthetics of the wild, with particular, loving attention to the quality of light on the high plains. Van Dyke saw wholeness as the *sine qua non* of beauty, and wholeness nowhere better represented than in wilderness. His writing recalls the Upper Mississippi thirty years earlier, when "all was quite as wild and primeval as one could wish, and every traveller standing on the deck of the river steamer, as he ascended that stream felt the freshness of the air, the brightness of the light, the unmarred, the unbroken beauty of forest, bluff, and shining water."

————. *The Open Spaces.* New York: Charles Scribner's Sons, 1922.
In part an autobiography, this book emphasizes the mysterious but undeniable sense of connectedness and meaning that the author felt in wild, open situations. It also laments the coming of the automobile (Van Dyke was one of the first to foresee what it would do to Yosemite, for example) and presents, offhand almost, a good deal of natural history. "What a strange feeling, sleeping under the wide sky, that you belong only to the universe. You are back to your habitat, to your original environment, to your native heritage."

Wallace, David Rains (1945–). *The Dark Range: A Naturalist's Night Notebook*. San Francisco: Sierra Club Books, 1978.
Night makes wilderness more challenging, and the little-visited Yolla Bolly Mountains of northern California tend to compound the effect. Narratives of animal nightlife in three habitat types are presented. The "Index to Animals and Plants" consists of wonderfully concise and informative definitions.

————. *Idle Weeds: The Life of a Sandstone Ridge*. San Francisco: Sierra Club Books, 1980; Columbus: Ohio State University Press, 1986.
Wallace narrates the natural history of a year on an ordinary wooded ridge in Ohio that has just recently been preserved. The opening and closing essays, characterizing the past and the possible futures of the ridge, are thoughtful.

————. *The Klamath Knot: Explorations of Myth and Evolution*. San Francisco: Sierra Club Books, 1983.
An essay on evolution, which Wallace calls "the great myth of modern times," illuminated and given specificity by the author's experience and study in the mountain wilderness of northwestern California. The reflections on evolutionary theory arise naturally from notes on the tangle of forested mountains described, making this one of the most definitely place-centered of books on biological theory.

————. *The Untamed Garden and Other Personal Essays*. Columbus: Ohio State University Press, 1986.
These rambles show a consistent, even-tempered sensibility. There is a good, nonrighteous investigation of an urban lake (Oakland's Lake Merritt), an interesting essay on the Absaroka-Beartooth Wilderness in Montana, and, in "The Nature of Nature Writing," a survey of the history of the genre and some reflection on its "quiet," revolutionary content.

Warner, William W. (1920–). *Beautiful Swimmers: Watermen, Crabs, and the Chesapeake Bay*. Boston: Little, Brown, 1976; New York: Penguin, 1977; Boston: Little, Brown, 1994.
Local history within the ecological context, built on detailed narratives of the blue crab fishery, the kinds of human life founded on the bay and its now-threatened abundance, and the natural history of the place itself.

Weidensaul, Scott. *Living on the Wind: Across the Hemisphere with Migratory Birds*. New York: North Point Press, 1999.
Beginning with reportage on several migratory species (many of them personal

accounts), and concluding with "Trouble in the Woods," the author has certainly done his homework. The truth is: "Migratory birds as a whole are being squeezed at every stage of their life cycle—summer, winter, and in transit." What is behind such a seemingly bland utterance is enormous complexity, and a willingness to go into it. Readers willing to go along with the author will feel rewarded.

Wheeler, William Morton (1865–1937). *Foibles of Insects and Men.* New York: Alfred A. Knopf, 1928.
The introduction to this collection of essays by the great entomologist discusses changing attitudes toward the study of insects, with observations on "Fundamentalists, spiritualists, anti-evolutionists and other confusionists with whom our modern world is so richly provided." "The Physiognomy of Insects" describes body and facial variation among insects, suggesting certain commonalities with human types. Of a variety of East Indian ant equipped with "huge eyes and clipping mandibles," Wheeler writes, "If there are Anthony Comstocks, movie censors and prohibition agents among the ants we might, perhaps, expect them to have just such faces." "Insect Parisitism and Its Peculiarities" and "A Study of the Guest Ant" similarly demonstrate the author's close observation and enlargement of his subjects with suggestive wit.

White, William Chapman (1903–1955). *Adirondack Country.* Edited by Erskine Caldwell. New York: Duell, Sloan and Pearce, 1954; Syracuse: Syracuse University Press, 1985.
Part of the American Folkways series, this survey emphasizes the history and local character of the region. It is also a record of human impacts, of course, and of at least partly successful preservation. Part 8, "Adirondack Year," is a calendar based on natural history.

Whitman, Walt (1819–1892). *Specimen Days.* Philadelphia: D. McKay, 1882; Boston: David R. Godine, 1971.
This autobiography-by-vignette includes some lovely, sun-filled descriptions of summer days at Timber Creek in southern New Jersey, where the poet was recuperating from serious illness.

Williams, Brooke (1952–). *Halflives: Reconciling Work and Wilderness.* Washington, D.C.: Island Press, 1999.
The author had the extreme good fortune to be self-critical and intelligent, and to realize there was more to life than money. He traced back over his path and

saw where there had been turning points that he hadn't quite made. In the end, he is on the way to a fulfilled state, still imperfect but happy.

Williams, Samuel (1743–1817). *The Natural and Civil History of Vermont.* **Walpole, N.H.: Thomas and Carlisle, 1794.**
A scientifically minded minister, Williams made measurements of soil and air temperature on a regular basis, watched the behavior of animals closely (though he fell into some traditional errors), organized his book to give first and fundamental importance to environmental factors, and espoused a broad, nonanthropocentric outlook. A literate and sophisticated early American text that is too often overlooked.

Williams, Terry Tempest (1955–). *Pieces of White Shell: A Journey to Navajoland.* **New York: Charles Scribner's Sons, 1984; Albuquerque: University of New Mexico Press, 1987.**
The journey of a museum curator whose "knowledge of earth is literal," into a land where things are not that simple. "I quietly kept on walking," the author writes, and the eventual enlargement of view that she gains makes even a museum collection take on life.

———. *Refuge: An Unnatural History of Family and Place.* **New York: Pantheon Books, 1991.**
In the early 1980s, as the Great Salt Lake rose to historically unprecedented levels, drowning bird-productive lakeside marshes in salt water, the author's mother sank toward death from cancer. Williams weaves these two dimensions together masterfully and movingly. The last chapter, "The Clan of One-Breasted Women," describes living in Utah as a cancer hazard because of open-air, atomic bomb testing in Nevada, upwind just to the west. This book, deservingly, has had wide influence.

———. *An Unpoken Hunger: Stories from the Field.* **New York: Pantheon Books, 1994.**
A collection of strong essays from diverse magazines, given unity by the author's uncompromising spirit. "Testimony," a statement given to a government committee, is typical: factual, hard, passionate. The final words of the book are "Anticipate resurrection."

Wilson, Alexander (1766–1813). *American Ornithology, or The Natural History of the Birds of the United States.* **9 vols. Philadelphia: Bradford and Inskeep, 1808–14; reprinted in 3 vols., New York: Collins & Co., and Philadelphia: Harrison Hall, 1828–29; North Stratford, N.H.: Ayer Company, 1970.**
The first large-scale, nearly complete treatment of American birds. Wilson's

enthusiasm shines through these pages, showing the springs of motivation of nature study. Donald Culross Peattie wrote of Wilson: "As an observer his patience was infinite, his attention faultless; he had the gift of accuracy that lifts him right out of the rank of the dilettante into the highest realms of science."

———. *The Poems and Literary Prose of Alexander Wilson.* 2 vols. Edited by Alexander B. Grosart. Paisley, Scotland: Alex. Gardner, 1876.
A compendious collection of Wilson's work, prefaced by an admiring introduction by the editor. Grosart says of Wilson's bird descriptions, several of which are included here, "You have painstaking technical accuracy; but besides, a tender, delicate, lingering over their habits which is most taking." Wilson's letters give interesting detail on American country life during the first decade of the nineteenth century.

Wilson, Edward O. (1929–). *Biophilia.* Cambridge: Harvard University Press, 1984.
Wilson's presentation of biology in a way that is simultaneously heartfelt and mechanistic will likely challenge some readers. His "rough map of innovation in science" begins thus: "You start by loving a subject." The starting point here is the author's tropical research, in particular his fascination with insect life.

———. *The Diversity of Life.* Cambridge: Harvard University Press, 1992; New York: W. W. Norton, 2000.
In the first ten chapters, full of color and detail, this book delivers one of the most coherent and seeable narratives of the not-always-smooth growth of biological diversity on earth. The last five chapters, likewise full of color and detail, present a scientifically overwhelming picture of recent decline—caused by humanity. The totality is epic in scale and urgent in its message.

———. *Naturalist.* Washington, D.C.: Island Press, Shearwater Books, 1994.
The autobiography of a scientist who is able to stand back and look at himself and his evolving ideas with objectivity, and to note well the larger, changing historical picture in which his life has occurred. The twentieth century's decline in biodiversity necessarily gives a certain sundown flavor to this book, but the author's native passion for learning gives light back to the account.

Wood, William (flourished 1629–1635). *New England's Prospect.* London: I. Bellamie, 1634; Amherst: University of Massachusetts Press, 1977, 1993.
A keen and judicious observer of wildlife, soil fertility, and Indians, Wood looked steadily outward beyond the literal pale of the infant Puritan

settlement. His account is refreshing for its point of view, which was quite unusual for the time, and is presented in sturdy, interesting prose. His description of a flight of passenger pigeons is a moving glimpse of the original America.

Wright, Billie (1902–1988). *Four Seasons North.* **New York: Harper and Row, 1973.**
The author describes the experiences she and her husband shared in the Brooks Range about a hundred miles above the Arctic Circle: living in a miner's cabin, laying in two or three caribou and a moose for their winter meat, trapping and shooting wolves that threatened to compete with them for food, picking berries, trying out new recipes. Wright attains what she calls *koviashuktok,* the quality of being here and now in her environment. She warns against others trying the same life on for size—she believes the Arctic's "delicately balanced ecological life" could not take the impact.

Wright, Mabel Osgood (1859–1934). *The Friendship of Nature: A New England Chronicle of Birds and Flowers.* **New York: Macmillan, 1894; Baltimore: Johns Hopkins University Press, 1999.**
The months of nature's year, lovingly recounted with homey details: "eight acres of rolling ground, and in the centre a plainly cheerful house. . . ." The author subscribes to the agrarian theme—"Farms near at hand, farms on the slopes, farms standing boldly against the horizon, and over all the white wings of the dove of peace are folded"—but the main thing here is her ready response to light and wind and color, and the songs of birds, all contributing to a great and enveloping friendship with nature.

Wright, Sam (1919–). *Koviashuvik: A Time of Place and Joy.* **San Francisco: Sierra Club Books, 1988.**
The author continues the story left off by his wife, Billie, in *Four Seasons North,* adding a portion on England and a portion on the Southwest. The result is occasionally blissful, but most readers will find the account strangely mixed. There is a good chapter on a family of Arctic terns.

Wright, William H. (1856–1934). *The Grizzly Bear: The Narrative of a Hunter-Naturalist, Historical, Scientific and Adventurous.* **New York: Scribner's, 1909.**
Part 1 is history and taxonomy, and includes an account of the remarkable James Capen "Grizzly" Adams; part 2 covers the author's own often amazing experiences with bears, including several hunting expeditions; and part 3, on the "character and habits of the grizzly," concludes with Wright's advice to the reader to go to the wilderness without a gun. "He will learn more about

[the grizzly] in one season than he will in a lifetime of hunting to kill." This admonition was founded in the author's own experience.

Young, Louise B. (1919–). *The Blue Planet*. Boston: Little, Brown, 1983; reprinted with subtitle *A Celebration of Earth*. New York: New American Library, 1984.
Young describes the earth as a whole, geophysically: "If we could watch a time-lapse movie of the planet's history, we could see an amazing drama of change and development: mountains being created and destroyed, seafloor ejected along ocean ridges and consumed again at the trenches, canyons being carved by turbulent rivers, new continents split from old ones and set adrift to wander around the planet." The author provides just such a time-lapse account.

Zwinger, Ann (1925–). *Beyond the Aspen Grove*. New York: Random House, 1970; New York: Harper and Row, 1981; Tucson: University of Arizona Press, 1988.
West of Colorado Springs, on forty acres at an elevation of 8,300 feet, the author and her husband built a summer place, and she began to learn the natural history of the area. This book is a pleasant mixture of family reminiscences and botany and zoology notes, illustrated by Zwinger's fine drawings.

———. *A Desert Country Near the Sea: A Natural History of the Cape Region of Baja California*. New York: Harper and Row, 1983.
The author wanders at a leisurely pace, but with intense attention, from mountaintop down to the undersea world, giving detailed accounts of several different habitats along the way. A land once regarded as barren is found to be astonishingly diverse and rich.

———. *Downcanyon: A Naturalist Explores the Colorado River through the Grand Canyon*. Tucson: University of Arizona Press, 1995.
It's all here—rapids, bald eagles, golden eagles, canyon wrens, speckled dace, more than three thousand Anasazi sites (60 to 70 percent unexplored), history, buffalo gnats, harvester ants, gray-blue gnatcatchers, humpback chub, the Tanner Trail, temperature change, and much else. Fifty-five pages of notes tell where you can find the background, though not the experience. The author looks at the natural scene almost exclusively, and though you won't know who rafted through Lava Falls, you'll share her goosebumps. A memorable book.

———. *The Mysterious Lands: A Naturalist Explores the Four Great Deserts of the Southwest*. New York: E. P. Dutton, 1989; Tucson: University of Arizona Press, 1996.
In command of a broad range of reference, much of it drawn from the history

of art, the author gives rich texture to her survey of the Chihuahuan, Sonoran, Mojave, and Great Basin deserts. Her own drawings of plants, mammals, birds, toads, and landscapes, among other subjects, and her narratives of explorations as well, add a personal dimension. We see these deserts through experienced but still wondering eyes.

―――. *The Nearsighted Naturalist.* Tucson: University of Arizona Press, 1998.
Twenty-one beautiful essays from various periodicals. You are surprised by the level of personal information and delighted by the natural history. "The Art of Wandering," from *Orion,* is a look inside the process of nature writing.

―――. *Run, River, Run: A Naturalist's Journey Down One of the Great Rivers of the West.* New York: Harper and Row, 1975; Tucson: University of Arizona Press, 1984.
The author walks and paddles the length of the Green River, from its origins high in the Wind River Range of Wyoming to its confluence with the Colorado River in Utah. Along the way, she describes interesting elements in the river's natural history, identifies and analyzes threats to its integrity, and responds to solitude and wildness.

―――. *Shaped by Wind and Water: Reflections of a Naturalist.* Minneapolis: Milkweed Editions, 2000.
Sequestered in a small cabin by Puget Sound, alone, a beneficiary of Hedgebrook's retreat for women writers—Zwinger sets down what has counted for her. This is probably as close as she will come to autobiography. She defends her methods: "We need to know that spiders are *not* insects, and sea cucumbers are *not* vegetables, or what we do in ignorance will come back to haunt our children's children." Readers will find that this little book tells just about everything that matters in writing, and enough about the real, outer world to tell why.

―――. *Wind in the Rock.* New York: Harper and Row, 1978; Tucson: University of Arizona Press, 1986.
Rambles into five dramatic canyons in southern Utah, with particular attention to solitude, quiet, the very interesting natural history of the area, and the impact of modern man. Illustrated by the author's delicate, precise drawings.

Zwinger, Ann, and Edwin Way Teale. *A Conscious Stillness: Two Naturalists on Thoreau's Rivers.* New York: Harper and Row, 1982.
Zwinger and Teale alternate, she concentrating on Thoreau's "river of ripples,"

the Assabet, and he on the "river of reflections," the Sudbury. They canoe together down one stream or the other, noting the geological, hydrological, botanical, and historical changes that have occurred over time. They see disheartening signs of pollution much of the way, but also remnants of wildness. Autobiographical passages by Teale are forthright and interesting.

Zwinger, Ann, and Beatrice H. Willard (1925–). *Land Above the Trees: A Guide to American Alpine Tundra.* New York: Harper and Row, 1972.
American alpine ecology, focusing on the plants of the tundra but also highlighting Zwinger's responses to the openness, the weather, and the light, and offering strong commentary on the alpine zone's vulnerability. A most useful text.

SECONDARY STUDIES

This section includes philosophical essays on humanity and nature, critical interpretations of nature literature, histories, and a few of the many anthologies. Some of the most far-reaching philosophical speculation on our species, as well as what seem to me the most useful scholarly sources, can be found here.

Abram, David (1957–). *The Spell of the Sensuous: Perception and Language in a More-Than-Human World.* New York: Pantheon Books, 1996.
An ambitious attempt to return language and thought, and with them the human self, to a more sensuous embrace with the natural world. Abram's critique of the present: "Caught up in a mass of abstractions, our attention hypnotized by a host of human-made technologies that only reflect us back to ourselves, it is all too easy for us to forget our carnal inherence in a more-than-human matrix of sensations and sensibilities." His hope for the future: "The recuperation of the incarnate, sensorial dimension of experience brings with it a recuperation of the living landscape in which we are corporeally embedded." The analysis makes interesting use of the author's background as a sleight-of-hand-magician.

Adams, Alexander B. (1917–1984). *Eternal Quest: The Story of the Great Naturalists.* New York: G. P. Putnam's Sons, 1969.
A history of the natural sciences, presented in narrative fashion through biographies of significant figures: Aristotle, Pliny, Copernicus, Linnaeus, Darwin, and others. Audubon and Wilson are included. The interpretive theme is that

creativity, curiosity, and intuition vie, often dramatically, with the inertia of authority.

Allen, Durward L. (1910–). *Our Wildlife Legacy.* **New York: Funk and Wagnalls, 1954.**
An excellent history of wildlife and wildlife management in the United States, folded into a presentation of the major principles of population study, ecology, and wildlife conservation. The study is marked by its emphasis on habitat health and its clear acknowledgment of the rightful place of predators in the natural scheme. Like Aldo Leopold's *A Sand County Almanac,* but with more supporting detail, it extends the lessons of American wildlife history to the realm of ethics: "I suspect that . . . curious, impartial sympathy toward *all* creatures, regardless of their diet, is an attitude of the cultivated mind. It is a measure of man's civilization."

Anderson, Edgar (1897–1969). *Plants, Man, and Life.* **Boston: Little, Brown, 1952; St. Louis: Missouri Botanical Gardens, 1997.**
An exploration of interrelationships, focusing on such aspects of economic botany as crops, weeds, monoculture, and diverse planting. Anderson presents a provocative discussion of efficiency in agriculture, based on his study of a low-maintenance, "primitive" garden in Guatemala.

Anderson, Lorraine, ed. *Sisters of the Earth: Women's Prose and Poetry about Nature.* **New York: Vintage Books, 1991.**
This is one of the great early anthologies, including poems, short stories, essays, novel excerpts, journal entries, autobiography, and natural history in its attempt to bring "women's voices into the circle of nature literature valued by our culture."

Bailey, Liberty Hyde (1858–1954). *The State and the Farmer.* **New York: Macmillan, 1908.**
Bailey saw that power had concentrated in the city and the national government, but he hoped that through skillful diversification and simple awareness (paying more attention to the value of woodlots, for example, and being wary of centralist moves like school consolidation) farmers could survive the great shift.

Bakeless, John (1894–1978). *The Eyes of Discovery: The Pageant of North America As Seen by the First Explorers.* **Philadelphia: J. B. Lippincott, 1950; New York: Dover Publications, 1961.**

Explorers' responses to the aboriginal American environment. Such records have remained alive, affecting our literature profoundly. Bakeless found the appreciators among the first Europeans here—Cartier, Radisson, and others— and he noted too the preoccupations that blinded so many.

Baron, Robert C., and Elizabeth Darby Junkin, eds. *Of Discovery and Destiny: An Anthology of American Writers and the American Land.* Golden, Colo.: Fulcrum, 1986. "In this anthology we have included what we think are whispers of the creation of this peculiar American character, this character that has always looked outside of itself for peace and in hope of ever more possibility."

Basso, Keith H. (1940–). *Wisdom Sits in Places: Landscape and Language among the Western Apache.* Albuquerque: University of New Mexico Press, 1996. A patient and humble ethnographer visits Cibecue, on the Western Apache Reservation, for several years and has his mind deepened. The topic is the sense of place, and all the curious flows of language involving it. The epilogue reveals that the sense of place is continuing, at least among inhabitants of Cibecue with the proper mindset.

Bates, Marston (1906–1974). *The Nature of Natural History.* New York: Charles Scribner's Sons, 1950; rev. ed., New York: Charles Scribner's Sons, 1962; Princeton: Princeton University Press, 1990. Natural history, which Bates describes as a "growing point of science," "an area of science of immediate concern to all of us," and also a reasonably accessible kind of knowledge, might be the means for developing an attitude attuned to ecological relationships and conservation. In this basic ecological essay, Bates discusses taxonomy, community, and evolution and enters a plea for the respectability of the term "naturalist."

Beebe, William (1877–1962). *The Book of Naturalists: An Anthology of the Best Natural History.* New York: Alfred A. Knopf, 1944; Princeton: Princeton University Press, 1988. The introduction presents events in chronological order, with no strongly developed theme, but the selections, ranging from Aristotle to Rachel Carson, give a sense of the growth and inherent adventure of natural science.

Bergon, Frank, ed. *The Wilderness Reader.* New York: New American Library, 1980; Reno: University of Nevada Press, 1994. An anthology of well-known and not-so-well-known selections, introduced by an overview of the literary history of American wilderness. Bergon presents a number of useful insights in this history and in the headnotes to the selections.

Berry, Wendell (1934–). *The Unsettling of America: Culture and Agriculture.* San Francisco: Sierra Club Books, 1977, 1996; New York: Avon, 1978.
Dealing with farming techniques as they manifest worldviews, Berry mounts as thorough and unsparing a critique of industrial agriculture as can be found. The central theme is the unity of land care, morality, health, education, public policy, and the indefinable essence of character. Berry's conclusion seems to be that fragmentation anywhere tends to spread like disease.

Bonta, Marcia Myers (1940–). *Women in the Field: America's Pioneering Women Naturalists.* College Station: Texas A&M University Press, 1992.
Thorough, groundbreaking research, establishing for the first time on this national scope the stories and contributions of female naturalists. This is a great work of restoration, uncovering and re-establishing women who themselves often had to work uphill for even grudging acceptance. Of the twenty-five covered, only Florence Merriam Bailey, Margaret Morse Nice, and Rachel Carson will be familiar to many readers. A true landmark of a book.

————, ed. *American Women Afield: Writings by Pioneering Women Naturalists.* College Station: Texas A & M University Press, 1995.
A sort-of sequel to the previous book. The biographies are brief and the writings are given prominence. Cordelia Stanwood (1865–1958) will perhaps stand as an example: "When the thrush sings, I desire to live in a small, scrupulously neat camp, open to the sun and the wind and the voices of the birds."

Borland, Hal (1900–1978). *The History of Wildlife in America.* Washington, D.C.: National Wildlife Federation, 1975.
A large-format book with many illustrations, surveying major happenings clearly. Its conclusion is that we have come to our senses to a degree, and through intelligent management may provide a livable world for wildlife.

————, ed. *Our Natural World: The Land and Wildlife of America as Seen and Described by Writers Since the Country's Discovery.* Garden City, N.Y.: Doubleday, 1965; Philadelphia: J. B. Lippincott, 1969.
A generous selection, organized by "The Scene" (Woodlands, Watery Places, Plains and Deserts, and Mountains) and "The Life" (Animals, Birds, Insects, and Plants and Trees).

Botkin, Daniel B. (1937–). *Discordant Harmonies: A New Ecology for the Twenty-First Century.* New York: Oxford University Press, 1990; Bridgewater, N.J.: Replica Books, 2001.
The author argues that our present approach to environmental issues is based on "faulty beliefs, mythologies, and religious convictions" that center on nature as static. We should adopt a more dynamic concept, so that we can "manage nature wisely and prudently."

————. *Our Natural History: The Lessons of Lewis and Clark.* New York: G. P. Putnam's Sons, 1995.
Botkin declares himself "puzzled by our inability to use our environmental sciences well" and believes that a dose of the realism of Lewis and Clark, as revealed in their journals and in their practical success, would be clarifying for us. He retraces their epic journey, giving lectures comparing our romantic, dualistic, wilderness-worshiping decadence with Lewis and Clark's pragmatism and respect for fact.

Bowden, Charles (1945–). *Killing the Hidden Waters.* Austin: University of Texas Press, 1977, 1985.
The modern-day mining of groundwater in Arizona and Texas, supported by fossil fuel energy and accompanied by a singular faith, is here contrasted with the old, unsubsidized ways of the Papago and Comanche.

Branch, Michael P., Rochelle Johnson, Daniel Patterson, and Scott Slovic, eds. *Reading the Earth: New Directions in the Study of Literature and the Environment.* Moscow: University of Idaho Press, 1998.
Twenty-one papers from a 1995 meeting of the Association for the Study of Literature and Environment, providing a cross section of mid-1990s ecocriticism.

Brooks, Paul (1909–1998). *The House of Life: Rachel Carson at Work.* Boston: Houghton Mifflin, 1972.
A moving study. Passages from many letters, together with personal reminiscence, give insight into Carson's philosophy and her difficult life as a writer. This biography rises to high drama in describing the genesis, writing, and reception of *Silent Spring*.

————. *The Pursuit of Wilderness.* Boston: Houghton Mifflin, 1971.
Crucial moments in the dawning environmental consciousness of the 1960s. Brooks records "certain key battles for wilderness" in the North Cascades,

Alaska, the Everglades, and Africa, showing how they illustrate the profound choices we must make. There are some hard, but unfortunately true, words here for the U.S. Forest Service and the Army Corps of Engineers.

―――. *Speaking for Nature: How Literary Naturalists from Henry Thoreau to Rachel Carson Have Shaped America*. Boston: Houghton Mifflin, 1980; San Francisco: Sierra Club Books, 1983.
Brooks surveys the careers and influence of some fifty-eight American nature writers since Thoreau's time, arguing for their large effect upon culture and public policy. Lesser-known figures such as Wilson Flagg and Florence Merriam are included, and there are fresh views of the greats. A valuable sourcebook, suggesting an interpretation of American history.

―――. *The View from Lincoln Hill: Man and the Land in a New England Town*. Boston: Houghton Mifflin, 1976.
Brooks presents the human-ecological history of Lincoln, Masssachusetts. In 1976 there were only four farmers left in Lincoln and the town had become a suburb of Boston. But through careful planning and a process whose roots went back all the way to the colonial era, open space and a degree of rural atmosphere had been preserved. Standards of value "traditionally associated with rural New England no longer look as quaint as they did a generation ago."

Buell, Lawrence (1939–). *The Environmental Imagination: Thoreau, Nature Writing, and the Formation of American Culture*. Cambridge: Harvard University Press, 1995.
A study of the importance of nature writing whose scale and approach recall the literary-cultural scholarship of F. O. Matthiessen and Lewis Mumford. Buell shows that an ecocritic needs to be capable of relational thinking and have knowledge of history, psychology, natural history, and philosophy. He legitimizes ecocriticism here by the weight and reasonableness of his scholarship. Thoreau is the natural reference point, and when Buell gets into topics like poststructuralist notions of nature (which he demolishes, in an understated, quiet way), he keeps to a standard of good common sense.

Burroughs, John (1837–1921). *Accepting the Universe: Essays in Naturalism*. Boston: Houghton Mifflin, 1920; reprinted in vol. 21 of *The Complete Writings of John Burroughs*. New York: Wm. H. Wise, 1924; Highland City, Fla.: Rainbow Books, 1987.
An eighty-year-old's lucid exposition of his semi-Darwinian, naturalistic, reverent philosophy. In the final chapter, Burroughs closed his writing career as he had opened it, with a marveling, yet perceptive, tribute to Walt Whitman.

Carson, Rachel (1907–1964). *Silent Spring*. Boston: Houghton Mifflin, 1962; New York: Fawcett Crest, 1964; New York: Ballantine, 1982, 1988, 1993.
A major text that is still valuable, still urgent. Carson assembled the evidence painstakingly, showing by careful reasoning and ecological insight just what a chemicalized environment would mean. History and further investigation have borne out her analysis. "How many a man has dated a new era in his life from the reading of a book," Thoreau wrote. This may one day be said of America and *Silent Spring*.

Clough, Wilson O. (1894–1990). *The Necessary Earth: Nature and Solitude in American Literature*. Austin: University of Texas Press, 1964.
The American land, and life on the frontier, are here seen as sources of the newness, vitality, and distinctiveness of American literature. Clough stresses the American habit of "direct reference to experience."

Coues, Elliott (1842–1899). *Biogen: A Speculation on the Origin and Nature of Life*. Boston: Estes and Lauriat, 1884.
"Biogen" means soul-stuff. It is the mysterious vital principle which, Coues writes, is "inscrutable." In this lecture we see a scientist, one of the important American ornithologists, placing limits on the scientific method. Pure reason, to the author, is "a lamp which finally serves not to light the way, but only to make the darkness visible."

Cronon, William (1954–). *Changes in the Land: Indians, Colonists, and the Ecology of New England*. New York: Hill and Wang, 1983.
Cronon offers documentation, and a carefully stated overview, on the transition from the diversity of pre-colonial New England to the more regularized systems under European management. He does not absolve the Indians of a certain complicity (perhaps circumstantially forced) in the new market system. This study might serve as a model for ecological histories of other areas affected by European conquest, or indeed any region undergoing profound transformations.

————, ed. *Uncommon Ground: Rethinking the Human Place in Nature*. New York: W. W. Norton, 1996.
A collection of postmodern essays deconstructing the traditional notion that wild nature is simply an objective reality. The editor's lead essay, "The Trouble with Wilderness; or, Getting Back to the Wrong Nature," argues that "the dream of an unworked natural landscape is very much the fantasy of people who have

never themselves had to work the land to make a living." The essays here are concerned with ideas, and do not address biological diversity or wilderness as anything more than concepts in the minds of humans. This book has aroused as much critical response as any text in the humanity-and-nature field since the "nature-fakers" controversy.

Cutright, Paul Russell (1897–1988). *Lewis and Clark: Pioneering Naturalists.* Urbana: University of Illinois Press, 1969; Norman: University of Oklahoma Press, 2001.
A narrative of the expedition, emphasizing the natural history aspects. Lewis's observations often contained minute detail (the number of feathers in a grouse's tail, for example), and also provided benchmark descriptions of unspoiled wilderness. Cutright believes Lewis "had a distinct flair for literary composition."

Dasmann, Raymond F. (1919–). *The Last Horizon.* New York: Macmillan, 1963.
Biome by biome, Dasmann examines the process of homogenization, by which the diversity of the earth's wilderness and culture are reduced to the industrial model, and contemplates the possibility of a thoroughly tamed world.

Devall, Bill (1938–), and George Sessions (1938–). *Deep Ecology.* Salt Lake City: Gibbs M. Smith, 1985.
Shallow ecology, devoted to intelligent management of natural resources, is anthropocentric at heart. It tends to cover over the fundamental problem—alienation from nature—with a confident gloss of purposeful activity. People are surprised when things keep getting worse. To practice deep ecology, the authors say, is to recover an old orientation to nature, one of belonging: "We need to accept the invitation to the dance." The authors mount a vigorous critique of the presently dominant worldview, leaving hardly a pillar unshaken, and they present a many-sided, carefully attributed introduction to the deeper position. One of the most useful features of this book is its command of bibliographic sources.

Diamond, Irene, and Gloria Feman Orenstein, eds. *Reweaving the World: The Emergence of Ecofeminism.* San Francisco: Sierra Club Books, 1990.
A collection of essays (most deriving from a 1987 conference) introduced with a strong attitude. The background of the conference was "many women [who] began to understand how the larger culture's devaluation of natural processes was a product of masculine consciousness." "Reweaving" means going beyond the dualistic and imperial mentality that the editors associate with males.

Durrenberger, Robert W. (1918–). *Environment and Man: A Bibliography.* Palo Alto, Calif.: National Press Books, 1970.
Emphasizes, but is not limited to, books and articles from the 1960s. Arranged alphabetically, then by means of numbers, into forty-six subject categories. Though "literature" is not one of these categories, the list's accent on environmental concern makes it a useful source for anyone tracing the recent literary history of humanity and the environment.

Egerton, Frank N. (1936–), ed. *History of American Ecology.* New York: Arno Press, 1977.
Pays tribute to Peter Kalm, Samuel Williams, Alexander Wilson, and Ralph Waldo Emerson as forerunners in the development of an ecological perspective.

Ehrenfeld, David (1938–). *The Arrogance of Humanism.* New York: Oxford University Press, 1978, 1981.
The preposterous claims of the anthropocentric-mechanist mentality, and the faith this religion inspires in the masses, are surveyed here with wit, logic, passion, and finally compassion. Against the specist cult of certainty the author proposes two humbling laws: "1. Most scientific discoveries and technological inventions can be developed in such a way that they are capable of doing great damage to human beings, their cultures, and their environments. 2. If a discovery or a technology can be used for evil purposes, it will be so used."

Eiseley, Loren (1907–1977). *Darwin's Century: Evolution and the Men Who Discovered It.* Garden City, N.Y.: Doubleday, 1958, 1961.
A course of lectures on the scientific and philosophical challenge that may have marked a watershed in human thought. An essential background text.

Ekirch, Arthur A., Jr. (1915–2000). *Man and Nature in America.* New York: Columbia University Press, 1963.
A history of American ideas about nature, and an account of the changing human ecology of this country that in some part results from those ideas. This is a cautionary book, calling for an examination of anthropocentrism. The vicious circle of "greater production and greater consumption" is discussed, and the author makes a reasoned plea for reviving the concepts of harmony and balance.

Elder, John (1947–), ed. *American Nature Writers.* 2 vols. New York: Charles Scribner's Sons, 1996.

A large-format, double-column, 1210-page compendium of criticism that sets a high standard for comprehensiveness and earnest, scholarly investigation. These volumes, among other accomplishments, announce and prove the academic legitimacy of nature writing. Focusing on the twentieth century and covering everyone of note, almost, from Abbey to Zwinger (oddly, Donald Culross Peattie is missing), and then adding a dozen essays on topics like bioregionalism and mountaineering literature, *American Nature Writers* is an indispensable reference.

Elman, Robert (1930–). *First in the Field: America's Pioneering Naturalists*. New York: Mason/Charter, 1977.
A well-informed survey of the careers and contributions of Catesby, the Bartrams, Wilson, Audubon, Agassiz, Powell, and Burroughs—the latter not for additions to scientific knowledge but for popularizing natural history at a crucial time in American history.

Evans, Howard Ensign (1919–). *Pioneer Naturalists: The Discovery and Naming of North American Plants and Animals*. New York: Henry Holt, 1993.
After a succinct introduction covering the beginnings of natural history in America, this book is arranged encyclopedia-style according to the species named: Baird's sandpiper, Bewick's wren, Lindheimer's Daisy, etc. The individual treatments are unfailingly interesting amalgams of human and natural history.

Ewan, Joseph (1909–), and Nesta Ewan. *John Banister and His Natural History of Virginia, 1678–1692*. Urbana: University of Illinois Press, 1970.
Banister, who had an M.A. from Oxford, spent fourteen years in Virginia and was, according to the Ewans, "America's first resident naturalist." His drawings, covering thirty-two pages here, are delicate and detailed, and his projected "Natural History of Virginia" might have been a landmark. The authors' chronology of American natural history, 1650 to 1753, complementing the one by Joseph Ewan in *William Bartram: Botanical and Zoological Drawings*, is most useful.

Feduccia, Alan (1943–), ed. *Catesby's Birds of Colonial America*. Chapel Hill: University of North Carolina Press, 1985, 1999.
A superb modern edition of Catesby's bird plates, with useful ancillary information on just how many species the early naturalists saw and how well they knew their birds.

Finch, Robert, and John Elder, eds. *The Norton Book of Nature Writing.* New York: W. W. Norton, 1990.
An unmistakable sign that the day of nature writing had come. This collection includes British writers.

Foerster, Norman (1887–1972). *Nature in American Literature: Studies in the Modern View of Nature.* New York: Macmillan, 1923.
Foerster treats Bryant, Whittier, Emerson, Thoreau, Lowell, Whitman, Lanier, Muir, and Burroughs as exemplary and influential nature writers. He presents interesting insights into Thoreau's sensuousness, and describes Burroughs's "temperamental laxity" and his "rudderless" books, while praising his sincerity. A dated but still significant study.

Frick, George Frederick (1925–), and Raymond Phineas Stearns (1904–1970). *Mark Catesby: The Colonial Audubon.* Urbana: University of Illinois Press, 1961.
Offering as much as we are likely to learn about Catesby's life, this study is particularly good on the place of his work in American natural history.

Fritzell, Peter A. (1940–). *Nature Writing and America: Essays Upon a Cultural Type.* Ames: Iowa State University Press, 1990.
"American nature writing contains, then, the early and classic American's quest both for a coherent sense of self and a coherent sense of place." "The characteristic persuasions of American nature writing have been evolutionary, metaphysical, and theoretically ecological rather than political, economic, or sociological." There are forty-one pages of notes.

Glacken, Clarence J. (1909–1989). *Traces on the Rhodian Shore: Nature and Culture in Western Thought from Ancient Times to the End of the Eighteenth Century.* Berkeley: University of California Press, 1967.
An immense, scholarly examination of three ideas: the notion that the earth was designed for man, the concept that the moral and social dimensions of human life are influenced by nature, and the realization that man is a significant agent of ecological change.

Glotfelty, Cheryll, and Harold Fromm, eds. *The Ecocriticism Reader: Landmarks in Literary Ecology.* Athens: University of Georgia Press, 1996.
Embodying a wide, eclectic, even adventurous, view of what should be encompassed by literary criticism of green coloration, this collection includes essays on the relationship of poststructuralism to ecology and on the "interiority of

outdoor experience," and a critique of "toxic consciousness" in the fiction of the 1980s, for starters.

Graber, Linda. *Wilderness As Sacred Space.* Washington, D.C.: Association of American Geographers, 1976.
Graber's thesis is that wilderness appreciation and the drive to preserve wildlands are basically religious phenomena. She asks why wilderness should generate religiously potent imagery and answers that it is because wilderness is "Wholly Other" to modern man. The analysis tends to be reductive, perhaps even hobby-horsical, but is nonetheless of interest.

Graham, Frank, Jr. (1925–). *Since Silent Spring.* Boston: Houghton Mifflin, 1970; New York: Fawcett Crest, 1970.
Graham pays tribute to the astuteness and courage of Rachel Carson, and brings the story of pesticides and herbicides eight years further along, giving evidence that the venality of pesticide promoters had not much abated and that the fence-sitting, and worse, of academics and bureaucrats continued. By 1970, though, there were indications of organized resistance to the mindless spraying of chemicals.

Griffin, Susan (1943–). *Woman and Nature: The Roaring Inside Her.* New York: Harper and Row, 1978; San Francisco: Sierra Club Books, 2000.
Griffin describes what she calls the unnatural history of patriarchy's alienated, abstract, egoistic, reductionist, world-fragmenting arrogance of power. The good side is the emergence of a feminine, natural outlook, answering to a "green and still living" possibility. "This earth is my sister. . . ."

Hanley, Wayne (1915–). *Natural History in America: From Mark Catesby to Rachel Carson.* New York: Quadrangle, New York Times Books, 1977.
Modestly describing himself as a compiler, Hanley intersperses longish passages from the works of great American naturalists with a running historical commentary. His remarks on the influence of Linnaeus and the major contributions of Wilson, Audubon, and Nuttall are helpful in building the historical overview.

Hazard, Lucy Lockwood (1890–1959). *The Frontier in American Literature.* New York: Thomas Y. Crowell, 1927.
A consideration of American writing in light of the "frontier thesis" of Frederick Jackson Turner, with interesting insights on transcendentalist

thought, which Hazard believed to be heavily influenced by the frontier condition of American life. Her linkage of John Winthrop, Ralph Waldo Emerson, and George F. Babbitt is a stimulating concept.

Hicks, Philip Marshall (1885–1977). "The Development of the Natural History Essay in American Literature." Ph.D. thesis, University of Pennsylvania, 1924.
Hicks argues that the natural history essay is properly limited to "scientifically accurate observations of the life history of the lower orders of nature," and does not include "the essay inspired merely by an aesthetic or sentimental delight in nature in general; the narrative of travel, where the observation is only incidental; and the sketch which is concerned solely with description of scenery." He covers nearly everyone of importance from Captain John Smith to John Burroughs, giving extremely high significance to Burroughs ("the chief contributor to the literature of this field") and, oddly, not mentioning John Muir at all.

Huth, Hans (1892–1977). *Nature and the American: Three Centuries of Changing Attitudes.* Berkeley: University of California Press, 1957; Lincoln: University of Nebraska Press, 1990.
Steps along the way, and influential thinkers, recounted in scholarly fashion: Jefferson, the Bartrams, Crèvecoeur, Wilson, Bryant, Cooper, the Hudson River School, the transcendentalists, Catlin, G. P. Marsh (with the publication of *Man and Nature* in 1864 seen here as a turning point), and so on. The author appears to accept dams and the Tennessee Valley Authority uncritically, as conservation measures, but the parts of this study covering the eighteenth and nineteenth centuries are eminently useful.

Jackson, John B. (1909–). *Landscapes: Selected Writings of J. B. Jackson.* Edited by Ervin H. Zube. Amherst: University of Massachusetts Press, 1970.
Humanist landscape-criticism, founded on impressive historical knowledge of our culture's relationship with nature. Includes an interesting comparison of the "anti-urbanism" of Thomas Jefferson and Henry David Thoreau.

Jones, Howard Mumford (1892–1980). *O Strange New World: American Culture: The Formative Years.* New York: Viking Press, 1964; Westport, Conn.: Greenwood Publishing Group, 1982.
This study of the formative years of American culture includes three chapters on the European encounter with American nature: "The Image of the New World" and "The Anti-Image," which open the investigation, and "American

Landscape," which concludes it with an analysis of the West and the influence of space upon American values.

Kastner, Joseph (1907–1997). *A Species of Eternity.* New York: Alfred A. Knopf, 1977. Impressively thorough research makes this account of the "virtuoso" period of American natural history a standard reference. Informing Kastner's biographies is a clear sense of American intellectual life and its development. An indispensable work.

——. *A World of Watchers.* New York: Alfred A. Knopf, 1986.
A chatty, anecdotal, informative history of birdwatching in America, written with good humor (on such subjects as bird clubs' exclusiveness, for example) and with a strong sense of what birding has meant, in all seriousness, to this nation historically.

Kohl, Judith, and Herbert Kohl (1937–). *The View from the Oak: The Private Worlds of Other Creatures.* San Francisco: Sierra Club Books, 1977; New York: New Press, 2000.
Classified as "juvenile literature," but containing sentences like "It is difficult to understand the umwelt of creatures that have different senses and sizes than ours," this book asks the reader to go beyond the usual perceptual borders. A useful educational guide for all ages.

Kolodny, Annette (1941–). *The Land Before Her: Fantasy and Experience of the American Frontiers, 1630–1860.* Chapel Hill: University of North Carolina Press, 1984. An analysis of symbolic landscapes and fantasies, showing women's responses to the American frontiers. For many women, the image of the garden was central: "The garden implied home and community, not [as for many of the male fantasies depicted in Kolodny's *The Lay of the Land*] privatized erotic mastery." This book offers a fresh look at American history with regard to the land.

——. *The Lay of the Land: Metaphor as Experience and History in American Life and Letters.* Chapel Hill: University of North Carolina Press, 1975, 1984.
This careful study examines the feminine personification of the New World landscape and ponders the effects of this continuing metaphor.

Krutch, Joseph Wood (1893–1970), ed. *Great American Nature Writing.* New York: William Sloane, 1950.
The eighty-page prologue to this anthology, an invaluable essay, describes the philosophical preconditions of modern nature writing. Krutch traces the

history of the idea of oneness with nature and the accompanying attitude of fellow-feeling. He finds the move toward an ecological view nothing less than an "intellectual revolution." There is analysis of the concept of the sublime, of mechanism, of Linnaean science versus Cartesian, and of the influence of certain divines like John Ray.

LaBastille, Anne (1938–). *Women and Wilderness.* San Francisco: Sierra Club Books, 1980.
An interesting study of how women in North America responded to wilderness in the era of settlement and westward movement, how they began in modern times to go to the wilderness for study and recreation, and what they now do there. It is the story of a kind of revolution. Profiles of fifteen contemporary women who have had extensive wilderness experience comprise a major portion of the book.

LaChapelle, Dolores (1911–1992). *Earth Wisdom.* Los Angeles: Guild of the Tutors, 1978; rev. ed., Silverton, Colo.: Finn Hill Arts, 1984; Skyland, N.C.: Kivaki Press, 1993.
A synthesis of anthropological and biological information, philosophy, and personal experience, focused by a provocative intuition. The author's theme is the healing reconnection that is, she believes, yet possible.

———. *Sacred Land Sacred Sex—Rapture of the Deep: Concerning Deep Ecology and Celebrating Life.* Silverton, Colo.: Finn Hill Arts, 1988; Skyland, N.C.: Kivaki Press, 1992.
A sequel to *Earth Wisdom,* deepening the treatment of our historical alienation and the archetypal roots of our consciousness. LaChapelle is a student of Taoism, C. G. Jung, and D. H. Lawrence, pre-eminently among other topics, but she offers an original philosophy that appears to both unify and transcend her sources.

———. *D. H. Lawrence: Future Primitive.* Denton: University of North Texas Press, 1996.
A fresh reading of Lawrence, concentrating on his experience of nature and the nature-centered quality of his outlook. An outstanding example of nonacademic ecocriticism.

Lillard, Richard G. (1909–). *The Great Forest.* New York: Alfred A. Knopf, 1947.
A narrative history of America from the standpoint of forests and forest products, including chapters on conservation and labor issues.

Limerick, Patricia Nelson (1951–). *Desert Passages: Encounters with the American Deserts*. Albuquerque: University of New Mexico Press, 1985, 2001.
Early travelers, up to about the time of John Charles Van Dyke, disliked the unimproved desert. Later, Limerick argues, "appreciation supplants dislike." She believes that improvements in transportation gave a "margin of safety," so that twentieth-century Americans "felt safe to appreciate the desert."

Linden, Eugene (1947–). *Silent Partners: The Legacy of the Ape Language Experiments*. New York: Times Books, 1986.
Within this account of the decline of the ape language research, and the subsequent diaspora of the apes themselves, there is a complex question. What is it that separates humans from other animals? (Language? And if so, what is *that*?) Seen from a chimpanzee's point of view, perhaps we appear as a "bizarre, moody species." This book is marked by strong, unsentimental compassion for the chimpanzees and gorillas who are the silent partners in a human quest for knowledge.

Little, Charles E. (1931–). *The Dying of the Trees: The Pandemic in America's Forests*. New York: Viking, 1995, 1997.
A sober, documentary survey of forest decline—apparently accelerating in the 1990s—in eight separate regions of America. The causes are as various as climatic change, pollution, introduced diseases, and fire suppression, but they all trace back to the industrial way of life. Little concludes, "I have learned things I wish I had not learned."

Marsh, George Perkins (1801–1882). *Man and Nature, or Physical Geography As Modified by Human Action*. New York: Charles Scribner, 1864; Cambridge: Harvard University Press, 1965, 1973.
Marsh analyzed the decline of Mediterranean and Near Eastern civilization in terms of watershed abuse and warned against a similar mistake in America. He showed that humans had become a major force with the ability to change the earth radically, and he proposed the protection of wilderness. This is an early, one might say prescient, text in ecological awareness. Lewis Mumford, writing in *The Brown Decades* (1931), described it as the "fountainhead of the conservation movement."

Marx, Leo (1919–). *The Machine in the Garden: Technology and the Pastoral Ideal in America*. New York: Oxford University Press, 1964.
Marx states that his purpose is "to describe and evaluate the uses of the pastoral

ideal in the interpretation of American experience. I shall be tracing its adaptation to the conditions of life in the New World, its emergence as a distinctly American theory of society, and its subsequent transformation under the impact of industrialism." A major study of gray and green in American art and thought.

Matthiessen, Peter (1927–). *Wildlife in America.* New York: Viking Press, 1959; rev. and updated ed., New York: Viking Press, 1987, 1995.
Still the most complete record of the impact of three-plus centuries of Euro-American settlement upon the wildlife of North America. Matthiessen allows the often-appalling facts to speak for themselves. Not a heartening book, but a necessary one.

McClintock, James I. (1939–). *Nature's Kindred Spirits: Aldo Leopold, Joseph Wood Krutch, Edward Abbey, Annie Dillard, and Gary Snyder.* Madison: University of Wisconsin Press, 1994.
Close, alert readings of writers constituting "an informal community of concern and experience" who have "integrated Thoreauvian Romanticism and twentieth-century ecological biology." In doing so, they offer a "critique of modernity and a positive vision." This book pays attention to the sense of renewal at the heart of much nature writing.

McKibben, Bill (1960–). *The End of Nature.* New York: Random House, 1989; New York: Doubleday, 1999.
Recognizing the brute facts of global warming, stratospheric ozone depletion, and other dimensions of world-scale environmental degradation, McKibben argues that humanity's pervasive effects have altered the very context of life on earth. Thus, in a real sense, nature as we have known it no longer exists. Still, the author finds a measure of hope, or at least possibility, in the contemporary growth of biocentric thought.

———. *Hope, Human and Wild: True Stories of Living Lightly on the Earth.* Boston: Little, Brown, 1995; St. Paul, Minn.: Hungry Mind Press, 1996.
Possibly one of the important early texts in the literature of restoration. McKibben describes three places where human beings have tried to live more humbly—more in line with ecological reality: Curitiba, Brazil; the state of Kerala, in India; and his own home ground in the Adirondack mountains of New York State.

McNeill, J. R. *Something New Under the Sun: An Environmental History of the Twentieth-Century World.* New York: W. W. Norton, 2000.
A painstakingly thorough account of a species following its star. The record is of a "specialized fossil fuel-based civilization so ecologically disruptive that it guarantees surprises and shocks, and promotes just the sort of flux that favors the adaptable and clever," which leaves us where we are. However, having read this book, we can no longer be mute through ignorance.

Meeker, Joseph (1932–). *The Comedy of Survival.* New York: Charles Scribner's Sons, 1974; rev. ed., Los Angeles: Guild of the Tutors, 1980; Tucson: Arizona University Press, 1997.
Literary analysis from an ecological standpoint, offering fresh insights into well-known works and, more significantly, setting up a new way of reading. The author associates the tragic hero with nature-indifference and general ecological irresponsibility, and the comic stance with humility and survival. A provocative departure.

Merchant, Carolyn (1936–). *The Death of Nature: Women, Ecology, and the Scientific Revolution.* San Francisco: Harper and Row, 1980, 1990.
From an egalitarian standpoint, Merchant argues, women's liberation and ecological consciousness have much in common. The intellectual revolution that established the modern, mechanistic worldview in the sixteenth and seventeenth centuries denied the traditional, organic world—the female world of nature. Now, "by critically reexamining history from these [egalitarian] perspectives, we may begin to discover values associated with the premodern world that may be worthy of transformation and reintegration into today's and tomorrow's society." This revisionist study will be taken into account in any serious examination of our culture's relationship with the natural world.

Mills, Stephanie (1948–). *In Service of the Wild: Restoring and Reinhabiting Damaged Land.* Boston: Beacon Press, 1995.
This affirmative book, detailing several ongoing rehabilitation projects, says that restoration needs to be both pragmatic landscape-scale work and at the same time, an inward practice to recover our own full range of consciousness and spirit. The two dimensions go together. During a visit to India she meets Dr. V. B. Mishra, who is working on restoring the polluted Ganges River. Mishra sums up the underforce in Mills's book: "If there is no love and commitment in this world, then this world will disintegrate like sand particles."

Murray, John A. *A Republic of Rivers: Three Centuries of Nature Writing from Alaska and the Yukon.* New York: Oxford University Press, 1990.
After a move from Colorado to Alaska, John Murray devoted himself to the lore and history, and to the actual terrain, of his new home. One of the results is this wide-ranging collection. Underlying the selection process: "These pristine arctic refugia, and the writings of those who love them, symbolize the common hope of humanity for a better future."

————, ed. *American Nature Writing 1994.* San Francisco: Sierra Club Books, 1994.
The first in a surprisingly rich series of short pieces and excerpts, taken from a wide variety of sources.

————, ed. *American Nature Writing 1995.* San Francisco: Sierra Club Books, 1995.
This is a well-selected series. Murray is awake to nature writing and seems to have a wide idea of its boundaries.

————, ed. *American Nature Writing 1996.* San Francisco: Sierra Club Books, 1996.
A good survey of the year's output. This one has essays by Kate Boyes and Dave Petersen, for starters.

————, ed. *American Nature Writing 1997.* San Francisco: Sierra Club Books, 1997.
A previously unpublished piece by Edward Abbey leads twenty-two voices.

————, ed. *American Nature Writing 1998.* San Francisco: Sierra Club Books, 1998.
The editor's introduction, "From the Faraway Nearby," as just one example, should not be missed.

————, ed. *American Nature Writing 1999.* Corvallis: Oregon State University Press, 1999.
Examples of young writers getting started, and pushing against whatever definition of nature writing you had.

————, ed. *American Nature Writing 2000.* Corvallis: Oregon State University Press, 2000.
Without belaboring the case or the cause, Murray gathers nineteen female authors, from Trudy Dittmar on the moose to Janisse Ray on the deer of Georgia.

Nash, Roderick (1939–). *Wilderness and the American Mind.* New Haven, Conn.: Yale University Press, 1967; rev. ed., 1973; 3rd ed., 1982.
An indispensable historical survey. The later editions make observations on recent developments such as the environmental movement in the 1960s and 1970s

and the contemporary crowding of wilderness areas. Nash appears to equate Western society with society in general regarding attitudes toward the wild, and he holds to what might be termed the "full-stomach" theory of wilderness appreciation (veneration of the wild arises *after* certain basic needs have been met). Both these views are debatable, but the book remains authoritative in its historical analysis.

Norwood, Vera. *Made from This Earth: American Women and Nature.* Chapel Hill: University of North Carolina Press, 1993.
An attempt to cover what had not been covered: the contribution of women. Norwood starts with the early nineteenth century and comes forward to the very late twentieth, covering, along the way, Almira Hart Lincoln Phelps, Jane Colden, Graceanna Lewis, Agnes Chase, and Diane Fossey, among others. The part on Carson is good, pointing out that men approached her book on gender lines.

Oelschlaeger, Max (1943–). *The Idea of Wilderness: From Prehistory to the Age of Ecology.* New Haven, Conn.: Yale University Press, 1991.
A comprehensive, green history of the philosophy and psychology of Western civilization, whose roots lie in the Paleolithic and Neolithic and whose concepts of the wild have been shaped classically by religious and historicist notions and, more recently, by modernist scientific ideas. This survey, which has affinities with Lynn White's and Dolores LaChapelle's understandings, is followed by excellent ecocritical readings of Thoreau, Muir, Leopold, Jeffers, and Snyder, showing, in one way or another, that our civilization may be preparing for a massive paradigm shift indicated today by the philosophy called Deep Ecology.

O'Grady, John P. (1958–). *Pilgrims to the Wild: Everett Ruess, Henry David Thoreau, John Muir, Clarence King, Mary Austin.* Salt Lake City: University of Utah Press, 1993.
The thesis is that a religious desire for the infinite/sublime/wild drives these writers. O'Grady's readings are appropriately adventurous, buttressing the analysis with sources ranging from Dogen to D. H. Lawrence. This book conveys the passion behind nature writing.

Osborn, Fairfield (1887–1969). *Our Plundered Planet.* Boston: Little, Brown, 1948.
A sobering work, written at the dawn of the postwar frenzy of development. A world population of some two billion worried Osborn, as did topsoil loss, the increase of degenerative diseases, and the curious faith that science will make everything turn out right.

Osborn, Henry Fairfield (1852–1935). *Impressions of Great Naturalists: Reminiscences of Darwin, Huxley, Balfour, Cope and Others.* New York: Charles Scribner's Sons, 1924. "I like a naturalist better than a scientist," Professor Osborn wrote, "because there is less of the ego in him, and in a naturalist like Darwin the ego entirely disappears and through his vision we see Nature with the least human aberration." The sketches of John Muir and John Burroughs are influenced by Osborn's ideas on heredity and race—Muir he saw as a representative "Scotch type of soul," and Burroughs as very English.

Owings, Loren C. (1928–). *Environmental Values, 1860–1972: A Guide to Information Sources.* Detroit: Gale Research, 1976.
This well-annotated reference work covers humans and nature in America, travelers' accounts by region, American landscape painting, conservation, nature writing and nature study, camping literature, and country living, and does so with a clear focus on philosophy and values. An excellent sourcebook.

Page, George. *Inside the Animal Mind.* New York: Doubleday, 1999.
A scientifically correct companion to the author's TV series, breaking down the human conceit of special creation. Page brings every significant item to consideration, leaving one to wonder what strange mechanisms keep that original notion so blithely intact.

Paul, Sherman (1920–1995). *For Love of the World: Essays on Nature Writers.* Iowa City: University of Iowa Press, 1992.
Professor Paul takes a leisurely, personal reading tour here, engaging Thoreau, Leopold, Lopez, Beston, Nelson, Eiseley, and Muir in essays that are ruminative. The author is willing to take the time to listen closely and read between the lines. He takes these writers at the top of their powers and has, as it were, deep conversations with them. The result is extraordinarily capacious criticism at its best.

Payne, Daniel G. (1958–). *Voices in the Wilderness: American Nature Writing and Environmental Politics.* Hanover, N.H.: University Press of New England, 1996.
From "nascent ecological sensibility" in early times to Edward Abbey, this survey covers some of the same ground as Paul Brooks's *Speaking for Nature* (1980), but offers more literary criticism, particularly in analysis of rhetorical strategies.

Peattie, Donald Culross (1898–1964). *Green Laurels: The Lives and Achievements of the Great Naturalists.* New York: Simon and Schuster, 1936.

Informative background on medieval and Renaissance concepts of nature, and on the life and work of Linnaeus, serve as a kind of prologue to this study of the Bartrams, the two botanists Michaux (father and son), Wilson, Audubon, the entomologist Thomas Say, and others important in American natural history.

―――. *Singing in the Wilderness: A Salute to John James Audubon.* New York: G. P. Putnam's Sons, 1935.
Peattie was highly sympathetic to his subject ("Audubon gave everything he had for the most beautiful thing he could see"), freely novelizing scenes and speaking forthrightly of Audubon's importance in his own life. But he was also clearheaded about his methods, astute in his art criticism, and knowledgeable about the middle America of 1805 to 1825. An honest, accessible biography, very modern in conception.

Phillips, Kathryn (1957–). *Tracking the Vanishing Frogs: An Ecological Mystery.* New York: St. Martin's Press, 1994; New York: Penguin USA, 1995.
Phillips became interested in the global mystery of declining frogs and attached herself to several scientists who held promising theories. In the course of the book, concentrating upon California and Costa Rica, she adds up the evidence, finding no obvious headline except for the hand of man. A well-written, scientific book.

Porter, Charlotte M. (1948–). *The Eagle's Nest: Natural History and American Ideas, 1812–1842.* Tuscaloosa: University of Alabama Press, 1986.
A survey of the naturalists of the early republic, centering on William Maclure (who completed the first geological survey of the United States in 1808) and the Philadelphia-based Academy of Natural Sciences. These naturalists were "sons of the Enlightenment," Porter says, and beneficent views of nature came easily to them.

Robertson, David (1937–). *West of Eden: A History of the Art and Literature of Yosemite.* Berkeley: Wilderness Press and Yosemite Natural History Association, 1984.
A model scholarly study of the expression of place. Robertson's criticism suggests the high level at which nature writing may be enjoyed. His treatment of Ansel Adams's work, in the section on photography, likewise elevates the level of discourse.

Ronald, Ann (1939–), ed. *Words for the Wild: The Sierra Club Trailside Reader.* San Francisco: Sierra Club Books, 1987.
The editor has chosen particularly resonant excerpts from twenty-three

American writers, from R. W. Emerson to Barry Lopez, which are accompanied by instructive statements on what these writers have meant to her.

Sauer, Carl Ortwin (1889–1975). *Sixteenth Century North America: The Land and the People as Seen by the Europeans.* Berkeley: University of California Press, 1971.
A recounting of explorations and attempts at settlement, in large part those of the Spanish, with ecological commentary. Sauer describes the Indians' sophisticated agriculture, noting that even on the high plains of present-day west Texas, Native Americans were not purely nomadic.

Savage, Henry, Jr. (1903–1990). *Lost Heritage.* New York: William Morrow, 1970.
Brief, fact-filled biographies of seven important naturalists: John Lawson, Mark Catesby, the Bartrams, André and Francois André Michaux, and Alexander Wilson. The text is enriched by a sense of the beauty and intactness (the "lost heritage") of the America these men saw and given a sharp point by the author's outspoken commentary on the present state of the American environment.

Schama, Simon (1945–). *Landscape and Memory.* New York: Alfred A. Knopf, 1995.
A monumental aggregation of evidence, most of it drawn from art history, showing that forests, rivers, and mountains have to the present day reverberated in the mythological imagination of Western culture. The corollary is that we are perhaps not as alienated as some might think. Paul Shepard's *Man in the Landscape* (1967), though far less prodigious in size, is likely to remain the most persuasive reading of the Western sense of nature as revealed in art.

Scheese, Don. *Nature Writing: The Pastoral Impulse in America.* New York: Twayne Publishers, 1996.
A clarifying study detailing the evolution of American pastoralism through the work of six major writers: Thoreau, Muir, Austin, Abbey, Leopold, and Dillard. Scheese provides a good overview of American nature writing, nature art and photography, and landscape appreciation in general. This book includes an appropriately wide-ranging bibliographic essay.

Schmitt, Peter J. (1947–). *Back to Nature: The Arcadian Myth in Urban America.* New York: Oxford University Press, 1969; Baltimore: Johns Hopkins University Press, 1990.
Various responses to the urbanization of America, ranging from the retreat to the suburb and hobby farm, to nature study in the schools, to the popular novel of the wilderness, analyzed as expressions of what the author terms the "Arcadian myth." The approach is patronizing, limiting the depth of the analysis, but the scope and sheer numbers of examples and illustrations are impressive.

Schwartz, William, ed. *Voices for the Wilderness.* New York: Ballantine Books, 1969.
A collection of papers from the Sierra Club's biennial wilderness conferences of the 1960s, including some strong essays by David Brower, Joseph Wood Krutch, and Wallace Stegner.

Shepard, Paul (1925–1996). *Man in the Landscape: A Historic View of the Esthetics of Nature.* New York: Alfred A. Knopf, 1967; College Station: Texas A & M University Press, 1991.
A historical consideration of views of nature, centered on Western civilization. Contains a spirited inquiry into the roots of our cultural estrangement from nature and an interesting account of the impact of wild, western landscapes upon the Euro-American sensibility.

———. *Nature and Madness.* San Francisco: Sierra Club Books, 1982; Athens: University of Georgia Press, 1998.
Describing the role played by encounters with wild nature in the development of personality, Shepard provides a challenging analysis of our culture's historically atypical situation. He traces the development of our estrangement from nature, or "madness," back into the Industrial Revolution, then further into the time of the desert fathers and further still into the time of the domestication of plants and animals. Each of these eras provided ideas and practices reinforcing the dualistic, "mad" view of the world, which Shepard describes as a kind of freezing of certain immature, normally superseded attitudes.

———. *The Tender Carnivore and the Sacred Game.* New York: Charles Scribner's Sons, 1973.
The author looks into the life of man before the Neolithic revolution to see if the hunting and gathering life might provide any useful references for the present crisis. He has harsh words for agriculture and domestication: "The myth that the practice of agriculture engenders respect for the soil does not stand careful examination." This book requires a rethinking of the term "primitive."

———. *Thinking Animals: Animals and the Development of Human Intelligence.* New York: Viking Press, 1978.
Far from being independent of the other animals, we are profoundly affected by them "in the shaping of personality, identity, and social consciousness." This book makes a many-sided argument for the symbiosis of our awareness and the natural world.

Shepard, Paul, and Barry Sanders (1938–). *The Sacred Paw: The Bear in Nature, Myth, and Literature.* New York: Viking, 1985.
Bears have entered deeply into human thought, ritual, symbology, language, and literature. The authors show how and why the bear "strikes a chord in us of fear and caution, curiosity and fascination."

Slaughter, Thomas P. *The Natures of John and William Bartram.* New York: Alfred A. Knopf, 1996.
"The Bartrams are unique and exemplary," the author writes, and proves the judgment many times over with a narrative account of their writings, architectural ideas, landscape awareness, aesthetic sensitivity, botanical and zoological acumen, business experiences, travel adventures, acquaintances and friends, and finally their complex relation with each other.

Slovic, Scott (1960–). *Seeking Awareness in American Nature Writing: Henry Thoreau, Annie Dillard, Edward Abbey, Wendell Berry, Barry Lopez.* Salt Lake City: University of Utah Press, 1992.
The writers treated are seeking equilibrium, Slovic argues, between self-possession and rhapsody, or science and aesthetics, and the hoped-for result is "the prized tension of awareness." A continuing interest of these writers is clarified consciousness.

Slovic, Scott, and Terrell F. Dixon (1940–), eds., *Being in the World: An Environmental Reader for Writers.* New York: Macmillan, 1993.
Eighty-three selections, representing a wide range of "the best American nature writing since Thoreau." Though nominally pointed toward composition courses, this anthology transcends textbook status. The notes on authors go into more detail, offer sharper critical judgment, and relate the writers more clearly to the environment than such headnotes usually do.

Smallwood, William Martin (1873–1949), and Mabel Sarah Coon Smallwood. *Natural History and the American Mind.* New York: Columbia University Press, 1941; New York: AMS Press, 1969.
A useful record of the advance of science, particularly informative on the influence, culturewide, of university curricula in natural history.

Soulé, Michael E., and Gary Lease, eds. *Reinventing Nature? Responses to Postmodern Deconstruction.* Washington, D.C.: Island Press, 1995.
A collection of essays critiquing the William Cronon-led deconstruction of

traditional concepts of nature (see *Uncommon Ground*). The essayists here include Paul Shepard and Donald Worster, and in the aggregate they agree with Stephen Kellert that deconstructive notions are "both biologically misguided and socially dangerous."

Stewart, Frank (1946–). *A Natural History of Nature Writing.* **Washington, D.C.: Island Press, 1995.**
Readings of Thoreau, Muir, Burroughs, Leopold, Carson, Abbey, and Gilbert White. Nature writers "seek to make our minds and hearts whole again." They are "in some fundamental way optimistic," exploring "how we might restore balance in our paradoxical selves...."

Thomas, Lewis (1913–1993). *Late Night Thoughts on Listening to Mahler's Ninth Symphony.* **New York: Viking Press, 1983; New York: Bantam Books, 1984; New York: Oxford University Press, 1985; New York: Penguin USA, 1995.**
Most of these essays are from *Discover,* and many are meditations on modern developments related to biology and medicine—heart pacemakers, atomic weapons and their possible use and consequences, the Gaia hypothesis, chemical treatments for mental illness, and fraudulent research publications, among others. The author conveys a humane view of our time and the human prospect. The shadow of the Bomb is over these essays, but they embody the inherent affirmation of an inquiring mind.

Tobias, Michael (1951–), ed. *Deep Ecology.* **San Diego: Avant Books, 1985.**
A wide-ranging collection of sixteen essays and several poems, most of them pointed toward a new and radically deeper understanding of our ecological situation. There is an excellent survey of the philosophical literature on the subject, by George Sessions, along with a sobering study of population and our pressure on the world, by William R. Catton Jr., and a provocative investigation of nature and sex, by Dolores LaChapelle, among other pieces of note. Perhaps the root distinction between "shallow ecology" and "deep ecology," at the level of self-concept and identity, will be most clearly seen by comparing the essay "Discriminating Altruisms," by Garrett Hardin, with "Identification as a Source of Deep Ecological Attitudes," by the Norwegian philosopher Arne Naess. Both essays are astute and, in their different ways, persuasive.

Torrance, Robert M. (1939–), ed. *Encompassing Nature: A Sourcebook.* **Washington, D.C.: Counterpoint, 1998.**
A 1,224-page anthology of pre-"nature writing" sources, given point by the

editor's spirited argument that writing about nature greatly predates the late-eighteenth-century dawn of the modern nature essay. Drawing from many cultures, and defending the Western tradition in particular against charges of antinature bias, Torrance performs a work of excavation, restoration, and perhaps revision. There was "no distinct genre of nature writing in such [non-alienated] cultures for the very reason that nature is always nearby. . . ."

Tracy, Henry Chester (1876–1958). *American Naturists.* **New York: E. P. Dutton, 1930.**
A history of American nature writing, with commentary on the genre's cultural significance and on individual writers' distinctive contributions. There are interesting insights here. Of John Muir: "It takes something more than, or other than literary criticism to find and assay the chief values in John Muir's prose." Of Mary Austin: "Deeper and deeper, as one proceeds, he is led into an inner seeing; by word-clues, by wands snatched from the Indian, by subduings of the clamant Western ego, by eye and hand contacts, by yieldings to the silent desert sense. One is ever on the edge of new-seeing."

Trimble, Stephen (1950–), ed. *Words from the Land: Encounters with Natural History Writing.* **Salt Lake City: Gibbs M. Smith, 1988; rev. ed., Reno: University of Nevada Press, 1995.**
An anthology of contemporary essays, prefaced by a most interesting gathering of comments from some of the authors on their research and writing methods. This wide-ranging introduction will be richly educative for anyone venturing upon criticism of the nature essay.

Turner, Frederick W. (1937–). *Beyond Geography: The Western Spirit Against the Wilderness.* **New York: Viking Press, 1980; New Brunswick, N.J.: Rutgers University Press, 1992.**
An essay in spiritual history, arguing that the loss of a mythic sense of life, and its replacement by a historical sense, were factors in Western civilization's alienation from nature. This study suggests origins for the seeming ethical indifference with which the New World was conquered and transformed.

———. *Spirit of Place: The Making of an American Literary Landscape.* **San Francisco: Sierra Club Books, 1989; Washington, D.C.: Island Press, 1992.**
Ecocriticism of nine authors who knew their places so deeply that they created reference points for the country as a whole, and thus helped form an American identity. Turner makes pilgrimages to the places of Thoreau, Twain, George Washington Cable, Cather, Sandoz, Faulkner, Steinbeck, William Carlos

Williams, and Leslie Silko. The high point is a climb of Mt. Katahdin in
Maine, accompanied by the naturalist and writer John Hay.

Vermes, Jean C. (1907–), ed. *The Wilderness Sampler: A Tonic of Great Writings about
the Moods of Nature.* **Harrisburg, Pa.: Stackpole Books, 1968.**
An anthology including Herman Melville on the "Enchanted isles" (the
Galapagos), Muir on the 1872 Inyo earthquake, and other familiar selections
from Powell, Audubon, Thoreau, and Burroughs, among thirty authors
represented.

West, Herbert Faulkner (1898–1974). *The Nature Writers: A Guide to Richer Reading.*
Brattleboro, Vt.: Stephen Daye Press, 1939.
An annotated booklist, brief but international in scope, preceded by the editor's introduction, which presents a historical overview of nature writing, and
a foreword by Henry Beston, which describes the nature writer's function
as being like that of the poet: "To give depth and color to the adventures of
human life, to touch the imagination of his readers, exalt their sense of beauty
and mystery, and fortify in their souls that power of intelligent awareness with
which they look out upon their world."

Wheeler, William Morton (1865–1937). *Essays in Philosophical Biology.* **Cambridge:
Harvard University Press, 1939.**
Twelve essays collected from various sources, giving a good idea of Wheeler's
range of interests and his philosopher's humane understanding. An antipedant
and a thinker whose insights into ecological relationships were carefully derived
and precisely formulated, Wheeler saw life in a manner both wittily satiric and
penetrating. His sense of the term "social" extended "down through the nonliving to the very atom with its organization of component electrons." Thus his
comparisons of ant and human societies go beyond the obvious deflation of
human pride to suggest the understanding that we live in and manifest great
natural patterns, greater by far than our narrow conceptions of politics or
economics.

Wild, Peter (1940–). *Pioneer Conservationists of Eastern America.* **Missoula, Mont.:
Mountain Press Publishing, 1987.**
Critical sketches of fifteen Americans whose proenvironment works have
helped shape history, opening up the possibility of a qualitative definition of
progress. Under this rubric, Wild treats Ralph Nader and Amory Lovins as
modern successors of the Marsh-Olmsted-Roosevelt line. It is by no means

sure that conservationists' minority views will ever prevail—"... fueled by economics and out of control, the destruction goes on at a far faster pace than the intense but limited efforts at restoration"—but these brief biographies do demonstrate the revolutionary power of ecological conscience. A forty-three-page bibliography helps make this a most serviceable reference.

————. *Pioneer Conservationists of Western America*. Missoula, Mont.: Mountain Press Publishing, 1979.
Profiles of fifteen people, among them John Muir, Mary Austin, Olaus Murie, and David Brower, whose work urges a postfrontier understanding. Introduced by an interestingly straight, philosophical essay by Edward Abbey.

Wilson, David Scofield (1931–). *In the Presence of Nature*. Amherst: University of Massachusetts Press, 1978.
An American studies approach to the significance of natural history in colonial America, concentrating on Jonathan Carver, John Bartram, and Mark Catesby. Wilson makes an interesting and useful distinction between natural history writing and nature reportage, and studies here an example of the latter, giving John Bartram's prose some of the "serious and sustained scrutiny" he believes it deserves.

Wilson, Edward O. (1929–). *Sociobiology: The New Synthesis*. Cambridge: Harvard University Press, 1975, 2000.
A comprehensive attempt to describe the links between biological evolution and social evolution, written with objectivity and wit. To many students of evolution, this book has Darwinian scope and weight.

Wise, Steven M. *Rattling the Cage: Toward Legal Rights for Animals*. Cambridge, Mass.: Perseus Books, 2000.
A surpassing legal argument, by a lawyer, for full rights of personhood for chimpanzees and bonobos. "But it should now be obvious that the ancient Great Wall that has for so long divided humans from every other animal is biased, irrational, unfair, and unjust."

Worster, Donald (1941–). *Nature's Economy: The Roots of Ecology*. San Francisco: Sierra Club Books, 1977; Garden City, N.Y.: Doubleday, 1979; Cambridge: Cambridge University Press, 1994.
In this fascinating intellectual history, Worster shows how ecological thought over the past three centuries has been shaped by large cultural currents,

including both Arcadian visions of nature and the stronger imperial traditions. His tracing of the interaction of these two streams of thought is masterly. A comprehensive and useful study, whose more philosophical focus makes it an essential text to be read alongside Roderick Nash's *Wilderness and the American Mind*.

———. *The Wealth of Nature: Environmental History and the Ecological Imagination*. New York: Oxford University Press, 1993.
A collection of brilliant individual essays, representing Professor Worster's prodigious scholarship and personal commitment to putting environmental realities into history writing and his desire to make a difference. Refreshingly unacademic (though rigorous in both logic and documentation) and engaged.

NOTES

A TAXONOMY OF NATURE WRITING

1. Roger Tory Peterson, *A Field Guide to Western Birds* (Boston: Houghton Mifflin, 1961), 223.
2. See Joseph Campbell, *The Hero With a Thousand Faces* (Princeton: Princeton University Press, 1949). I am grateful to Professor Joe Gordon of Colorado College for pointing out this pattern's ubiquity in nature writing.

THE AMERICAN SETTING

1. Jean Ribaut, *The Whole & True Discouerye of Terra Florida* (Deland, Fla.: Florida State Historical Society, 1927), 72–73 (facsimile reprint of 1563 London edition).
2. Walter Prescott Webb, *The Great Frontier* (Austin: University of Texas Press, 1979), 13. Originally published by Houghton Mifflin, 1952.
3. Henry David Thoreau, "A Natural History of Massachusetts," in *The Portable Thoreau,* ed. Carl Bode (New York: Viking, 1964), 56.
4. William Bartram, *The Travels of William Bartram,* ed. Francis Harper, Naturalist's Edition (New Haven: Yale University Press, 1958), li, lvi.

5. Paul Brooks, *Speaking for Nature* (San Francisco: Sierra Club, 1983), 285. Originally published by Houghton Mifflin, 1980.
6. Edwin Way Teale, always careful with numbers, estimated that by 1951, 100 million acres of America's marshes had been drained or filled in the course of the country's history. See *North with the Spring* (New York: Dodd, Mead, 1951), 134.

BEGINNINGS

1. Carl O. Sauer, *Sixteenth Century North America: The Land and the People As Seen by the Europeans* (Berkeley: University of California Press, 1971), 57, and also William Cronon, *Changes in the Land* (New York: Hill and Wang, 1983), 25–26.
2. Cecil Jane, ed. and trans., *The Voyages of Christopher Columbus: Being the Journals of His First and Third, and the Letters Concerning His First and Last Voyages* (London: Argonaut Press, 1930), 153, 160.
3. Thomas Heriot, "A briefe and true report of the new found land of Virginia," in Richard Hakluyt, *The*

Principal Navigations, Voyages, Traffiques and Discoveries of the English Nation, vol. 6 (New York: E. P. Dutton, 1927), 181–82.

4. Thomas Morton, *New English Canaan* (London: Charles Green, 1632), reprinted in *Tracts and Other Papers, Relating Principally to the Origin, Settlement, and Progress of the Colonies in North America from the Discovery of the Country to the Year 1776* (Washington: Peter Force, 1838), 47.

5. Ibid., 48.

6. Ibid., 50.

7. Henry David Thoreau, *Journals,* vol. 7 (Boston: Houghton Mifflin, 1906), 109.

8. William Wood, *New England's Prospect,* ed. Alden T. Vaughan (Amherst: University of Massachusetts Press, 1977), 48. Originally published by I. Bellamie, London, 1634.

9. Ibid., 46.

10. Cronon, *Changes in the Land,* 27.

11. Peter Matthiessen, *Wildlife in America* (New York: Penguin, 1977), 281. Originally published by Viking, 1959.

12. Philip Marshall Hicks, *The Development of the Natural History Essay in American Literature* (Philadelphia: unpublished doctoral thesis, 1924), 15.

13. John Josselyn, *New England's Rarities Discovered,* in *Transactions and Collections of the American Antiquarian Society,* ed. Edward Tuckerman, vol. 4 (Boston: John Wilson and Son, 1860), 216.

14. See Tuckerman's opinion in *Transactions and Collections,* 112.

15. Josselyn, *New England's Rarities,* in *Transactions and Collections,* 144.

16. For more on this matter, see chapter 5, "Commodities of the Hunt," in William Cronon, *Changes in the Land.*

17. John Josselyn, *An Account of Two Voyages to New-England, Made During the Years 1638, 1663* (Boston: William Veazie, 1865), 107. Originally published by G. Widdows, London, 1674.

18. Ibid., 71.

19. Ibid., 72.

20. Ibid., 99.

21. John Ray, *The Wisdom of God Manifested in the Works of the Creation* (London: Innys and Manby, 1735), 175. Originally published by Samuel Smith, London, 1691.

22. Keith Thomas's *Man and the Natural World: A History of the Modern Sensibility* (New York: Pantheon, 1983) traces the widening of man's views of nature during the crucial time period from 1500 to 1800, in one of the major source countries for that widening, England.

23. Joseph Ewan and Nesta Ewan, *John Banister and His Natural History of Virginia, 1678–1692* (Urbana: University of Illinois Press, 1970), 63.

24. Joseph Kastner, *A Species of Eternity* (New York: Knopf, 1977), 12.

25. George Frederick Frick and Raymond Phineas Stearns, *Mark Catesby, the Colonial Audubon* (Urbana: University

of Illinois Press, 1961), 7. See also
Robert Elman, *First in the Field:
America's Pioneering Naturalists* (New
York: Mason/Charter, 1977), 9–25.

26. Alan Feduccia, *Catesby's Birds of
Colonial America* (Chapel Hill:
University of North Carolina Press,
1985), 10.

27. Ibid., 138.

28. Mark Catesby, *The Natural History
of Carolina, Florida, and the Bahama
Islands*, vol. 2 (London: "Printed at
the Expence of the Author," 1743),
xxxvi.

29. Ibid., 56.

30. Ibid., Appendix, 13. For an analysis
of Catesby's contribution, see David
Scofield Wilson, *In the Presence
of Nature* (Amherst: University of
Massachusetts Press, 1978), 123–59.

31. Peter Kalm, *Peter Kalm's Travels in
North America*, ed. Adolph B. Benson
(New York: Wilson-Erickson, 1937), 152.

32. Ibid., 300.

33. Ibid., 153.

34. Ibid., 48.

35. Ibid., 698.

36. Ibid., 707.

37. Hector St. John de Crèvecoeur, *Sketches
of Eighteenth Century America*, ed.
Henri L. Bourdin, Ralph H. Gabriel,
and Stanley T. Williams (New Haven:
Yale University Press, 1925), 39.

38. Ibid., 41–42.

39. Ibid., 46.

40. D. H. Lawrence, *Studies in Classic
American Literature* (New York:
Thomas Seltzer, 1923), 33.

41. Crèvecoeur, *Sketches*, 77.

42. Ibid., 106–7.

43. Crèvecoeur, *Letters from an American
Farmer* (New York: Fox, Duffield,
1904), 253–54.

44. Thomas Jefferson, *Notes on the
State of Virginia*, ed. William Peden
(Chapel Hill: University of North
Carolina Press, 1955), 58–59.

45. Joseph Kastner, *A Species of Eternity*, 4.

46. John Bartram, *John and William
Bartram's America: Selections from the
Writings of the Philadelphia Naturalists*,
ed. Helen Gere Cruickshank (New
York: Devin-Adair, 1957), 13

47. William Bartram, *The Travels of
William Bartram*, ed. Francis Harper,
Naturalist's Edition (New Haven: Yale
University Press, 1958), 133.

48. Ibid., lvii, 38.

49. Ibid., 71.

50. Ibid.

51. Samuel Williams, *The Natural and
Civil History of Vermont* (Walpole,
N.H.: Thomas and Carlisle, 1794), viii.

52. Ibid., 121, 86–87, 73.

53. Ibid., 131.

54. Meriwether Lewis, *Original Journals
of the Lewis and Clark Expedition,
1804–1806*, ed. Reuben Gold Thwaites,
vol. 1, part 2 (New York: Dodd, Mead,
1904), 335.

55. Paul Russell Cutright, *Lewis and
Clark: Pioneering Naturalists* (Urbana:
University of Illinois Press, 1969), vii.

56. Alexander Wilson, *The Poems and
Literary Prose of Alexander Wilson*, ed.
Alexander B. Grosart (Paisley,

Scotland: Alex. Gardner, 1876), xl.
Robert Cantwell's *Alexander Wilson,
Naturalist and Pioneer* (Philadelphia:
Lippincott, 1961) is the most detailed
biography.

57. Wilson, 1.

58. Wilson, *American Ornithology*, vol. 4
(Philadelphia: Bradford and Inskeep,
1811), 20.

59. Alan Feduccia, *Catesby's Birds of
Colonial America*, 101.

60. Biographical information is found in
Jeannette E. Graustein's study, *Thomas
Nuttall, Naturalist: Explorations
in America, 1808–1841* (Cambridge:
Harvard University Press, 1967).
References to Nuttall may be found
in Washington Irving, *Astoria*, ed.
Edgeley W. Todd (Norman: University
of Oklahoma Press, 1964), 143, 144, 170,
201, 215; and in Richard Henry Dana,
Jr., *Two Years Before the Mast* (Boston:
Houghton Mifflin, 1911), 359–61, 412.
Astoria was first published in 1836, and
Two Years Before the Mast in 1840.

61. Jeannette E. Graustein, ed. *Nuttall's
Travels into the Old Northwest: An
Unpublished 1810 Diary*, vol. 14 of
Chronica Botanica (Waltham, Mass.:
Chronica Botanica Company,
1950–1951).

62. Thomas Nuttall, *A Journal of Travels
into the Arkansa Territory, During the
Year 1819*, in *Early Western Travels*, ed.
Reuben Gold Thwaites, vol. 13
(Cleveland: Arthur H. Clark, 1905),
109. Originally published by Thos. H.
Palmer, Philadelphia, 1821.

63. John D. Godman, *American Natural
History*, vol. 1 (Philadelphia: R. W.
Pomeroy, 1842), 44. Originally published by Carey and Lea, Philadelphia,
1826.

64. Ibid., 205.

65. Ibid., vol. 2, 291. *Rambles of a
Naturalist* is included in this edition
of *American Natural History*.

66. John James Audubon, *Ornithological
Biography*, vol. 1 (Edinburgh: Adam
Black, 1831–1834), vii.

67. Ibid., vol. 2, 242.

68. Ibid., vol. 1, 29.

THE AGE OF THOREAU, MUIR, AND
BURROUGHS

1. Jonathan Edwards, *The Works of
President Edwards*, ed. Samuel Austin,
vol. 1 (Worcester, Mass.: Isaiah
Thomas, Jr., 1808), 34–35.

2. Ralph Waldo Emerson, "Nature," in
*The Selected Writings of Ralph Waldo
Emerson*, ed. Brooks Atkinson (New
York: Random House, 1940), 6.
Originally published by J. Munroe,
Boston, 1836.

3. Thoreau's original subtitle for *Walden*
was "or, Life in the Woods."

4. Bradford Torrey, ed., *Journal*, in
The Writings of Henry David Thoreau,
vol. 1 (Boston: Houghton Mifflin,
1906), xli.

5. William Howarth, *The Book of
Concord* (New York: Viking, 1982), 9.

6. See Robert D. Richardson Jr., *Henry
Thoreau: A Life of the Mind* (Berkeley:

University of California Press, 1986), 116, 123, 224.

7. Henry David Thoreau, "A Natural History of Massachusetts," 34.

8. Ibid.

9. Thoreau, *Journals*, vol. 1, 265.

10. Walter Harding, *The Days of Henry Thoreau* (New York: Knopf, 1965), 457. This remark has a Buddhist flavor, and it may be pertinent that Rick Fields, in *How the Swans Came to the Lake: A Narrative History of Buddhism in America* (Boulder: Shambhala, 1981), writes that Thoreau was "perhaps the first American to explore the nontheistic mode of contemplation which is the distinguishing mark of Buddhism" (62–63). Reginald H. Blyth, the British student of Zen in literature, considered Thoreau a great man in world history, ranking him only behind J. S. Bach and the Japanese Haiku poet Bashō. "The order is the order of Zen," Blyth explained. R. H. Blyth, *Mumonkan*, in *Zen and Zen Classics*, vol. 4 (Tokyo: Hokuseido, 1966), 7.

11. Thoreau, *Walden*, ed. J. Lyndon Shanley (Princeton: Princeton University Press, 1971), 312.

12. Nuttall, *A Manual of the Ornithology of the United States and Canada* (Boston: Hilliard, Gray, 1840), 392. Originally published by Hilliard and Brown, Cambridge, 1832.

13. Thoreau, *Journals*, vol. 4, 190–91.

14. Thoreau, "Walking," *Atlantic Monthly* 9 (June, 1862): 659, 662, 667.

15. Ibid., 661, 674, 665.

16. Thoreau, *Walden*, 129.

17. Ibid., 329.

18. John H. White Jr., "Railroads: Wood to Burn," in *Material Culture in the Wooden Age*, ed. Brooke Hindle (Tarrytown, N.Y.: Sleepy Hollow Press, 1981), 199–201, 215.

19. Betty Flanders Thomson, *The Changing Face of New England* (New York: Macmillan, 1958), 31.

20. The most thorough history of American extinctions and extirpations is found in Peter Matthiessen, *Wildlife in America*, rev. and updated ed. (New York: Viking, 1987). Originally published by Viking, 1959.

21. John Muir, *The Story of My Boyhood and Youth* (Boston: Houghton Mifflin, 1913), 53

22. John Muir, *John of the Mountains: The Unpublished Journals of John Muir*, ed. Linnie Marsh Wolfe (Madison: University of Wisconsin Press, 1979), 8. Originally published by Houghton Mifflin, 1938.

23. Muir, *My First Summer in the Sierra* (Boston: Houghton Mifflin, 1979), 131.

24. Ibid.

25. Muir, *John of the Mountains*, 79–80.

26. Linnie Marsh Wolfe, *Son of the Wilderness: The Life of John Muir* (Madison: University of Wisconsin Press, 1978), 166. Originally published by Alfred A. Knopf, 1945.

27. Muir, *John of the Mountains*, 95.

28. Thoreau, *The Maine Woods* (New York: Crowell, 1966), 83. See also

Roderick Nash, *Wilderness and the American Mind,* 3rd ed. (New Haven: Yale University Press, 1982), 91.

29. William Frederic Badé, *The Life and Letters of John Muir,* vol. 1 (Boston: Houghton Mifflin, 1923), 326.

30. Wolfe, *Son of the Wilderness,* 158.

31. Muir, "Wild Wool," *Overland Monthly* 5 (April 1875): 364.

32. Ibid.

33. Muir, *John of the Mountains,* 138.

34. Muir, *The Mountains of California* (Garden City, N.Y.: Doubleday, 1961), 93. Originally published by Century, 1894.

35. Muir, *The Yosemite* (New York: Century, 1912), 262.

36. Wolfe, *Son of the Wilderess,* 188–91.

37. Ibid., 344.

38. Thoreau, *Walden,* 138.

39. John Burroughs, *Accepting the Universe: Essays in Naturalism* (Boston: Houghton Mifflin, 1920), 304.

40. William Sloane Kennedy, *The Real John Burroughs* (New York: Funk and Wagnalls, 1924), 122.

41. Burroughs, *Accepting the Universe,* vii.

42. Clara Barrus, *The Life and Letters of John Burroughs,* vol. 2 (Boston: Houghton Mifflin, 1925), 319.

43. Burroughs, *Notes on Walt Whitman, As Poet and Person,* 2d ed. (New York: J. S. Redfield, 1871), 46. Originally published by American News Company, New York, 1867.

44. Burroughs, quoted in Clara Barrus, *The Life and Letters of John Burroughs,* vol. 1, 256.

45. Burroughs, *Accepting the Universe,* 146.

46. Burroughs, quoted in Clara Barrus, *The Life and Letters of John Burroughs,* vol. 2, 336.

47. Burroughs, *Ways of Nature,* in *The Writings of John Burroughs,* vol. 14 (Boston: Houghton Mifflin, 1905), 80.

48. Ibid., 30–31.

49. Thoreau, *The Correspondence of Henry David Thoreau,* ed. Walter Harding and Carl Bode (New York: New York University Press, 1958), 489.

50. Wilson Flagg, *The Woods and By-Ways of New England* (Boston: James R. Osgood, 1872), vii.

51. Ibid., 80.

52. Ibid., 111, 142.

53. Ibid., 427, 433.

54. Flagg, *Studies in the Field and Forest* (Boston: Little, Brown, 1857), 258–59.

55. Clarence E. Dutton, *Tertiary History of the Grand Cañon District* (Washington: U.S. Government, 1882), 90, 56.

56. John Charles Van Dyke, *The Desert* (New York: Scribner's, 1901), 53.

57. Ibid., 129.

58. Ibid., ix.

59. Mary Austin, *Earth Horizon* (Boston: Houghton Mifflin, 1932), 198.

60. "I-Mary" came into conscious existence at age six: "It was a summer morning, and the child I was had walked down through the orchard alone and come out on the brow of a sloping hill where there were grass and a wind blowing and one tall tree reaching into infinite immensities of

blueness. Quite suddenly, after a moment of quietness there, earth and sky and tree and wind-blown grass and the child in the midst of them came alive together with a pulsing light of consciousness. There was a wild foxglove at the child's feet and a bee dozing about it, and to this day [1931] I can recall the swift inclusive awareness of each for the whole—I in them and they in me and all of us enclosed in a warm lucent bubble of livingness." See Mary Austin, *Experiences Facing Death* (London: Rider, 1931), 24–25.

61. See Rae G. Ballard, "Mary Austin's *Earth Horizon:* The Imperfect Circle," unpublished dissertation, Claremont Graduate School, 1977, for an analysis of Austin's preoccupation with pattern.

62. Lawrence Evers, "Mary Austin and the Spirit of the Land," in Mary Austin, *The Land of Journeys' Ending* (Tucson: University of Arizona Press, 1983), xviii.

63. Austin, letter to D. T. MacDougal, 1922, quoted in Augusta Fink, *I-Mary* (Tucson: University of Arizona Press, 1983), 202.

64. On the influence of the Indians, see Mary Austin, *The American Rhythm* (New York: Harcourt, Brace, 1923), 27–28, 39, and *Earth Horizon*, 289. The aid given by Lummis is covered in Fink, *I-Mary*, 96–112.

65. Austin, *The Land of Little Rain* (Cambridge, Mass.: Riverside Press, 1950), 6. Originally published by Houghton Mifflin, 1903.

66. Ibid., 25.

67. Austin, *The Land of Journeys' Ending*, 40, 442.

68. Ibid., 40.

THE TWENTIETH CENTURY

1. John Hay, *In Defense of Nature* (Boston: Atlantic Monthly Press, 1969), 120.

2. Hay, *The Undiscovered Country* (New York: Norton, 1981), 15.

3. Aldo Leopold, *A Sand County Almanac* (New York: Oxford University Press, 1949), 130.

4. Susan L. Flader, *Thinking Like a Mountain: Aldo Leopold and the Evolution of an Ecological Attitude Toward Deer, Wolves, and Forests* (Columbia: University of Missouri Press, 1974), 60–61, 79–80.

5. Ibid., 153.

6. Leopold, *A Sand County Almanac*, 224–25.

7. Joseph Wood Krutch, *The Modern Temper* (New York: Harvest, 1956), 169. Originally published by Harcourt, Brace, 1929.

8. Ibid., 168.

9. Krutch, *The Voice of the Desert* (New York: William Sloane, 1954), 218.

10. Krutch, "If You Don't Mind My Saying So," *American Scholar* 39 (Spring 1970): 204.

11. Linda Lear, ed., *Lost Woods: The Discovered Writing of Rachel Carson* (Boston: Beacon Press, 1998), ix.

12. Rachel Carson, *Silent Spring* (Boston: Mifflin, 1962), 56.

13. Ibid., 162.

14. Henry Beston, *The Outermost House* (Garden City, N.Y.: Doubleday, Doran and Company, 1929), 10.

15. Ibid., 24.

16. Ibid., 216.

17. Ibid., 221–22.

18. Edward Abbey, *Desert Solitaire* (New York: McGraw-Hill, 1968), 135.

19. Ibid., xiii.

20. Ibid., xiv.

21. Ibid., 51.

22. Jan Wojcik, "The American Wisdom Literature of Farming," *Agriculture and Human Values* 1, no. 4 (Fall 1984): 30.

23. Liberty Hyde Bailey, *The Country-Life Movement in the United States* (New York: Macmillan, 1911), 20.

24. Bailey, *The Holy Earth* (New York: Scribner's, 1915), 29, 30.

25. Loren C. Owings, *Environmental Values, 1860–1972: A Guide to Information Sources* (Detroit: Gale, 1976), 243.

26. Wendell Berry, *The Long-Legged House* (New York: Harcourt, Brace and World, 1969), 149.

27. Berry, *A Continuous Harmony* (New York: Harcourt Brace Jovanovich, 1972), 45.

28. Berry, *The Unsettling of America* (San Francisco: Sierra Club, 1977), 21.

29. Berry, *The Gift of Good Land* (Berkeley: North Point, 1981), 210.

30. Edward Hoagland, *Notes from the Century Before: A Journal from British Columbia* (New York: Random House, 1969), 13.

31. Ibid., 40–41.

32. Ibid., 265.

33. Ibid., 271.

34. Ibid., 272.

35. Barry Lopez, *Arctic Dreams* (New York: Scribner's, 1986), xxiv.

36. Lopez, in "Barry Lopez," *Antaeus,* no. 57 (Autumn 1986): 297.

37. Irene Diamond and Gloria Feman Orenstein, eds., *Reweaving the World: The Emergence of Ecofeminism* (San Francisco: Sierra Club, 1990), ix.

38. Janisse Ray, *Ecology of a Cracker Childhood* (Minneapolis: Milkweed, 1999), 8.

39. William Cronon, *Uncommon Ground: Rethinking the Human Place in Nature* (New York: Norton, 1995), answered by debate in the journal *Wild Earth,* eventually resulting in a book, *Reinventing Nature? Responses to Postmodern Deconstruction,* ed. Michael Soulé and Gary Lease (Washington, D.C.: Island Press, 1995), and by *The Great New Wilderness Debate,* ed. J. Baird Callicott and Michael P. Nelson (Athens: University of Georgia Press, 1998).

40. Ray, *Ecology of a Cracker Childhood,* 15.

41. Don Scheese, *Nature Writing: The Pastoral Impulse in America* (New York: Twayne Publishers, 1996), 54–55.

42. Ann Zwinger, *Downcanyon: A Naturalist Explores the Colorado River through the Grand Canyon* (Tucson: University of Arizona Press, 1995), 80.

43. Ibid., 81.

44. Zwinger, *The Nearsighted Naturalist*

(Tucson: University of Arizona Press, 1998), 192.

45. Ibid., 193.

46. Rick Bass, *Brown Dog of the Yaak* (Minneapolis: Milkweed, 1999), 14.

47. Ibid., 44.

48. Ibid., 66.

49. Rick Bass, *The Book of Yaak* (Boston: Houghton Mifflin, 1996), 71.

50. Ibid., 74.

THOMAS J. LYON taught at Utah State University from 1964 to 1997, where he also edited the journal *Western American Literature*. He was senior editor of *A Literary History of the American West* (1987) and *Updating the Literary West* (1997), and he edited *This Incomperable Lande* (1989), *The Literary West* (1999), and *A Frank Waters Reader* (2000). He enjoys walking and reading.

MORE BOOKS ON THE WORLD AS HOME
FROM MILKWEED EDITIONS

To order books or for more information, contact Milkweed at (800) 520-6455 or visit our website (www.worldashome.org).

BROWN DOG OF THE YAAK:
ESSAYS ON ART AND ACTIVISM
Rick Bass

SWIMMING WITH GIANTS:
MY ENCOUNTERS WITH WHALES, DOLPHINS, AND SEALS
Anne Collet

THE PRAIRIE IN HER EYES
Ann Daum

WRITING THE SACRED INTO THE REAL
Alison Hawthorne Deming

BOUNDARY WATERS:
THE GRACE OF THE WILD
Paul Gruchow

GRASS ROOTS:
THE UNIVERSE OF HOME
Paul Gruchow

THE NECESSITY OF EMPTY PLACES
Paul Gruchow

A SENSE OF THE MORNING:
FIELD NOTES OF A BORN OBSERVER
David Brendan Hopes

TAKING CARE:
THOUGHTS ON STORYTELLING AND BELIEF
William Kittredge

A WING IN THE DOOR:
LIFE WITH A RED-TAILED HAWK
Peri Phillips McQuay

AN AMERICAN CHILD SUPREME:
THE EDUCATION OF A LIBERATION ECOLOGIST
John Nichols

THE BARN AT THE END OF THE WORLD:
THE APPRENTICESHIP OF A QUAKER, BUDDHIST SHEPHERD
Mary Rose O'Reilley

WALKING THE HIGH RIDGE:
LIFE AS FIELD TRIP
Robert Michael Pyle

ECOLOGY OF A CRACKER CHILDHOOD
Janisse Ray

THE DREAM OF THE MARSH WREN:
WRITING AS RECIPROCAL CREATION
Pattiann Rogers

THE COUNTRY OF LANGUAGE
Scott Russell Sanders

OF LANDSCAPE AND LONGING:
FINDING A HOME AT THE WATER S EDGE
Carolyn Servid

THE BOOK OF THE TONGASS
Edited by Carolyn Servid and Donald Snow

HOMESTEAD
Annick Smith

TESTIMONY:
WRITERS OF THE WEST SPEAK ON BEHALF OF UTAH WILDERNESS
Compiled by Stephen Trimble and Terry Tempest Williams

SHAPED BY WIND AND WATER:
REFLECTIONS OF A NATURALIST
Ann Haymond Zwinger

OTHER BOOKS OF INTEREST TO THE WORLD AS HOME READER

ESSAYS

ECCENTRIC ISLANDS:
TRAVELS REAL AND IMAGINARY
Bill Holm

THE HEART CAN BE FILLED ANYWHERE ON EARTH
Bill Holm

SHEDDING LIFE:
DISEASE, POLITICS, AND OTHER HUMAN CONDITIONS
Miroslav Holub

CHILDREN'S NOVELS

TIDES
V. M. Caldwell

NO PLACE
Kay Haugaard

THE MONKEY THIEF
Aileen Kilgore Henderson

TREASURE OF PANTHER PEAK
Aileen Kilgore Henderson

THE DOG WITH GOLDEN EYES
Frances Wilbur

CHILDREN'S ANTHOLOGIES

STORIES FROM WHERE WE LIVE—THE CALIFORNIA COAST
Edited by Sara St. Antoine

STORIES FROM WHERE WE LIVE—THE GREAT NORTH AMERICAN PRAIRIE
Edited by Sara St. Antoine

STORIES FROM WHERE WE LIVE—THE NORTH ATLANTIC COAST
Edited by Sara St. Antoine

ANTHOLOGIES

SACRED GROUND:
WRITINGS ABOUT HOME
Edited by Barbara Bonner

URBAN NATURE:
POEMS ABOUT WILDLIFE IN THE CITY
Edited by Laure-Anne Bosselaar

VERSE AND UNIVERSE:
POEMS ABOUT SCIENCE AND MATHEMATICS
Edited by Kurt Brown

POETRY

TURNING OVER THE EARTH
Ralph Black

BOXELDER BUG VARIATIONS
Bill Holm

BUTTERFLY EFFECT
Harry Humes

EATING BREAD AND HONEY
Pattiann Rogers

FIREKEEPER:
NEW AND SELECTED POEMS
Pattiann Rogers

JOIN US

Milkweed publishes adult and children's fiction, poetry, and, in its World As Home program, literary nonfiction about the natural world. Milkweed also hosts two websites: www.milkweed.org, where readers can find in-depth information about Milkweed books, authors, and programs, and www.worldashome.org, which is your online resource of books, organizations, and writings that explore ethical, esthetic, and cultural dimensions of our relationship to the natural world.

Since its genesis as *Milkweed Chronicle* in 1979, Milkweed has helped hundreds of emerging writers reach their readers. Thanks to the generosity of foundations and of individuals like you, Milkweed Editions is able to continue its nonprofit mission of publishing books chosen on the basis of literary merit—of how they impact the human heart and spirit—rather than on how they impact the bottom line. That's a miracle that our readers have made possible.

In addition to purchasing Milkweed books, you can join the growing community of Milkweed supporters. Individual contributions of any amount are both meaningful and welcome. Contact us for a Milkweed catalog or log on to www.milkweed.org and click on "About Milkweed," then "Why Join Milkweed," to find out about our donor program, or simply call (800) 520-6455 and ask about becoming one of Milkweed's contributors. As a nonprofit press, Milkweed belongs to you, the community. Milkweed's board, its staff, and especially the authors whose careers you help launch thank you for reading our books and supporting our mission in any way you can.

Interior design by Dale Cooney
Typeset in Minion 11/15.5
by Stanton Publication Services, Inc.
Printed on acid-free 55# Frasier Miami Book Natural Recycled paper
by Friesen Corporation